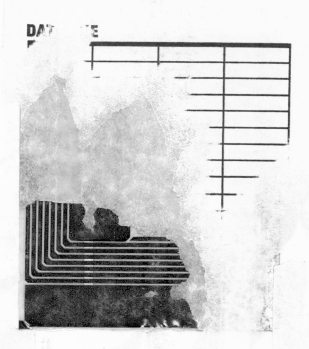

MAKING AMERICA WORK

Other Books of Which
James O'Toole is Principal Author or Editor:

Work in America (1973)

Watts and Woodstock: Identity and Culture in the United
States and South Africa (1973)

Work and the Quality of Life (1974)

Energy and Social Change (1976)

Work, Learning and the American Future (1977)

Tenure (1979)

MAKING AMERICA WORK
Productivity and Responsibility

JAMES O'TOOLE

CONTINUUM · New York

1981
The Continuum Publishing Company
575 Lexington Avenue
New York, N.Y. 10022

Printed in the United States of America

Library of Congress Cataloging in Publication Data

O'Toole, James.
  Making America work.

  Includes index.
  1. Labor productivity. 2. Industrial organization.
3. Employees' representation in management. I. Title.
HD57.08   658.3'14   81-766
ISBN 0-8264-0045-0   AACR2

CONTENTS

ACKNOWLEDGMENTS

I WISH to thank my colleagues at the Center for Futures Research, and the sponsors of the center's study on the "Future of Worker and Social Entitlements," for allowing me to piggyback much of the research that went into this book on similar efforts for that study. In particular, I wish to acknowledge the helpful criticisms, insights, and inspiration contributed by Kenneth Brousseau, Richard Drobnick, Selwyn Enzer, Burt Nanus, and August Ralston.

Ivar Berg, William Herman, and Robert Schrank offered scathing (and deserved) criticisms of an earlier draft of this book; I appreciate their wisdom and candor. In addition, Bob Schrank contributed in other ways: He assembled a conference of experts on the quality of work life, the purpose of which was to reeducate me on that subject, and he wrangled a small summer grant from the Ford Foundation that allowed me to reimmerse myself in the literature of work after a six–year hiatus. I gratefully acknowledge that grant.

Parts of this book have appeared in substantially different forms in articles in *The Harvard Business Review* and *The Wilson Quarterly,* and as contributed chapters in the C. Stewart Sheppard and Donald C. Carroll volume, *Working in the 21st Century,* and Cary L. Cooper's *Behavioral Problems in Organizations.* Many of the ideas in these pages came from my Mitchell Prize–winning paper in *Towards Sustainable Growth,* edited by Harland Cleveland.

Unless otherwise indicated, all the data cited in this book are from the U.S. Department of Labor, Bureau of Labor Statistics. The sources of the data are: *The Human Resources Report of the President* (1978 and 1979 editions), *Monthly Labor Review* (1978 and 1979 volumes), and *Occupational Outlook for College Graduates,* 1978–1979 Edition.

1

THE WEALTH OF THE NATION

THERE are three basic sources of productivity: labor (the mental and physical efforts of workers), management (the activities of planning, coordinating, motivating, and controlling), and technology (the contribution of machines transferring energy into useful work). Historically the greatest improvements in the productive powers of workers came about through the division of labor. In the 1700s, for example, one man working alone could not make as many as twenty pins in a day; by dividing the task into eighteen distinct operations, ten men could make upwards of forty-eight thousand pins in a day. The organization of these workers was the first purely managerial contribution to productivity. The next major increase in productivity resulted from the introduction of technology. By the twentieth century—thanks to the assistance of high-speed machines—a worker in a pin factory could easily produce several hundred thousand pins a day. Unlike the eighteenth century worker, the modern worker "makes" no pins—rather he or she tends the machines that, in fact, make the pins. Nevertheless it is said that the modern worker is several hundred times more "productive" than his counterpart was at the dawn of the industrial age. Therein lies the source of the wealth of the advanced nations.

It is comforting to assume, as most futurists are wont to do, that this trend of increasing productivity will continue unbroken into the future. It is often said that machines will increasingly replace the labor of men and women, all to the benefit of the American standard of living. Certainly if the pattern established during the Industrial Revolution were to continue, progress would ultimately triumph over poverty.

But things are not going as predicted. The constantly rising productivity trend appears to have leveled and even started to fall. Perhaps this is just a temporary setback. Then again, it could be that a point of radical disjuncture has been reached in the American economy.

Clearly America isn't working as well as it once did. Evidence of this decline can be glimpsed daily on the covers of national newsmagazines ("U.S. Lags in Industrial Innovation"), on the front pages of newspapers ("Productivity Down Sixth Quarter Running"), and in articles in scholarly journals that seek to document the causes and effects of the decreasing ability of the nation to compete in international markets. There is little doubt that many American products no longer sell abroad as successfully as they did ten years ago, and are losing out domestically in competition with foreign-made goods. Moreover when American products do sell, the presumption often is that they won't work as advertised, and will not be as up to date or well made as comparable Japanese and German products. As if to rub salt in America's wounds, the nation's chief competitors, Japan and Germany, have low rates of inflation and unemployment—while at home escalating prices and burgeoning unemployment lines have become chronic.

Many explanations for America's new economic woes are being advanced: There is inadequate investment in new plants and machines; government is overregulating industry; excessive taxation saps the incentive to produce. No doubt there is truth to such explanations. Increased incentives for savings and capital investment along with reduced regulation and taxation probably would have positive effects on the interrelated problems of low productivity and innovation and high inflation and unemployment. But is it realistic to expect that such changes in industrial policy would *solve* the nation's economic problems? Recent experience should give us pause. British Prime Minister Margaret Thatcher has altered her country's policies in the manner prescribed by the disciples of Adam Smith, but the bitter medicine has not produced the desired effects. Why? The reasons are many, but basically it would seem that a nation's economic woes are rooted in human attitudes and behavior—that is, in the values and culture of a people. In Britain, for example, the class conflict that is acted out daily in industrial strife cannot be corrected by changes in tax policy. America's economic malaise is rooted in changing demographics and social values, in alterations in such fundamental social institutions as the family, church, and community, and in such basic shifts as the enormous growth of the services sector and the new knowledge industries. Clearly, such external factors as the energy crunch have grossly distorted the nation's economic performance. But, in the final analysis, patterns of energy consumption—and failures of conservation—also are grounded in social behavior. In short, most economic problems are only *symptoms* of underlying social and cultural patterns.

Changes in economic policy, of course, can give symptomatic relief. Inflation can be wrung out of the patient by introducing stringent monetary and fiscal measures, but the effects of such measures are short-lived and often contraindicated by severe social side effects (economists call these trade-offs). For example, the cost of reducing inflation by inducing recession is often unemployment, and subsequently increased class conflict.

Admittedly, it seems likely that the current pattern of stagflation can be overcome temporarily by an appropriate mix of tax incentives, reductions in federal spending, selective deregulation and tight money. But as surely as there are business cycles and changes in national leadership, the chronic, underlying problems of unemployment, inflation and low productivity will resurface. It is not that such changes in economic policy are necessarily wrong, or that these should not be tried. But it should be recognized that these changes are short-term in nature and superficial in effect. Such changes seldom alter structure and never alter culture. And it is at the basic level of societal structure and culture where the roots of the nation's economic problems are to be found and, one hopes, eradicated.

What is needed is exploratory social surgery to find a cure for America's malaise, and not merely short-term relief of symptoms. In search of the real but hidden causes of the low-productivity epidemic, the surgeon might begin by putting the scalpel to the body economic. In search of common, causal patterns of dysfunction, he might examine the body's vital organs —the work organizations that make it function. That is what I have attempted to do over the last few years. In eviscerating about one hundred American work places through both direct observation and the analysis of descriptions carefully prepared and documented by others, I have identified a common pattern of behavior among companies that rank low on common measures of productivity. Significantly this pattern of behavior could not be altered greatly by changes in national economic policy; it would require, in addition, changes in managerial philosophy about work—changes in "culture," if you will. While my case-by-case analysis is more art than science, the pattern of behavior found among dysfunctional firms is too similar to be random. Consider four examples of organizations with low productivity.

In Organization A managers have stubbornly retained the product mix, technology, and work processes that were appropriate in the 1950s but have now become obsolete as the result of increasing foreign competition.

Ironically, as a consequence of the failure of managers to meet the exigencies of the market, the official measure of *labor* productivity has fallen in the company. Moreover, workers have borne the brunt of the costs of the mismanagement: about half the labor force in the company has been laid off.

In Organization B there is extremely high productivity in but one of the company's many plants. The unusual record of performance in this one plant has been achieved by "self-management" (giving workers full responsibility for the quantity and quality of their work). But managers in central headquarters discover that the plant has been operating outside of company staffing norms: there is an insufficient number of supervisors and middle managers. Several layers of managers are then introduced, and productivity in the plants drops to the company average.

In Organization C (this is a government office) productivity is running about 50 percent higher than in the agency as a whole. Top management investigates and discovers that the office manager assigns a heavy work load to his staff on Monday, then permits them to take off work for the rest of the week whenever they have completed their assignments. The agency head orders a cessation of this practice: "You can't give people five days' pay for four days on the job." Productivity in the office then regresses to the agency mean: two and a half days' output are rewarded with five days' pay.

Organization D operates in England (we search there because one might learn a great deal about disease in a body where it has spread to nearly every organ). In this company thousands of workers face the threat of imminent layoff. To avoid this fate, the workers take the initiative and prepare detailed plans, programs, and budgets to make dozens of new products that not only are they skilled to produce but that the company can produce without new capital investment. The managers refuse to consider the plans on the grounds that workers have no experience in product design, development, or finance. The workers are laid off. Eventually other companies adopt many of the workers' ideas and successfully and profitably manufacture and market products they invented.

These examples are not typical of the behavior of American managers. For the sake of illustration, I have chosen extreme cases where poor managerial decisions clearly can be seen to have led to low worker productivity. Usually the consequences of managerial decisions are not so apparent, which is why correcting the problem of low productivity is so difficult. Moreover the purpose of these cases is not to set the stage for scapegoating. There are no villians or heroes to this piece.

Nor are these examples typical of the behavior of American workers.

Indeed we should be careful not to generalize about the behavior, values, desires, and satisfactions of the labor force. A major mistake that observers of the work place have repeatedly made is overgeneralizing about what people want from work (for example, industrial engineers have assumed that all workers seek higher pay and security, and humanists have assumed that all workers seek "self-actualization"). At work, as in life, a full spectrum of attitudes and behavior is found. There are workers who are ambitious and dedicated, and others who are sullen and uncooperative. There are those who hate work, and those who would rather work than play. Some workers are interested in the intrinsic rewards of their jobs, and others care only for security—even though their security needs appear to have been satisfied. Some workers are selfish and concerned only with guarding their "rights," but many are committed to their employers and dedicated to their jobs as any Japanese or German worker. This *diversity* is the single most important fact about the American work force. Indeed, by aggregating the countless studies of worker attitudes, values, and satisfactions that were conducted in the 1970s, one arrives at a singularly significant conclusion: *Workers are not all alike; they have different needs, interests and motivations. Moreover, these characteristics constantly change over the career of each worker, much as the modal work values of the society as a whole shift over time.*

The failure of scholars, managers, and union leaders to recognize that worker values are diverse and changing is at the heart of the inappropriate philosophy and organization of work prevalent in America today—and at the core of the problem of declining productivity. Ignoring diversity, management theorists have assumed there is one best way to organize work—whether that assumption has been that workers are lazy and irresponsible, or that they are noble and in search of self-actualization. Ignoring the changing nature of work values, managers and unionists have sought to organize work for the generation that came of age in the turbulent 1960s and 1970s in a fashion that was appropriate for the generation of workers that came of age during the Depression.

The implications of diverse and changing work values are of enormous significance to the task of increasing productivity. For one thing, it means that it is impossible to design a single plan that is appropriate at all times, for all workers, in all organizations. Another implication is that managers will have to develop a philosophy and organization of work that is appropriate for the social conditions of the 1980s. Happily a number of enlightened managers have begun to develop a philosophy and organization of work that is flexible and bridges the social disjunctions of the era. In a few instances union leaders have similarly altered their philosophy. To illustrate by example, let us enter a healthy plant, one relatively free of the disease of low productivity.

In 1977 one of the nation's larger industrial corporations opened a new chemical processing plant in Texas. For the plant to operate efficiently, the managers realized that it would be necessary to have great flexibility in the assignment of the work force: That is, all three hundred workers would have to be ready and able to do any job in the plant at any time. This need for flexibility ran up against one of the basic tenets of unionism: the need to uphold rigid craft lines in order to protect workers in one job classification from being replaced by less skilled workers from a lower wage classification. The corporation had little hope of gaining the reforms it sought because the union involved, the United Steel Workers of America, held job/wage classifications sacrosanct. Furthermore the union had a firm policy of pursuing uniform provisions in all its contracts with various employers.

Consequently company executives were astonished when the union expressed willingness to negotiate. The enlightened union official responsible for the plant explains why they were willing to talk: "Adversarial relationships often deteriorate into economic warfare. We felt there ought to be a better way." The better way that the union had in mind was industrial democracy ("the elimination of the master/servant relationship") and participative management ("the right of workers to participate in managerial decisions and in company profits"). After thus stating their position in words that normally cause managers to see red, the union officials were equally surprised when the company still expressed willingness to negotiate.

In negotiating the details of the contract the union and the employers moved out of the "smoke-filled room" and into the open where workers could have an input into the various provisions being carved out. The preamble to this contract is especially significant. It states that neither the union nor management has given up its traditional rights and responsibilities, but both have agreed to "exercise these cooperatively." That spirit informs the entire contract, and makes possible the following provisions, which have scant precedent in the adversarial history of American labor relations:

· There is a no layoff agreement.
· There are no time clocks.
· There are no company rules.
· Foremen have no authority to assign or to discipline workers.
· The only discipline available to the company is to send a worker home

(but it must continue to pay his salary, and he is presumed innocent until proved guilty). The first step in resolving a problem that leads to such a suspension is counseling by the union and management. If this isn't successful, the worker is entitled to counseling by an outsider. If the problem still isn't resolved, the worker is entitled to a hearing before a jury of his peers: The names of five workers are drawn from a hat, and they have the final say on whether the worker will be permanently dismissed or not.

There is a single wage classification for all production workers, and a single classification for all maintenance workers (this is *not* utopia: the company and the union failed to find a way to get one classification for all workers, but they did come rather close). The salaries of the workers are about $1.55 an hour above the industry average.

There is a two-year training program for all workers (including classes on problem solving, communications, leadership, and conflict resolution).

There are no grievance or arbitration procedures.

Grievance and arbitration procedures were seen as unnecessary because the plant is governed democratically by a series of *joint* worker–manager committees, starting at the shop-floor level with problem-solving committees made up of every member of every work crew, and spreading to elected plant-wide committees, such as the Common Interest Committee, which has the power to take on any issue it chooses to consider. The plant Safety Committee not only sets rules, but has the authority to make expenditures to improve physical working conditions as well. Another committee develops manuals to show how to repair the plant's complex machinery. Another joint committee has authority to make contributions to local community activities (a function that is considered particularly important by the racially-integrated work force). To deal with unusual problems, a union official is permanently available at the plant's personnel office. In case of emergency, there is a direct telephone "hot line" linking union and corporate headquarters.

Most important in terms of productivity and worker commitment, each self-managing crew has *full* responsibility for accomplishing its own work. It is up to the crew to decide who will do what tasks, and how those tasks will be done. (Reflecting the different interests and styles of the crews, each has developed its own work methods and procedures.)

Union and management have agreed not to disclose the name or location of this plant in order to keep pesky media types from turning it into a fishbowl. And while the company is unwilling to disclose how profitable the plant is, it admits that productivity has far outpaced the predictions engineers had made based on the capabilities of the technology employed. (The company nevertheless has a policy of full disclosure to the workers and the union of all managerial and financial information.)

For their part, workers apparently like what is happening. In two and a half years of operation the absenteeism rate in the plant has been less than 1 percent and there has been no measurable turnover. Given that the average age of the workers in this plant is in the low twenties, this is a remarkable record of responsibility and stability. The company and the union seem to think so: They are now making plans to adopt similar practices in other plants.

In comparing this organization to the sick ones described above, certain observations can be made and tentative conclusions drawn (these conclusions are buttressed by the arguments in the chapters that follow).

In all organizations the effort and output of workers is governed by decisions made by managers. When work is organized in traditional ways, many workers are quite willing to slide along, producing at low levels, watching the clock, and waiting to collect their paychecks. But when managers organize work appropriately, worker effort and output are high. While it is not possible to define what is "appropriate" for all workers and all work places, it does appear that productivity increases when workers are given full responsibility for the quantity and quality of their work. Although workers have a wide variety of interests, needs, desires, and motivations, they almost all seem to respond when managers tie responsibilities to rights, for this, in effect, "individualizes" each job. Changing the philosophy and organization of work to make this tie—while in itself a complex and difficult task for managers—isn't sufficient. Workers seem willing to accept responsibilities only when they share directly in the financial gains that result from their increased output—or when they indirectly benefit as shareholders of stock in the companies in which they work.

Thus the prescription for increased productivity is simple: Managers must increase the responsibilities of workers, and give them a real stake in the enterprise. The effort this would entail is considerable. Not only does it mean that managers would have to work harder themselves, but they would also have to adopt an entirely new way of thinking about their role. In effect, *the culture of management must change,* a task far more difficult to accomplish than changing national economic policies.

But it can be done. When the Quasar division of Motorola was making televisions in its Chicago plant in the early 1970s, the predominantly minority work force labored in dirty conditions with inappropriate equipment. For example, there was an old belt-type assembly line that ran continuously—even if a worker had left his station and had not installed his part of the set. Consequently the TV set would continue down the line, into retail stores, and finally into homes, *sans* an essential part. The quality of the TV sets was so poor that there was a 60% in-plant rejection rate. That is, about two-thirds of the sets produced were sent to "rework" departments. This cost the company about $22 million annually. Reviewing the situation, the company concluded that it was impossible to make televisions economically in the United States. In their wisdom, Motorola's managers decided that there was nothing they could do to compete successfully with "cheap and docile" foreign labor. They therefore sold the division.

When Matsushita purchased the division in 1974, the new Japanese managers cleaned up the work environment and made some relatively simple changes in the equipment. For example, they added a foot pedal at each work station that allowed workers to stop the assembly line when they left their stations or had not completed their assignments. Another major change was to involve workers in managerial processes. Each day all assembly operations halt for a meeting during which workers are asked if they have any problems completing their tasks or have any ideas for improving productivity or quality. Under Japanese management there is only a 1 percent rate of quality rejection, and production of TV sets has increased from one thousand to two thousand a day with the same size work force.

There is an important lesson here: Japanese and German products have captured American markets not because foreigners are better workers or are paid less. The real advantage that foreign competitors enjoy is workers who feel a greater loyalty toward the company that employs them and a greater commitment to making quality products. This is the case in part because social values are different abroad than at home, and because Japanese and German workers are still responding to the aftermath of World War II. But as the Quasar case illustrates, these factors do not explain the entire difference. The key is that Japanese and German managers give their workers both appropriate equipment to do their jobs and responsibility for quality control and other key decisions that affect productivity. Significantly these appropriate tools are, in many instances, not expensive high technologies that American companies could not afford without changes in national tax policy. And the responsibilities are ones that are particularly important to young, educated Americans and to women and minority workers who have just joined the work force and are said to be less productive than older, white, men workers. These responsibilities give these new workers a say in the "system" that they correctly or incorrectly feel excludes them from full participation.

Thus Japanese managers have no magic formula for success. They adhere to no scientific principles of management, nor do they believe in any universal psychology of human needs, values, and satisfactions. Instead they are willing to leave their offices for the shop floor, to roll up their sleeves, and to work closely with their employees to help them solve problems. Above all, Japanese managers solicit and carefully consider the ideas that workers offer for improving quality and productivity. While this book is not about the Japanese system of management, it is about the need for American managers to roll up their sleeves and help their employees find better and more productive ways to organize work. (In fact, the key to the success of Japanese corporations has been that they rely on banks as their prime source of financing, whereas U.S. corporations rely on the stock market. Since banks take a long-term perspective on business, and stock markets are driven by short-term considerations, Japanese managers thus enjoy a greater luxury in planning ahead. The second key to the success of the Japanese is their national culture. Thus, it is impossible for America to transfer, or even translate for domestic use, the two major sources of Japanese success. Nonetheless, worker participation in decision-making was originally an *American* idea—we merely have not practiced it to the extent the Japanese have in imitation.)

Fortunately for the country, some American managers are starting to accept this challenge. One of the first to do so was Rene McPherson, recently retired chief executive officer of the Dana Corporation, whose business philosophy reflects a realistic appraisal of where managers have gone wrong and what they should do about it. McPherson says, "I am opposed to the idea that less government, fewer regulations, capital-formation incentives, and renewed research and development activity are what are needed most to improve productivity. My suggestion: Let our people 'get the job done.' " In the pages that follow, we shall see how McPherson—and a few dozen like-minded managers in other successful American corporations—have created work environments that allow their employees to "get the job done."

In brief, here is the message of this book: Underlying America's economic problems of the 1980s are deep and massive movements along a societal fault line, including (1) changes in demographics that have brought into the work force a generation of young workers—the largest cohort in the nation's history—whose prime social experience has been the trauma of the Vietnam era; (2) changes in the family that have forever altered the relationship of men and women, and have brought millions of women into the work force with a heightened sense of what is their due; and (3) radical changes in the society in general that have altered the nature of what is acceptable authority in all institutions, including work places. These and other changes in social values have led to new expectations about work, expectations that managers have thus far been unable to meet. As a result, there has been a decline in the willingness to work hard, productivity has decreased, and the seemingly endless escalator to affluence has ceased its steady upward progression. Unfortunately worker expectations are predicated on economic progress, growth, and the assumption that things will be better next year than they are this year. Thus negative reinforcement is built into the system: Less effort at work leads to lower productivity, lower productivity leads to unfilled expectations, and unfilled expectations lead to even less effort at work.

The managerial challenge of the 1980s is to find ways to break this syndrome by creating a philosophy and organization of work that is responsive to the underlying shifts in social values and expectations. What makes this task so difficult is that no single monolithic solution will be appropriate. People, companies, and work tasks are too complex and varied in modern America to lend themselves to simple or ideological solutions.

While the challenge is formidable, it cannot be ignored without running the risk of unraveling the fabric of democracy. The challenge must be met if America is to achieve its promise of a high standard of living and high quality of life for all its citizens. Those goals simply cannot be achieved in a just and fair fashion without increased productivity.

Such a challenge is not for the faint-hearted. For those willing to accept it, a convenient place to start the process of rethinking the philosophy and organization of work is at the place of greatest confusion: the misunderstood concept of productivity.

2

DECLINING GROWTH AND
DECLINING PRODUCTIVITY

AT the most abstract level the issue of work in America is synonymous with the issue of what kind of society America wants in the future. Thus it is appropriate to begin an inquiry into the problems of work on the high plane of inquiry about social justice. The greatest political economists of the last two centuries have all addressed themselves to a common question: How can a just society be created? Although Adam Smith, Karl Marx, J. S. Mill, Lord Keynes, and such contemporaries as J. K. Galbraith and Milton Friedman have real and obvious differences of opinion about what constitutes justice, these economists all agree that the ultimate goal of the "dismal science" is to find the best way for society to satisfy the basic needs of all its members. And not merely their physical needs. Recall that Smith cared about restoring to consumers the sovereignty that had been lost to state-granted monopolies; Marx was concerned with ending work-place alienation; Mill sought to create equality of opportunity for women and for people of all social classes; and Friedman's highest aim is to secure political liberty. The great economists have thus all placed noneconomic goals higher than purely physical or monetary goals.

Although most contemporary economists have forsaken this great tradition of political economy in favor of econometrics and other scientistic pursuits, a few still continue to ask the ultimate question. But during the last decade a twist has been added to that question. Today we ask: How can a just society be created *in a world of limited natural resources?*

THE GROWTH PROBLEM

This little addendum seems almost insignificant given the immensity of the basic question, but the added clause has had the effect of bringing traditional economic thinking into question. For all traditional economists, regardless of their ideological proclivities, believe that *societies must grow their way to justice.* If Marxists can't have economic growth, they cannot achieve their cherished egalitarian dreams. If libertarians can't have economic growth, they can't have their cherished freedom. And so on down the line, the achievement of the primary goal of every traditional political/economic philosophy is predicated on the efficient utilization of the factors of production to maximize growth. Growth, in sum, is seen by all economists as the means to the higher ends they pursue.

While the ideas of economists are seldom right, they are, alas, invariably influential. We recall Lord Keynes's famous (and only slightly hyperbolic) statement that the notions of economists

> both when they are right and when they are wrong, are more powerful than is commonly understood. Indeed the world is ruled by little else. Practical men, who believe themselves to be quite exempt from any intellectual influences, are usually the slaves of some defunct economist. Madmen in authority, who hear voices in the air, are distilling their frenzy from some academic scribbler of a few years back.[1]

And, Keynes might have added, the content and organization of work created by industrial engineers, corporate managers, trade unionists, and psychologists also is ruled by the basic assumptions of economists. In particular, nearly every major theory about work-place organization, worker motivation, and job satisfaction is predicated on the unstated assumption of economic growth. Indeed these theories *depend* on growth for their successful application.

I challenge the skeptical reader to examine any leading philosophy of work to see if the goals of that philosophy could be achieved without high rates of economic growth. To illustrate my point, let me take the most difficult case, that of B. F. Skinner. Arguably, the industrial applications of his theory of "behavior modification" are unconsciously predicated on a future of growing resources, for Skinner's brave new world *depends* on an overflowing cornucopia of goodies from which to bribe workers to do good. Even Maslow's humanistic hierarchy of needs is based on continuing economic growth. To Maslow, scarcity was a thing of the past, assumed away as America entered a new era of affluence and abundance. And the trade unionist psychology, expressed eloquently and precisely by Samuel Gompers in one word, "More," requires no elaboration on its attitude towards growth. Finally, consider the clearest case: F. W. Taylor's scientific management, the sum and substance of which is the efficient maximization of output. Taylorism is merely the translation of economics into psychology.

With the notable exception of E. F. Schumacher, all major writers who have addressed the issues of the structure and functions of work have assumed economic growth as the basis for funding the alternative systems of rewards and incentives they have proposed. Look closely, and I suggest the reader will find the unstated assumption of continued economic growth underlying even the writings of the last two generations of organizational theorists, including Peter Drucker, Douglas MacGregor, David McClelland, Warren Bennis, Frederick Herzberg, and Rensis Likert. Like political economists, these scholars are interested in creating greater social justice. Their specific concern, of course, is justice in the work place. And as with the economists, growth is the means to the higher goals they pursue. Whether their goal is self-actualization, job satisfaction, individual development, greater equality, or whatever, economic growth is unconsciously factored into their thinking as the means to pay for the greater justice they envision. For example: One simply cannot imagine workers achieving self-actualization in a stagnating economy or in a firm that is retrenching. At any rate, no student of work has ever advanced a theory of organizational development or behavior on the assumption of declining growth, hard times, or the end of abundance.

While it is a matter of considerable controversy whether America's economy can or should grow again at the rates that were common before the 1970s, it nevertheless is a fact that few economists *expect* America to return to these high rates of growth. The U.S. economy is currently not experiencing much real growth, and economists argue that it is highly unlikely that the country will soon return to the boom conditions of the 1950s, primarily because those good times were fueled by cheap and abundant energy. And no expert is forecasting cheap and abundant energy to flow again in the next two decades.

We are now getting close to defining the central work-place problem that arises in America as the result of slowing economic growth: *There is a mismatch between the philosophy and organization of work on the one hand, and economic reality on the other.* The symptoms of the mismatch abound: high inflation, low productivity, declining innovation, a drop in the relative value of the dollar, the increasing export of jobs to foreign competitors. While this mismatch is not the simple, proximate cause of these symptoms, it is a major contributing factor to them all.

The current system breeds demands for more money, benefits, and entitlements from work, while at the same time ensuring that less and less time and effort will be expended at work. This is admittedly a strong assertion that will require the entire next chapter to make convincingly. But first, are there any clear economic indicators of this hypothesized mismatch?

Importantly, this phenomenon is not restricted to the much-publicized unionized workers who demand and receive more for doing less—and in the process price the products they make out of world markets. In fact, almost all American workers are joyful riders of the same economic escalator. For example, doctors who once engaged in solo practice now organize themselves into partnerships, the purposes of which are to reduce financial risk and individual responsibility, while increasing income, benefits, and, in particular, time off from work. This game is played in different ways to achieve similar ends by every occupation from accountant to zoologist. Blue collar and white collar, laborer and manager, service worker and professional, we *all* want more pay for working and producing less.

While this pattern is a "normal" outcome of affluence, in turn it generates a series of undesirable by-products. For example, the liberal economist Sidney Weintraub has recently written that the major cause of inflation in America is that everyone—from workers on the shop floor to corporate chief executives—is demanding hefty raises, even while he or she is working less or producing less. Writes Weintraub:

> Average pay increases for the year may hit about 8 percent for 1979, while employee productivity has been declining by about 2.5 percent. An inflationary price upheaval must invariably ensue to fill the void. The income-productivity tug-of-war is the inexorable fact blithely ignored as we castigate the Arabs, the Ayatollah, Government largesse, Government regulation, lax money policy, rapacious business firms or aggressive labor unions. It is a mad assault on the laws of arithmetic to grab 8, 10, 25 percent more while productivity inches by slight 1 percent doses, as it has done throughout most of the 1970's in this country. Money incomes in England leaped by about 20 percent in 1974, and prices followed suit. Similar experiments in squaring the circle were performed in Australia and Canada. . . .
>
> Everybody wants more money, and enough people are now in a position to get it, regardless of whether they have increased their productivity, to create severe economic problems.[2]

While it is rare to find agreement among economists, Weintraub's views are shared by the conservative economist, Irving Friedman, who ties together the problems of inflation and productivity, and shows that they are rooted in changes in social values:

The basic causes of modern inflation differ greatly from whose of classic inflation. They are not confined to the economic field of human activity only, but are now deeply rooted in society and in its political, social, and psychological structures. For these reasons I call them societal causes. The single most important cause is . . . [that] demand is no longer strictly related to contributions to the productive process. . . .

The fact that societies are simply not producing enough to meet the[ir] requirements has begun to be more generally realized, but it has not yet been translated into major redefinitions of expectations and priorities. People continue to expect more than can be effectively given by their economy.[3]

THE PRODUCTIVITY PROBLEM

The clearest single indicator of the problem at hand is a *decreasing national productivity/labor cost ratio.* Note that I did not write *the* ratio, for unfortunately there are no reliable national measures of productivity. In fact, productivity is the fuzziest economic concept in common use. Common sense tells us that productivity is the measure of how efficiently management uses all resources—people, machines, materials—to make a product or deliver a service. But in practice, when the government measures productivity, it focuses its attention solely on one of these resources, people. "Labor productivity" is officially defined as output per hour worked. Let us briefly review how the government keeps its famous productivity accounts, starting with the agricultural sector where output is easiest to measure.

For example, in 1977, 4 percent of the nation's work force directly produced more tons of food than 16 percent of the nation's work force had in 1947. This reduction in the number of American farm workers—and the increase in their output—is a clear example of a gain in real productivity. The increase resulted from the automation of planting and harvesting, from more scientific breeding of animals and plants, and from better management of use of fertilizers, herbicides, and insecticides. Output in this example is easy to measure: in tons of grain per worker, in numbers of chickens slaughtered per worker, etc.

But the oft-quoted industrial productivity figures are not based on the output of things. Rather these famous numbers represent the dollar value of output, which is used as a proxy for the output of things (this is necessary because it is impossible to find another standard measure for the output of such diverse things as automobiles, books, and pigs). This homogenization leads to absurdities in the national accounts. For example, in Corporation X it might have taken the equivalent of ten workers one day to build a car that sold for $4,000 over cost of inputs in 1976. But in 1977 fashions might have changed so that the company found itself with another Corvette Sting Ray or T-Bird on its hands that it could sell for $8,000 over the cost of inputs. In the national accounts the productivity of these ten workers would have doubled, even though it still would take them a day to build the same car, at the same wages.

There are even greater distortions with the measures of the output of the majority of workers—those who produce services rather than things. The output of teachers, doctors, musicians, janitors, and bureaucrats is also measured in terms of its dollar value. Thus a pop singer who earns $2 million for a single concert is considered to be a hundred times more productive than a garbage collector who works six days a week for $20,000 a year.

As if this weren't bad enough, there is no way of measuring the relative importance of the various factors of production—land, labor, and capital —to increases in manufacturing productivity. In their *1979 Report* the president's Council of Economic Advisers claimed that only one-half the decline in productivity growth in the 1970s could be accounted for by (1) lower rates of investment in new capital, (2) the entry of women and youth into the work force, and (3) the increase in governmental regulation of business. They could not explain the cause of the other half of the decline. Edward F. Denison of the Brookings Institution suggested such explanations as the decline in the number of hours worked, the costs of employee crime, and the changing economies of scale—still he admitted that he couldn't account for one-half of the observed drop in productivity.[4]

Moreover international comparisons of productivity are all but meaningless. For example, because Mexico has not started from the same base point as the United States, it is easier for Mexico to increase its productivity (a few new plants and a spurt in oil production will send their figures through the roof) than it is for the United States, where thousands of factories would have to be modernized to get the same relative effect. It even is difficult to compare one advanced country with another: Neither Japan nor Germany have a services sector anywhere near as large as America's. It may also turn out that Japanese workers are willing to work hard now only because they recently lived at a subsistence level—they may ease off when they, like Americans, have been affluent for a generation. A meaningful relative comparison would be to wait until a Japanese or European worker is paid exactly what an American worker in the same industry using the same technology is paid, then measure their productivity in terms of the output of *things* over time.

At this point, a key question arises.

To What Extent Is Labor a Factor in Productivity?

Ironically, even though labor is the only factor that the official rates of productivity purportedly measure, many economists go so far as to argue that workers have little or nothing to do with productivity. While this is somewhat accurate for many of the 1–2 percent of workers who "man" machine-paced technologies (such as assembly lines), it is not fully accurate for almost all white-collar service, professional, technical, clerical, and managerial workers, nor for most blue-collar construction, skilled, and semiskilled workers. Most machines depend on humans: There are typists capable of low productivity on even the latest $8,500 IBM typewriter. Paradoxically, capital-intensive high technologies are particularly sensitive to human performance. For example, in multimillion-dollar chemical plants and other facilities that use continuous-process technologies in which machines "do all the work," proactive human intervention is required to avoid expensive (and sometimes dangerous) downtime: witness Three Mile Island. In fact, it is nearly impossible to design the human factor out of any work system. Tom Wolfe documents the efforts of NASA engineers to design spacecraft that could be operated, literally, by a monkey.[5] Nonetheless pilot error led to the only major manned space mishaps, and pilot initiative and skill led to successful flights in several instances of machine failure. Workers also find ways of designing themselves into automated processes. For example, workers discovered how to insinuate themselves into "foolproof" processes on the world's most highly automated auto assembly line at Lordstown (see Chapter 5). And Wolfe reports that when the astronauts started their training, they redesigned the pilot right back into the system to the consternation of the engineers. Significantly, when productivity is measured on a micro or plant level, the human factor looms large. For example, in organizations with multiple plants—all using the same technology, all the same size—there are almost always observable differences in the amount of things produced per worker per hour. It is accurate to say, then, that humans are still more important than machines in most work environments—particularly in a postindustrial economy like ours where, by definition, more workers work with their heads than with their hands. Much of the recent decrease in official rates of productivity is to be found in the *non*manufacturing, *non*agricultural sectors. In retail trade and services productivity is about 40 percent below the average for the entire economy. (Nonetheless even brain workers need more productive machines. One shouldn't just assume that a machine will miraculously design, run, and repair itself.)

The decreasing productivity/labor cost ratio can also be explained by the rapid influx of "marginal" workers into the American labor force. What

makes these workers (youth, women, and minorities) "marginal" is *not*
that they are lazy or untrained (youth and women, in particular, are better
educated—if not trained—than the average "nonmarginal" worker), but
that they have different work values and expectations. While I return to
examine this important point in detail later, it requires a brief explanatory
note here. What must be understood is that the productivity of these new
workers is greatly influenced by the decisions made by—and examples set
by—managers and executives. Given the proper work environment, there
is considerable evidence that most of these "marginal" workers can
become fully productive. Curiously, while almost all workers seem to
believe that they can be more productive given appropriate working
conditions, few managers believe this to be the case. What is particularly
strange, is that while managers deny that proper conditions will elicit
greater *worker* productivity, they believe that proper conditions will elicit
greater managerial productivity.

In a recent survey by the newsletter *Productivity,* 80 percent of 221
managers polled cited "poor management" as the prime cause of low
productivity.[6] Characteristically, these managers did not see workers
making an important contribution either way to output. Without engaging
in too much amateur psychology, one might posit that managers have ego
needs that require them to believe that only they have wisdom or power to
affect output, or *should* have such wisdom and power. That only they have
the power is undeniable. It is over the issue of the allocation of wisdom
where workers and managers find themselves in disagreement.

Perceptions of Personal Productivity

In 1978 pollster Louis Harris asked 1,047 office employees—managers,
supervisors, and clerical workers—if they could work harder if they tried,
and if they would be more productive if their work were redesigned.[7]

Q: Being honest with yourself, do you feel you and your work colleagues certainly
do as much work as you reasonably can, probably do as much as you can, or do you
ever feel you could probably do more work?

(Number of respondents)	Total (1047)	Management (221)	Supervisory (205)	Regular Worker (597)
	%	%	%	%
Certainly do as much as can	42	36	43	43
Probably do as much as can	22	24	23	22

		Job Level		
(Number of respondents)	Total (1047)	Manage- ment (221)	Super- visory (205)	Regular Worker (597)
Could probably do more	34	39	32	32
Not sure/no answer	2	—	2	3

Q: Well, if the conditions and circumstances you work in were changed, then do you think you could certainly do more work in a day than you do now, or not?

		Job Level		
(Number of respondents)	Total (1047)	Manage- ment (221)	Super- visory (205)	Regular Worker (597)
	%	%	%	%
Could do more	74	67	71	77
Could not	23	32	25	19
Not sure/no answer	3	1	4	4

Harris found that in addition to feeling their jobs were designed in such a way as to limit their output, workers believed they had little incentive to work harder. In the same survey 73 percent of the office employees felt that management benefited "a lot" from increased productivity, but only 44 percent felt that workers benefited "a lot." In 1972 Harris polled the general public and found that 67 percent believed "companies benefit from increased productivity at the expense of workers," and only 20 percent believed that "employees benefited a lot from increased productivity."[8]

Professional, Technical, and Managerial Productivity

Management consultant James A. Fields estimates that the average worker is productive only 55 percent of the time he is on the job.[9] About 15 percent of his effort is lost to "normal personal time," but 30 percent is lost through scheduling problems, unclear assignments, improper staffing, and poor discipline. With the possible exception of the last reason given, all these causes of low productivity are amenable only to *managerial* actions.

The contribution to output of some higher-salaried workers could be viewed in an even harsher light. There are those who would argue that many corporate accountants, lawyers and finance people are mere "over-head"—that is, they contribute nothing to the process of production and should be treated only as costs of doing business. While I personally find this view rather harsh, there is no doubt that measuring the productivity of people whose only product is paper is nearly impossible, and leads to some zany accounting procedures at the Bureau of Labor Statistics. Let me cite a wild, but nonetheless instructive, illustration: If my hometown Los Angeles is any example, the actual amount of working and producing among professional, technical, and managerial workers is probably lower than Fields' estimate for the work force as a whole. Apparently a prodigious amount of output is lost because extramarital liaisons are conducted on company time.[10] Interestingly, the time spent in such affairs is counted as productive time in the national accounts because high-level workers are paid their salaries whether or not they are engaged in their jobs during work hours. Contrariwise, if a plumber or secretary (or any other worker who is paid by the hour) philanders between eight and five on a weekday, official productivity is reckoned to fall. If nothing else, this invidious distinction requires some readjustment of the national productivity figures!

Is Productivity a Meaningless Term?

In short, the official measures of productivity are nearly valueless, particularly for services, because where salaries are used as proxies, productivity measures are no more than tautologies. *Nevertheless productivity is a real and important concept.* Even if we can't define it or measure it, we spot it in a rising standard of living when it is going up, and we recognize its reflection in a declining standard of living when it is going down. Today many American products are being priced out of world markets, unemployment and inflation are rising, and the American standard of living is not improving as rapidly as the standards of living in Japan and northern Europe. Using their traditional measures, economists can only identify the causes of half of this problem. A great part of the half that is unaccounted for must be due to the existing philosophy and organization of work (and to such related issues as unions holding productivity down from fear of potential job losses). The burden of the subsequent four chapters is to present evidence that this is the case.

To make this case, a working (or workable) definition of productivity is required. At the least, there must be some agreement about what is *not* meant when the concept is employed in the analyses that follow.

Since the *official measure of productivity* is constantly confused with the more concrete concepts of *producing* and *working,* it is useful to sort out these three terms in order to clarify just what is meant when the word productivity is used in these pages.

Official Productivity. As defined by the Bureau of Labor Statistics, this is the dollar value of output per employee per hour. This is *not* what is meant by productivity in this book because, as I have explained, it is impossible to tell if an increase in dollar value represents an increase in the volume of goods produced or some other factor unrelated to how hard or efficiently employees or machines are working. Indeed when dollar value of output is the measure, official productivity can actually fall even though workers and machines are producing at a constant rate and cost; witness the decline in the official rates of productivity when an auto manufacturer gives a $500 rebate to the purchasers of new cars.

Producing. This is the output of "things" per employee per hour. "Things" includes ideas, services, and managerial inputs as well as goods. It is thus the measure of the actual work that is accomplished, not the dollar value of that work. For the reasons given in the definition of official productivity, a worker's *official productivity* may not rise even if he is *producing* more. Moreover a worker might produce more, but actually be *working* less—as when some of his labor is replaced by a machine.

Working. An increase in *working* occurs when an employee puts in more time or effort, or higher-quality time or effort on the job. For example, when a worker finds ways to reduce costs or waste, he is increasing the amount he is working. While increases in *working* will almost always lead to increases in *producing,* they may not lead to increases in *official productivity.*

This book is concerned only with working and producing, and not with the official rates of productivity (that is why the reader will search in vain for those famous charts showing a drop in productivity over the last decade; we must not be concerned here with what may be no more than a statistical artifact that has nothing to do with the efforts of workers and managers.) When the word *productivity* appears in these pages, it never refers to the dollar value of output or to any measure other than of working and producing.

While it is impossible to *prove* that too many Americans demand (and receive) more money for working less and producing less, most economists and observers of the labor scene nevertheless have a strong gut feeling that this is a major and growing problem in America. Significantly this conclusion comes not from antilabor sources, but from such prolabor economists as Sidney Weintraub (see above) and John Kenneth Galbraith. Writes Galbraith:

> With industrial maturity and increasing affluence, people like hard work less and work less hard. Worker productivity declines. The effect is greatest in industries such as textiles, automobiles, crude steel and ship-building, which are characterized by simple, tedious and repetitive work.
>
> In the younger industrial countries like Japan, the change in attitude is less marked than in older ones such as Britain and the United States. But even Japan feels pressure from the more eager workers of South Korea and Taiwan. Germany, France and Switzerland have been able to compensate for the drop in productivity by bringing in foreign workers from Yugoslavia, Italy, Spain and Portugal. For these migrating workers, industrial work compares favorably with their previous harsh rural existence.[11]

Galbraith is careful *not* to say that American workers are being paid too much per se, or even that their salaries are going up at too fast a rate. For the fact of the matter is that the salaries of workers in Japan and Europe have risen faster over the last decade than those of American workers, and total compensation costs in most of these countries is now about on a par with America. Nor is this to say that American workers are lazy, greedy, or culpable for the sorry state of the American economy. No, to make any sense out of what is happening in American industry, it is necessary to analyze worker expectations, compensation, productivity, and working conditions *simultaneously*. As I illustrate in the next three chapters, to treat these parts as if they were unrelated to one another will not lead to a real comprehension of what is going on in American work places or to an understanding of how to turn the problem around. For the problem is a *relational* one: The total output of workers has been decreasing *relative* to their total compensation.

In summary, there are many reasons why America is experiencing a decreasing productivity/labor cost ratio. Some of these reasons are technological, some are due to unwise governmental policies, and some to exogenous factors such as rising oil costs that make once-productive machines (like Boeing 707s) prohibitively expensive to operate. Moreover mismanagement contributes to the nation's low productivity when corporations like Chrysler choose to produce goods that will not sell either at home or abroad. But though these are all important factors, the truth of the matter is that nobody knows how much new machines would raise productivity or what the impact of rising energy prices has been. Using official measures of productivity, we cannot tell how much worker efforts could reverse it. The only facts we have in hand are the cases presented later in this book which demonstrate marked increases in the efficiency and effectiveness of workers when managers design jobs to capture workers' full productive capacities. This is not to say that energy and machines are unimportant factors in productivity but, taken together, they explain only a fraction of the problem—albeit the most easily measured part (which economists too often treat as if it were the whole). *In addition to these factors I suggest that America has an inappropriate philosophy and organization of work for an era of declining growth.* America is now in a double-bind. As its workers become more affluent, they want to work less. Less work lowers real productivity and economic growth. But affluence also creates demands for higher salaries and higher benefits. Thus in the decade ahead it is highly *un*likely that we will experience the productivity and economic growth needed to finance the higher compensation demanded by workers.

The next two chapters explore how the nation got into this bind and examine some of the future consequences of a continuation of the current philosophy and organization of work.

3

RIGHTS WITHOUT RESPONSIBILITIES

AMERICAN workers have been conditioned by experience constantly to expect more from work—more money, more fringe benefits, better working conditions—while producing less and putting in less time and effort on the job. Wanting more for less is not a problem if the engine of economic growth is running in fine tune. But the engine has started to knock. Productivity has faltered. Now the nation seems no longer able to sustain the level of output necessary to satisfy the ever-rising level of worker expectations.

There would thus seem to be a need for a philosophy and an organization of work that do not depend on rapid and constant economic growth. But herein lies the double-bind: The search for such an alternative is immediately frustrated by the fact that *worker expectations* are predicated on growth.

A simple way out of the bind suggests itself: change worker expectations. Unfortunately there is nothing simple about changing social attitudes and expectations. Of course such values do change, but slowly and only when workers are confronted with a reality that consistently demonstrates the inappropriateness of their present values. Because American workers are currently receiving go-go signals—particularly from the media, employers, unionists, and elected officials who deny the need to switch to policies consistent with slower growth—they see no convincing reason to change their values. Change is particularly difficult in this case because worker expectations have been transformed into rights; during the last two decades a host of personal needs have been translated into entitlements. These new entitlements include health care, cost-of-living allowances, vested pensions, maternity benefits, educational tuition remission, job security, promotions, and even the right to the job itself in the face of plant closings and redundancies. Although it is possible to alter a privilege, rights are by definition guaranteed, inalienable, and unalterable.

Paradoxically this new rights consciousness among American workers waxed just at the time America's economic fortunes began to wane. Once the wealthiest nation in the world, America now stands ninth in per capita income, behind Switzerland, Denmark, Sweden, West German, Norway, Belgium, Luxemburg, and Iceland. Seemingly impervious to this relative slippage, Americans demand not only (1) new rights but also (2) "zero risk," and (3) increased "selfishness" even as the national economy falters. Let me quickly review these three complementary components of the peculiar value system of the 1970s, to understand better how work has come to be thought of as it is, and how it is likely to be viewed in the future.

THE ENTITLEMENTS CONSCIOUSNESS

The late Arthur Okun[1] divided the "things" provided by a society into two categories: (1) entitlements, or things due to all individuals as rights by virtue of their membership in the society; and (2) market goods and services, or things that are distributed unequally by virtue of individual preferences, luck, hard work, merit, or intelligence. In general, then, entitlements promote equality, while the marketplace promotes inequality. Significantly, several changes are occurring in the composition and characteristics of both these categories.

· The dimensions of rights have expanded *horizontally* to include larger and larger portions of the total population. Consider how the notion of what defines a citizen with full and equal social and political rights has expanded in the United States over the last two hundred years. At the time of the Revolutionary War the only people with full rights were white male property owners over the age of twenty-one. By the Civil War property qualifications for the right to vote were disappearing, and black males started to become full citizens shortly thereafter. By the middle of the twentieth century women started to achieve full rights. Now one hears talk about the rights of children, of the handicapped, of aliens, of prisoners, of homosexuals, and even of fetuses.

· The dimensions of rights have also expanded *vertically,* so that *every* individual is now entitled to a greater number of things that were formerly in the realm of individual obligations. As this occurred, the focus of rights shifted from the traditional domain of *personal liberties* (the right to vote, to marry, to procreate, to emigrate, to equal justice before the law, and to freedom of speech and religion) to the broader area of *social entitlement* (the right to food, clothing, shelter, education, housing, health care, and an income).

· The concept of what constitutes a right underwent a radical transformation. In the Roosevelt era rights were tied to responsibilities; by the Lyndon Johnson era the tie between these concepts was broken. Okun suggests that it is instructive to look at changes in the old-age benefit laws to understand this transformation in the notion of rights. Under Roosevelt, the basic philosophy of Social Security was *contributory*, "stressing the obligation of people to provide for themselves."[2] But today contribution has been reduced as a requirement from most national social welfare programs. Contribution—that is, individual responsibilities—has become a quaint anachronism. The new values of entitlement—freed completely from the notion of individual responsibility—have spread from Social Security to almost every other aspect of working life.

· Whereas traditional rights were relatively cheap for society to provide (it costs the taxpayer little if his neighbor votes, goes to church, or decides to get married), the new social entitlements can be *extremely costly*. For example, if health care came to be defined as a right (as it is in England), its provision could cost the American taxpayer in excess of $200 billion (roughly $2,000 per each employed person). Admittedly the size of the current national bill for entitlements is problematic and controversial. But if one includes every service and benefit provided by government, the bill runs as high as one-third the gross national product. While this figure clearly overstates costs that most people consider social entitlements (it includes, for example, the entitlement to security against foreign aggression), it also *understates* the total bill because it excludes entitlements provided directly by employers to employees.

· There has been a trend toward *employer-provided* entitlements. These are mandated by the government (e.g., the minimum wage), voluntarily provided (e.g., private pensions), or contractually provided as the result of collective bargaining (e.g., dental plans). The total cost of fringe benefits (the most easily measured entitlements) went from 17 percent of the total compensation of workers in the private sector in 1966 to 21.8 percent in 1974. The figure for organized workers in 1974 was 24 percent.[3] In large corporations in the chemicals and primary metals industries, the figure was 43.3 percent in 1977.[4] The U.S. Chamber of Commerce reports that employee benefits cost a total of $310 billion in 1977, up from $100 billion in 1967.[5]

· The size of the entitlements domain has grown drastically at the expense of the market domain. Indeed, according to Burnham Beckwith (a quirky California sociologist), if current trends continue, over 50 percent of all *consumer* goods will be entitlements within the next century. Beckwith believes that entitlements "depend far more upon the degree of industrialization than upon the ideology of the government"[6] Because he sees growth in entitlements as an inevitable by-product of economic growth, Beckwith argues that the United States and the Soviet Union are both progressing towards the same mean of entitlements, and both societies will eventually provide the same kinds of free goods and services, with the same kinds of goods and services for sale in the market.

   · There are new demands for purely *social* employee entitlements, including:

The right to "blow the whistle" on illegal and unethical practices of employers.
The right to privacy (e.g., confidentiality of personnel files).
The right to conscientious objection to unethical orders.
The right to freedom in outside activities (e.g., political activities).
The right to sexual freedom (e.g., homosexual rights).
The right to freedom from sexual harassment by superiors.
The right to individual choice of appearance (e.g., for men to wear long hair and hippy beads in a bank teller's cage).
The right to vote on plant relocations.
The right to participate in all decisions directly affecting one's job.
The right to self-actualization on the job (i.e., the right to develop one's full productive potential).
The right to adequate leisure time (e.g., adequate time to spend with one's family).
The right to reject a cross-country transfer.
The right of all employees to full access to information about corporate activities.

   These expansions of, and changes in, the nature of worker and social entitlements do not, by themselves, constitute a problem. In fact, the manifest benefits of entitlements in reducing poverty, ill-health, discrimination, and inequality, and in increasing personal freedom and equality of opportunity, have been so great that few Americans bothered to question the costs involved when entitlements were being expanded prodigiously in the 1950s and 1960s. But recently a growing number of observers have been calling attention to the following kinds of problems or costs associated with the expansion of entitlements:

   · Entitlements are often in *conflict* with each other. Some firms are simultaneously faced with antidiscrimination and reverse discrimination suits. Other companies experience conflict between affirmative action and seniority rights.

· Entitlements, particularly such new rights as national health insurance, come at *high economic costs.* These are ultimately borne by taxpayers and consumers when entitlements reduce the nation's productivity and international economic competitiveness. For example, the National Planning Association has claimed that entitlements in Europe have pushed up production costs in some countries to the point where governments must subsidize certain domestic industries and impose import barriers.[7]

· Entitlements often require *government interference* with personal liberty and managerial prerogatives.

· Entitlements are *inefficient,* as is anything that by definition is given to all without regard to market constraints and that cannot be bought, sold, or traded. Because entitlements come without charge, people don't "economize" in their use.[8]

· Entitlements don't allow for *comparative advantage.* Since they go to everyone, they are used (or misused) by incompetents as well as by competents.[9]

· Entitlements do not serve as *incentives* because they are not distributed as rewards for performance.[10]

· Entitlements often reduce employee *loyalty, commitment,* and *discipline,* as I illustrate below. In the National Planning Association study referred to above, it was concluded that the high rate of entitlements in Europe increases absenteeism, turnover, and idleness, and adversely affects productivity.

· Entitlements add *administrative burdens or overhead costs.*

· Entitlements are a *fixed or uncontrollable cost* that can get out of hand rapidly, both in the public sector (e.g., Medicare) and in the private sector (e.g., pensions).

Whether such costs outweigh the benefits of a particular entitlement is a subjective value choice. Okun offers a neat little test, "The Leaky Bucket Experiment," for helping to decide how one feels about the cost of a particular entitlement.[11] Suppose a tax and income transfer program required that the money be carried from the rich to the poor in a leaky bucket (the leaks being, of course, all the inefficiencies described in the above list). The test is this: Would you favor the program if 10 percent of the money leaked out? Would you still favor it if 50 percent leaked? As Okun points out, Milton Friedman probably wouldn't tolerate much more than a 10 percent leakage, while John Rawls would keep filling the bucket even at a rate of 100 percent leakage! Though there is clearly no objective answer to how much leakage should be tolerated, it is probably within the realm of objectivity to claim that the total leakage from public and private entitlements is increasing in the United States. The reason for this increase in leakage (or social overhead, if you will) is simply that *demands* for new rights have increased dramatically in the last decade.

Daniel Bell was the first to identify, and Daniel Yankelovich has spent the last decade trying to measure, this new rights consciousness that transforms personal needs and privileges into social entitlements. The two Daniels entered a political lion's den when they took up the issue. For they argued that what was once viewed as a valuable benefit to be earned is today seen as an indispensable right, not given but *owed*. This is not an argument that is particularly appreciated by the New (or Old) Left, for it implies a kind of welfare-state paternalism and a corresponding erosion of moral fiber.

Yankelovich has found a distinct difference in attitudes about entitlements between the Baby Boom generation and their parents (whom I'll call the Depression Kids).[12] The under-thirty-fives are most concerned about purely social and psychological rights. For example, young workers feel they are entitled to self-actualization on the job and to a greater voice in the decisions that affect their jobs. Older workers, in contrast, tend to stress purely economic rights, such as pensions and job security.

For purposes of clarity, Yankelovich divides the work force into two broad but distinct categories:

1. *Traditionalists* are the shrinking majority (56 percent) of workers who are still motivated by money, status, and security. Included in this category are the older blue-collar workers for whom work is a habit, the older "silent majority" white-collar workers with conservative values and life-styles, and a small number of young "go-getters" who have traditional goals and life-styles (Jaycees, for example).
2. *Nontraditionalists* are the growing minority (44 percent) of the work force, almost all of whom are under thirty-five. This category includes the "turned-off," hedonistic, poorly educated, unencultured working-class and poverty youths. But most attention—perhaps unfairly—is paid to the larger category of highly educated, bright, creative, under-employed young people who have turned to leisure and nonwork avocations for the challenge and fulfillment they can't find at work.

Yankelovich found that only 21 percent of the nontraditionalists state that work means more to them than leisure.[13] The nontraditionalists' strongest demand for change in working conditions is more time away from the job. In fact, University of Michigan researchers have recently found that one-half of employed Americans report that they have problems with the inflexibility of their working schedules, and that the demands of work leave them with inadequate time for leisure activities.[14] One-third of these workers report that inconvenient or excessive working hours interfere with their family life. In a separate study, Fred Best of the Department of Labor found that 70 percent of American workers would be willing to give up 2 percent *or more* of their income for less time at work.[15] In particular, the workers said they would like to take this additional free time in the form of a sabbatical or a longer vacation.

Employers find that motivating this growing population of nontraditionalists is difficult. The threat of being fired doesn't work because welfare, unemployment compensation, food stamps, and other sources of income provide a cushion that turns brief spells of joblessness into vacations. Moreover because many young people have two-career marriages (and no children), one partner is always free to quit his or her job without a consequent severe drop in the family standard of living. (In 1977 fully 63 percent of the U.S. work force lived in multi-wage-earner families.) Often the carrot of money is not much of a motivator in these two-career marriages because, for example, a raise means only half as much as it does in a one-career marriage. All these factors add to the erosion of loyalty, motivation, and job commitment.

For predictive purposes, Yankelovich's findings add more to complexity than to clarification. For there are at least two reasonable interpretations. The first is that young people can be expected to follow in their parents' footsteps as they "mature," leaving behind youthful concerns for the quality of life and embracing "adult" concerns for security. The second interpretation is that values are determined more by experience than by age. Those who were at an impressionable age during the Depression (including all corporate executives aged sixty to sixty-five) had their values formed by the fact that they had trouble finding first jobs, that they had to postpone their educations and forgo the purchase not only of luxuries but also, in many instances, of necessities. Worse, they saw their adult relatives suffer the terror and humiliation of economic insecurity. It is not surprising that people who had so suffered would place security as the Sirius in their firmament of values.

In contrast, the postwar Boom Babies (the twenty-four to thirty-five-year-olds who are now on the bottom rungs of the organizations headed by the Depression Kids) were at an impressionable age during an era of incredible affluence. They saw blacks and women arguing to restructure centuries-old social patterns and, most excruciatingly, they were on the front line during the Vietnam protests. The brightest stars in their heaven of values are flexibility, choice, options, variety, and diversity. This is not to argue that they don't like money—human nature hasn't changed, just work values—but they see plenty of different avenues to material security.

If this second explanation is accurate, it could mean that the Boom Babies' values will dominate the work place of tomorrow, for by 1985 this postwar generation (the largest age cohort in the nation's history) will represent nearly a third of the entire U.S. work force.[16]

Indeed there is some evidence—although it is far from conclusive—that instead of young people growing out of their values, older Americans are growing into the Boom Babies' values. David Ewing of the *Harvard Business Review* has discovered a growing concern for the social rights of workers among the nation's business leaders.[17] Comparing the 1977 attitudes of corporate executives about employee rights to their attitudes in 1971, Ewing found a marked tendency among executives to be more tolerant of such rights as whistle blowing, privacy of personnel files, conscientious objection to unethical orders, "nonbusinesslike" dress and appearance on the job, employee voting on plant relocation, and the need for corporate ombudsmen. Clearly some values are contagious.

ZERO RISK

At the same time that this rights consciousness raising was going on, there was also a trend toward what Aaron Wildavsky calls the "chicken little" mentality—or the avoidance of all risk.[18] The clearest example of this is the famous Delaney Clause that requires the banning of any substance that is found to produce cancer in humans or animals. While zero risk has been applied most frequently to environmental and consumer issues, the notion has recently been extended to the work place, most notably and clearly in the area of occupational health and safety. For example, it used to be that a steeplejack assumed all the risks of his dangerous job. Today he is protected by OSHA (Occupational Safety and Health Administration), workers' compensation, health insurance, and disability insurance, all of which seem only fair to most people. But workers can't take risks even if they want to: Witness the safety lines and nets that circus high-wire acrobats are now forced to use. Most controversially, the reduction of risk goes beyond physical safety. Because of unemployment insurance and so forth, individuals today bear far less economic risk or job insecurity. For example, recent court rulings have made it increasingly difficult to fire even the most undeserving employees. A Brooklyn College professor is suing his college on the grounds that he was fired because he is an alcoholic, and the government is arguing that it is illegal for colleges to prefer sober professors to alcoholics because alcoholics are considered handicapped persons under the 1973 Rehabilitation Act.

Government regulations dealing with affirmative action also reduce the risks of workers. Indeed affirmative action can be viewed as the ultimate in risk reduction because it provides insurance against the "bad luck" of having been born black or female. Add to these trends the power of labor unions, unemployment benefits, and cost-of-living adjustments[19] and it is clear that the vast majority of workers are more secure today than ever before in America's history.

Thus a major reason why young people are apparently *un*concerned with material security may well be that they already have all the security they could possibly need. Indeed it is this security that makes possible both rights consciousness and zero risk. Today individual risk is socialized. As Wildavsky points out, this does not mean that risks are reduced; they are merely displaced. Health insurance doesn't make people any healthier, or reduce the overall costs of health care. In fact, what is controversial about such programs of social insurance is that they put bystanders, third parties, or society in general at risk. For example, there is evidence that individuals covered by workers' compensation behave more irresponsibly on the job than they would if they didn't have this accident insurance (or if there were a penalty for fault).[20] And recent studies show that individuals with unemployment insurance are less likely to look for work than those without it.[21]

What is significant about zero risk is its cost. Economists demonstrate rather convincingly that the marginal costs of reducing risk increase exponentially as the zero state is approached. For example, the costs of providing due process for employees is manageable, acceptable, and justifiable on a cost/benefit basis. But experience in Italy, where *every* employee has tenure, shows that the costs of zero risk of termination are unacceptably high in terms of lost labor force mobility and productivity. (See pp. 41) Ironically, in the United States demands for zero risk are increasing just as the economic growth that might have paid for it is giving out.

THE "CULTURE OF NARCISSISM"

Christopher Lasch has recently described "American life in an age of diminishing expectations."[22] He notes that for the first time in recent American history there is pessimism about the future, and that when the future looks bleak, one tries "to grab all the gusto one can." After all, "If

I've only one life, let me live it as a blonde." In such an era citizens become narcissistic. The signs of such selfishness abound in the "self-awareness" movement: EST, gestalt therapy, rolfing, massage, jogging, health foods, and meditation are all manifestations of the new self-consciousness.

The most fully documented aspect of the behavior of the "Me Generation" is the contemporary unwillingness to have children. The percentage of single-person households doubled over the last decade, and the number of childless households increased by over 6 percent between 1970 and 1977. Since one cannot have a movement in America without having a national organization to legitimize it, childless couples have formed antikid clubs across the nation. (There is now even a vogue, German term for the dislike of children, *kinderfeindlichkeit.*) And there is some evidence that Americans are spending less time with the children they have; employed women spent 20 percent less time on child rearing and housework last year than in 1965, and even full-time housewives spent 12 percent less time on these domestic activities.[23] Child abuse among the working class rose at about the same time it became faddish for upper-middle-class women to "get some space of their own." These women liberated themselves from their children to the surprise of their ex-husbands (these men then found themselves part of the "single parent" statistic).

What is important about all this is that the Me Generation may be missing out on an essential stage of human development. What has occurred to nearly everyone who has thought seriously about the child-rearing process is that it has unique benefits *for parents*. Particularly, parenting helps to make one into an adult, because it makes infantile selfishness rather difficult to maintain. One simply has to make some sacrifices in terms of time and money for one's children.

But the "Looking Out for No. 1" philosophy eschews self-denial in favor of self-indulgence. This may produce prodigious consumers, *but it makes for lousy workers*. The new narcissism, like zero risk and the rights consciousness, stresses entitlements without concomitant responsibilities.

I admit that this is a strong assertion, especially because it is impossible to offer scientific evidence to support it. Nevertheless the impression that many young workers are frequently irresponsible is broadly shared among American employers in particular, and the older half of the population in general. Witness the following story from the Associated Press:

> Boulder, Colorado, July 18, 1979—Employers in this college town have horror tales to tell about today's young workers, a survey by the Denver *Post* found.

Home builder Bob White says he is quitting the construction business because of his frustration with the work habits of area residents. Restaurant owner Pete Brophy says he loses $700 a month in dishes and silverware because of careless employees.

Absenteeism is another general complaint of Boulder employers, the *Post* reported. . . .

Boulder's average employee is between 20 and 35, well-educated and too often not well-trained to work, office managers said. Several employers said 10% of those hired for jobs fail to show up for the first day of work.

White said the construction pace in Boulder is about half that in the East, where he grew up in the building trades of New York City.

"There were crews of Lithuanians, Latvians, Russians . . . all kinds of people who took pride in their work," White said of New York. But he said that Old World work ethic is missing in Boulder. . . .

"These young guys are saying 'Look at me. I'm a carpenter. I have a pickup truck,' but they don't really want to know how to do the work. I can't deal with it. I can't accept it anymore," White said.

Brophy said he uses a crew of 70 in his restaurant. Last year he hired 192 employees.

Like other employers, he blamed problems with the workforce on reluctance to settle down, the ease of group living in a university town, unemployment-pay and food stamps.

"They're single. It isn't like being 25 and married with a baby and a house payment and a car payment. They just don't have any responsibilities," he said.

Coincidentally the same week this article appeared, I received a phone call from the chief operating officer of one of the largest corporations in the country. I can't say if his tone was one more of exasperation or desperation, but my notes confirm that he said roughly the following:

My managers—even the top one—don't seem to care about their work anymore. There is no real dedication, no commitment, no sense of obligation. I've tried giving them everything—money, long vacations, big bonuses —but nothing seems to motivate them like it used to. . . . How long can the nation keep going on like this?

Permit me one more anecdote: While waiting for my wife in a large department store, I recently witnessed an encounter that seems to sum up the present problems of work in America. Three clerks—all under thirty, I would guess—were standing, idly chatting, while about a half dozen customers waited for service. Finally a customer approached one of the clerks and politely asked for help. The clerk reluctantly and sullenly agreed. As it turned out, the customer wanted an article that had to be ordered from the stockroom. In a desultory manner the clerk sent the order to the stockroom and went back to chatting with her fellow clerks. The customer waited patiently for about twenty minutes (punctuality is not my wife's strong suit, so I was able to watch this little drama unfold in its entirety), then asked the clerk to please check if anything was wrong with her order. The reply came back with the sting of a razor strap: "Are you kidding, lady? If you don't want to wait, that's cool with me. But I'm sure as hell not going to run around finding out what's holding up your order."[24]

Of course anecdotes by themselves "prove" nothing. But such stories add up: A secretary takes a day of "sick leave" to go to the beach during the busiest week of the year. Managers buy luxury limousines and executive jets for themselves with company money, while failing to provide clean restrooms for their workers. A worker refuses to walk fifteen yards to pick up an essential piece of material that has not been delivered to his work station; he assembles the product without the key piece. A worker in a factory, or office, or store—it doesn't matter which—is temporarily overloaded with work, but his underutilized co-workers will not help by picking up a larger share of his load. The new American credo seems to be: "Who gives a damn?"

This is a dangerous argument to advance. It can easily be misinterpreted as a cranky, right-wing attack on contemporary culture. What is significant is that the argument is coming from the left, from the likes of Christopher Lasch and Barbara Tuchman. Historian Tuchman recently outlined the decline in the national dedication to quality on- and off-the-job:

> In labor and culture, standards of quality are certainly lower. Everyone is conscious of the prevalance of slipshod performance in clerical, manual and bureaucratic work. Much of it is slow, late, inaccurate, inefficient, either from lack of training or lack of caring or both . . .
>
> The decline has been precipitate, perhaps as one result of the student movements of the 1960's, when learning skills was renounced in favor of "doing your own thing" or consciousness-raising and other exercises in self-fulfillment.[25]

The evidence of growing irresponsibility is so pervasive that it has gone largely unnoticed. Just as Japanese workers don't run around constantly commenting, "My, how *responsible* we are," irresponsible behavior is becoming so ingrained in the fabric of work in America that it is accepted as an intergral part of our nature. But occasionally this seldom-noticed trait will manifest itself forcefully—as when the postal clerk slams the window in one's face at the first strike of five o'clock, or when an able-bodied individual turns down a job in favor of an unemployment compensation check, or when a fireman goes on strike, or when a schoolteacher gives a true–false exam because she can't be bothered with correcting essays. The postal clerk, the welfare recipient, the fireman, and the teacher are each acting within the scope of their rights as they have come to be defined in the late 1970s. Indeed one might view the history of labor relations over the last decade in terms of the expansion of rights.

According to Gary Bryner, president of Local 1112 of the United Automobile Workers, the famous 1972 strike at the General Motors plant in Lordstown, Ohio, was over workers' *rights:* Bryner argues that the young worker on the assembly line at Lordstown

> had to have some time. The best way is to slow down the pace. He might want to open up a book, he might want to smoke a cigarette, or he might want to walk two or three steps away to get a drink of water. He might want to talk to the guy next to him. So he started fighting like hell to get the work off of him. He thought he wasn't obligated to do more than his normal share. All of the sudden it mattered to him what was fair. . . . The reason might be that the dollar's here now. It wasn't in my father's young days. I can concentrate on the social aspects, my rights. And I feel good all around when I'm able to stand up and speak up for another guy's rights. [26]

Fair enough. But what of the worker's responsibilities on the line? Bryner answers this question, albeit indirectly:

> Talking to guys. You get into a little conversation. You watch this guy, 'cause you don't want to get in his way, 'cause he'll ruin a job. Occasionally he'll say, "Aw, fuckit. It's only a car." It's more important to just stand there and rap. I don't mean for car after car. He'd be in a hell of a lot of trouble with his foreman. But occasionally, he'll let a car go by. If something's loose or didn't get installed, somebody'll catch it, somebody'll repair it, hopefully. [27]

So the line is drawn between workers' rights and their responsibilities—and it is drawn increasingly on the side of workers' rights. As workers' rights expand, their responsibility for the quantity and quality of their work diminishes, their responsibility for taking the initiative on the job decreases, their attitudes toward their fellow workers, supervisors, customers, and subordinates grow less considerate, more selfish. When the workers at Lordstown complained about filth in their plant, GM responded by putting many more trash barrels around the plant. But as a senior officer in the UAW explained to me, "The young workers didn't even bother to throw their trash in the cans. In fact, the area around the cans was littered with garbage." Whose responsibility was it to keep the area policed? The workers', the managers', the union's?

MANAGERIAL RESPONSIBILITY COMES FIRST

The facile answer to the question of responsibility is that *workers* are to blame for failing to assume responsibility for their behavior on the job. But my argument leads to the conclusion that *managers* have created institutional structures that make it almost impossible for workers to assume responsibility for the quantity and quality of their work. Ivar Berg has recently argued that these managers exhibit highly irresponsible behavior in their financing, marketing, production, and planning tasks.[28] And Robert Schrank argues that it is mismangement that is often at the root of the irresponsible behavior exhibited by workers at Lordstown and other industrial settings.[29] This state of affairs should not be a surprise, for most managers in large corporations have as much job security as union members. In the five hundred largest corporations there is cradle-to-grave welfare for most top and middle managers (with the exception of Chief Executive Officers in some industries). Managers, after all, are not capitalists or entrepreneurs, they are employees, with almost as much job security as government employees. There is thus little more incentive for responsible behavior among managers than there is among workers—both are simply "hired hands."

Indeed, the case can be made that worker irresponsibility is merely the mirror-image of managerial irresponsibility. For example, in 1978 Hay-Huggins management consultants published what came to be known as the "hit parade of executive perks." In surveying 468 major corporations they found that the Remington subsidiary of Du Pont has a 3,000-acre hunting retreat in southwest Illinois, and that McCormick and Company owns a 185-acre island in Chesapeake Bay—all for the benefit of these companies' executives (and prime customers). Executives in the companies surveyed were offered the following perquisites:

83 percent were offered executive physicals.
79 percent were offered special parking.
79 percent were paid for spouse travel when on company business.
69 percent were provided with company cars.

55 percent were provided with luncheon club memberships.
53 percent were provided with country club memberships.[30]

One must be careful not to offer a blanket condemnation of such benefits, for many are no doubt justified. Nevertheless these executive perks have the same effect on corporate leaders as lesser entitlements have on shop-floor workers. They offer no motivation for harder work. These benefits come not as rewards for productivity, but as rights of office. Moreover such benefits invite invidious comparisons among noneligible employees and set examples of behavior that are likely to be emulated at the time of contract bargaining.

THE SECURITY/IRRESPONSIBILITY NEXUS

The current generation of top corporate management has extremely high security needs as the result of their painful experiences during the Depression. But how would acting responsibly threaten the security of a manager? How would it threaten the security of a top corporate executive to, say, advocate the end of bank "red-lining," or to argue against providing company-sponsored memberships in social clubs with discriminatory policies, or to fight against selling Kepone in Latin America? As John De Lorean found at General Motors when he advocated small safe cars (see Chapter 7), or as Lyman Ketchum found at General Foods when he advocated improving the quality of work (see Chapter 5), the only unforgivable sin in corporate life is to *appear* disloyal to the prevailing norms or culture of the firm. Incompetence is tolerated, breaking the law is seldom punished, but questioning the values of the organization can lead to ostracism or even to expulsion. Breaking ranks with accepted norms is thus about the only way that a manager risks his security in a large corporation. Nothing better explains the behavior of the sixty-year-olds who run large corporations than the fact that they were impressionable teenagers during the Depression who, as a consequence, have high security needs. Knowing that the only way they could ever lose their jobs is to appear disloyal, they seldom risk the enmity of their peers by moving proactively to correct defects in the industrial order. (It is permissible to move reactively to legal or social pressures to clean up pollution, hire women and minorities, or make safe products—so long as one appears to have been dragged into such activities kicking and screaming!)

The security/irresponsibility connection has causes and effects that extend far beyond the work place. As Hannah Arendt points out in *Jew as Pariah,* there has been a long-term secular trend in Western society from the individual as *citoyen* ("a responsible member of society, interested in all public affairs") to the individual as *bourgeois* (who "for the sake of his wife and children . . . was prepared to do literally anything"). While Arendt goes so far as to claim that the behavior of the Nazis was "normal bourgeois behavior," I wish only to claim that it is possible to create a social structure in which irresponsibility to neighbors, co-workers, and fellow citizens is the norm, and in which the *search for security actually compels such irresponsibility*. For example, union leaders behave irresponsibly to protect their security and the security of their members. To protect the jobs of middle-aged males, union leaders will unquestioningly exclude women, minorities, or youth from the work force. On another plane, unionists actively support the production of dangerous chemicals, polluting products, and unsafe consumer goods—all in the name of job security.

This line of reasoning leads to a dilemma: Is there an inescapable trade-off between security and responsibility? Since both concepts are held to be socially desirable, choosing one social good to the exclusion of the other will be unacceptable to the vast majority of the citizenry.

It is important to recognize that America is *unconsciously* choosing more security at the cost of reduced responsibility. Legislatures and courts seem to be moving to guarantee security without adequately analyzing the consequences and costs of a risk-free environment. For example, in a case involving a doctor who sued for the right to staff privileges in a private hospital, the California Court of Appeals recently handed down the sweeping ruling that "every citizen has the right to practice his profession."[31] Since future actions are justified by reference to legal precedent, it will no doubt soon be claimed that *no* professional worker can be fired. Moreover if professionals have unlimited rights, doesn't this mean that the employers (clients) of doctors, lawyers, and professors end up having no rights?

To take another example, the current generation seems to feel that it has unlimited rights to exploit the air, water, land, fossil fuels, and other natural resources of the nation to guarantee its economic security. This society therefore behaves irresponsibly towards subsequent generations in order to secure the high standards of material consumption that it takes as its birthright. (Of course, nothing in American political and social life is so simple; on the other side are those who claim that the snail darter has a "right" to live. One lawyer has even argued that "Trees have standing" in reply to lumbermen who claim that they have a right to cut down trees to ensure their livelihoods.[32] That loud crash you hear is not falling timber; it is the clash of opposing rights.)

Is There an Italy in our Future?

"The Italians work little and, above all, badly," says Gianni Agnelli, President of Fiat. If American society continues on the trip it is currently on, trends point to a future that resembles contemporary Britain or Italy. And, there is no getting around it, Italy is a future that doesn't work.

Italy presents a case in which the costs and benefits of perfect job security can easily be measured. Italian workers face a risk-free environment in that they *all* have job security. Not even the laziest, nastiest, and most thieving domestic worker can be fired in Italy without the prohibitive investment of time and expense involved in showing cause in court. The effects on individual workers, organizations, and national economics of maintaining a fully tenured labor force are striking: Italy leads the industrialized world in such dubious categories as absenteeism, low productivity, labor unrest, managerial sloth, and worker dissatisfaction. The average rate of absenteeism in Italy is 14 percent, the highest in Europe (the U.S. rate is about 2.9 percent). In the first two months of 1979 absenteeism cost Fiat over five thousand units in lost production.[33]

In England, where workers still can be fired, they nevertheless face a relatively secure working environment, protected by belligerent unions and cradle-to-grave welfare measures. The effects are pretty much the same as they are in Italy. (For those Americans who haven't had the personal displeasure of being treated with pluperfect disdain by a typical English salesperson, I can only assert that this behavior runs a spectrum ranging from supercilious to rude. By comparison, American service workers are still considerate gems!)

The overriding characteristic that distinguishes Italian and British workers and managers from their counterparts in, say, Japan, is *irresponsibility*. This attitude is best illustrated by what is undoubtedly the most frequent saying in the British Isles: "I'm all right, Jack." Translated into American, this means: I've got what I need, and if my getting it transgressed your rights or needs, well, screw you. British labor union leaders frequently and proudly express this sentiment when they proclaim that they would rather bring Britannia to her knees than cooperate with management to increase productivity, or cooperate with government to reduce inflation. And U.K. managers complement the union stance with disdain for the fact that all British social classes are ultimately in the same leaky tub.

Such attitudes provide a ready definition of worker and managerial irresponsibility: These are actions that destroy the sense of community and weaken a nation's economy and polity by sacrificing the public interest through single-minded pursuit of self-interest. In short, the kinds of irresponsible acts with which we should be concerned are those that lead to a breach of the social contract.

All the behavior I have described in this chapter could be dismissed as trivial were it not for the mounting evidence that the world will no longer "buy" the behavior of American workers and managers. Because of increasing balance-of-payments deficits and the declining dollar, American managers may no longer be able to afford to play golf on company time, and American workers may no longer be able to afford to goof off. The nation can only afford such behavior if it doesn't want Arabian oil, Jamaican bauxite, Brazilian coffee, French wines, and Japanese radios. Workers and managers can only behave this way if they don't want zero risk, and if they don't want rising entitlements.

I am arguing that the mismatch between the behavior of workers and the new economic realities threatens the long-term viability of the American economy. As the American economy becomes more labor-intensive as a result of the shift toward service, clerical, and knowledge work, the *attitudes* of workers become central factors in national productivity. In our mature, postindustrial economy the success or failure of the national enterprise rests on the willingness of individual workers to take responsibility for the quality and quantity of their work, to take initiative in those increasingly frequent work situations that cannot be routinely handled, to show a real interest in the welfare of customers, suppliers, and fellow workers—in short, to *care* about their work.

Trade unionists deny the existence of this problem: It is, after all, "illiberal" to suggest that workers need more self-discipline. And managers wrongly assume that the problem can be corrected by the workers: It is, after all, dangerously "leftish" to suggest that it is the responsibility of *managers* to organize work in a way that elicits greater worker self-discipline. Of all those who have studied work, only E. F. Schumacher saw what was happening, and more important, recognized that it was *the result of the existing philosophy and organization of work:* "the result [of which], not surprisingly, is a spirit of sullen irresponsibility which refuses to be modified by higher wage."[34]

The problem with the current state of work in America is *not* simply the rising costs of entitlements. Rather it is that entitlements are demanded and granted without the productive wherewithal to afford them. The problem is *not* simply workers who have too little commitment to their jobs. Rather it is the current organization and philosophy of work that does not tie responsibilities to rights.

Nor is the problem simply that the values of young workers are "bad" from the perspective of organization needs. In fact, *the dominant values of young workers may be more appropriate to the economic challenges of the 1980s than are the values of their parents.* Almost every pollster from Harris to Yankelovich has used the following words to characterize the values of the Boom Babies: change, flexibility, choice, options, variety, and diversity. One can make the case that these values are more appropriate to an uncertain future than the values of security and rigidity that characterize older generations of workers and managers. *The problem is that the current organization and philosophy of work does not tap the positive values and traits of young workers.* Instead it encourages the counterproductive traits of narcissism, irresponsibility, and selfishness.

We may well ask how long America can go on with the expectations of an affluent nation and with an organization of work that prevents it from affording these entitlements.

4

THE HISTORY
OF THE FUTURE

THE new values described in the previous chapter all surfaced in the early 1970s, suggesting that a watershed may have been reached at that time. Indeed a strong case can be made that the 1968–1975 period witnessed the most significant historical disjunction in the United States since the Great Depression. In contrast, the postwar 1945–1968 period was relatively free of revolutionary value change. Although this era included such momentous events as the Korean War, the McCarthy era, the Kennedy assassination, and several severe (but short) recessions, in general it was characterized by economic progress and social stability. Even the traumas of the McCarthy period and the civil rights protests might be seen in hindsight as affirmations of the nation's ultimate commitment to do what was right in the long run.

It may well be that the nation was able to absorb the potentially devastating blows of such events in the 1950s and 1960s because they were played out against the backdrop of high rates of economic growth, low rates of unemployment and inflation, cheap and abundant energy, and rising individual affluence and educational attainment. During this period the United States was master of the world both politically and economically. With unshaken faith that the country faced an ever-rosier future, Americans believed that their personal fortunes would rise along with the nation's. Not surprisingly, it was during this era of ever-rising affluence that corporations greatly increased the benefits they offered workers and government entitlement programs grew like weeds on a surburban lawn. By the end of this period security was taken for granted by young, educated workers, according to the first national Survey of Working Conditions undertaken in 1969.[1] It was thus no accident that Abraham Maslow's "Hierarchy of needs"—with all the basic security needs fulfilled for the typical worker—enjoyed such popularity during this era. Maslow's theory can be viewed as a historically valid description of the effects of rising affluence, educational levels, and social expectations of the post–World War II era. This era ended appropriately with an event that symbolized the faith in the progress that had characterized it: the landing of two Americans on the moon.

In 1968, when the first members of the super-large Baby Boom generation graduated from college, Robert Kennedy and Martin Luther King were assassinated and we had riots in the streets of Chicago during the Democratic convention. Two years later America bombed Cambodia and four students were shot at Kent State University. Things fell apart, the nation's center failed to hold, and anarchy was loosed upon the land. In quick succession the country experienced the following morally debilitating events: Watergate, the oil embargo, and corporate bribery and political contribution scandals.

In the economic sphere the value of the dollar declined, rates of unemployment and inflation rose simultaneously to the highest levels in recent history, national productivity and technological innovation dropped, and international economic competition became intense for the first time in over thirty years. Most immediate to the American worker, real per capita disposable income of the average household fell during 1978 to 1981—something that had not occurred since the Depression. In short, the era beginning in 1968 has been characterized by the marked relative decline of the United States as a world economic and political power.

Domestically the social arena was strewn with the bodies of bloodied contestants as the nation rejected two decades of consensus, centrist politics to engage in interest group mayhem. The participants in the discord can be listed as litigants, for it was in the courts that they fought their battles:

Men v. Women
Blacks v. Whites
Public Sector Employees v. Local Government Employers
Students v. Teachers
Enlisted Men v. Officers
Guards v. Prisoners
Homosexuals v. Heterosexuals
Environmentalists v. Corporations
Landlords v. Tenants
Consumers v. Producers
Workers v. Managers

As a result of this considerable tearing of the social fabric, social expectations fell, faith in institutions declined, and Americans became more pessimistic about the nation's future. No wonder Maslow's hierarchy fell into disrepute. When the blood-dimmed tide is loosed and the ceremony of innocence drowned, nobody puts much store in a universal prescription based on economic growth, collective progress, and individual self-betterment!

A FUTURE SCENARIO

Are these new conditions that have arisen in the last dozen years merely passing phenomena? Or are we witnessing the first stage in the decline and fall of the American Republic? It all depends. In particular, the shape of the next two decades will depend on how the *values* of American workers and the policies and the practices of corporations, unions, and the government respond to declining growth. No one can predict how Americans or their institutions will respond to this challenge, but if the national response during the last seven years to the energy problem is any indication, optimism about the future would seem to be on the same gossamer footing as faith in the Second Coming.

If I read their forecasts correctly, American corporations are predicating their human resources planning on a return to the kind of economic growth that characterized the 1950s and 1960s. I too hanker for the good old days of the 1950s and 1960s, but I would not bet on a return to levels of economic performance experienced in the United States only twice in the last hundred years. I suggest that there is more than theoretical value in exploring what worker behavior might be like in a slow or no-real-growth scenario. For instance, we might assume that the next decade will not see any real increase in the gross national product. No decrease, either, for this is not a doomsday scenario; rather it incorporates trends the nation has grown accustomed to over the last few years. It just assumes that things will get a little worse with time, that the next decade will witness slightly higher inflation and interest rates, much higher energy prices, lower corporate profits, more debt, less saving, less investment—all for the same interrelated reasons that such conditions exist today. Since these characteristics tend to feed on one another, with time they will naturally grow worse, not better. Even if national economic policies are shaped to encourage more investment, the short-term effect will be painful from the point of view of the average worker. Achieving adequate levels of reinvestment would necessitate as many as ten years of decreased consumption for Americans.

Mind you, this scenario does not hold disasters. For example, OPEC will keep selling oil. Gas will be available at about $3.50 a gallon toward the end of the decade. International trade competition will continue to stiffen but not destroy such American industries as autos and steel. Domestically the main effect of this particular congeries of development would be unemployment: not depression-type unemployment, rather, a decade of stagflation.

Worker Perceptions of the Future

Daniel Yankelovich reports that Americans expressed the following opinions about the economic future in public polls conducted between 1977 and 1979:

70 percent believe that "there is likely to be a recession in the country in the next five years."

50 percent believe that "there is likely to be a depression in the country in the next five years."

66 percent expect the economy during the next ten years to grow more *slowly* than it did during the 1950s and 1960s—*or not at all.*"

53 percent "expect that in the country as a whole over the next five years there will be *periods of widespread unemployment or depression.*"

62 percent "believe that our current standard of living may be the highest we can hope for."[2]

How might American workers respond to a prolonged period of high inflation, high unemployment, a declining standard of living, and diminished national ability to cope with the international conditions that exacerbate those domestic problems? While an examination of such a future can be no more than speculation, it would be reasonable to expect the following kinds of developments:

· Workers would "hunker down" and their primary goal would become economic security.
· Unionization would increase.
· Industrial unions would negotiate a guaranteed number of work days per year; nonindustrial unions would demand lifetime job security.
· Unions would demand legal restrictions on the freedom of corporations to close uneconomical plants, divisions, and facilities. These regulations might include:
  1. A required one-year advance notice before closing a plant.
  2. A required filing of a statement of economic justification and economic impact of a closure.

3. Sufficient opportunity for workers and local communities to purchase a plant.
4. Indemnities to affected workers and communities.
5. A requirement that the corporation find alternative employment for affected workers.

· The problem of the distribution of wealth would become more acute. The political system that functions well when dividing the fruits of increased productivity would break down under the pressure of claimants competing for shares of a smaller pie.
· Federal restrictions would be placed on the introduction of labor-saving technology.
· National manpower planning would be introduced. Inflation would wipe out the value of most pension funds, leading to the federalization of all pensions in the one fully-indexed system, Social Security.
· Permanent wage/price controls would be enacted (or alternatively, wages would be indexed).
· Unemployment benefits would be greatly increased, as would workers' compensation benefits, and both programs would be federalized.
· An American Labor Party would be formed.

Although this future might be desirable to a minority of Americans, from the point of view of the majority, it would be repugnant. It would lead to British-style labor unrest, ideologically based class conflict, and low productivity. It would satisfy neither the economic needs for greater efficiency and higher productivity, nor the admirable humanistic aspects of the new values of young workers. It would cause government to become more bureaucratically centralized and force unions to downplay collective bargaining and to stress a political role.

Unhappily the soil of present conditions nurtures the seeds of such a future. In the past Americans had incentives to work hard to increase their share of an ever-expanding economic pie. This behavior, in turn, caused the pie to expand. Now the material needs of the majority of Americans may be becoming sated. If this is the case, there will be inadequate incentives to promote continued growth and economic efficiency. And this, in turn, will cause the pie to stop growing. While the majority may no longer be willing to work as hard as they did in the past, the demands for a fair share of the pie will doubtless continue to grow—for, as I argued in the previous chapter, larger shares of the economic pie have now been transmitted into *rights*. The crash we may hear in the future will be the collapse of our political system into a black hole of unmet and unaffordable expectations. If this pessimistic scenario develops, then the trends I have been describing will poison the body politic and economic. For it has been economic growth that has bankrolled the risk-free work place and socially secure nation. If growth stops, some sacrifices would have to be made.

Herein lies the rub: The American system offers no mechanism for retrenchment. There is no process by which workers and managers can give up some of the benefits they have won. There is no mechanism for retreating even one step from the levels of security that are presently enjoyed. California's Proposition 13 is a current demonstration of this unfortunate fact. While revenues will inevitably shrink over the next few years in California, politicians have failed to significantly alter a single major public program. Take the largest single item in the Los Angeles City budget: pensions for police and firemen (which account for about 50 percent of all property tax revenues). The L.A. police and fire pension fund is undoubtedly the most generous in America.[3] Benefits include a provision that bases benefits on the salary of the worker on the last *day* before retirement—a provision that encourages the eleventh-hour promotion of patrolmen to captaincies shortly before "retirement" at age thirty-eight.

The pension plan could serve as a paradigm of the irresponsibility I have been analyzing. It has created a kind of contempt of the public among those in the uniformed services. It has encouraged law enforcers to behave immorally, if not illegally. But that is not why I cite the case. What is germane here is the way the police and firemen are fighting attempts to bring their pension benefits into line with the fiscal realities created by Proposition 13. There is no process of negotiation to establish reasonable pension benefits. Instead there is unreasoned conflict. The police claim that they are "entitled" to the benefits they have won and that they will fight to keep these "rights." The police are organized in a powerful union, they have a war chest, and they do not propose to give an inch. It is not unthinkable that they will go on strike if they feel their pensions are significantly threatened.

Thus when forced to retrench even slightly, this group of American workers, at least, seems completely unwilling to make some sacrifices for the greater good. On the contrary, they are willing to engage in the kind of industrial "warfare" that characterizes modern Britain and Italy. If America is forced into a period of belt tightening, it could be concluded that its social prospects would be bleak. Since the time of the Depression, the nation has been adopting policies that create the belief that every benefit workers, managers, and professionals have won (and more) is theirs as a matter of right. Since it is much more difficult to take away a right than it is to take away a privilege, the nation can only hope that there will be no limits imposed on growth.

Even if the economy continues to expand, however, growing entitlements will still present risks to the society, for even with growth it seems impossible for the nation to keep pace with the expectations of the work force. While the entitlement consciousness grows exponentially, the economy can only grow arithmetically—particularly in a future devoid of incentives to produce and sacrifice. America is at the point where social, political, economic, technological, and demographic trends are interacting in untoward ways, leaving us without the wherewithal to afford a risk-free society. In short, that with which we would be satisfied we cannot afford. This is true on the national level—we probably cannot afford national health insurance, clean air, adequate defense and a high material standard of living (most certainly we cannot afford all three at the same time). And it is true on a personal level—we cannot afford the house, car, and education for our children that we want. Of course, there is no fixed amount of what we can afford. But surely we cannot afford all these things, given our reluctance to save, to be productive, and to be as committed to our work as the Germans and Japanese are to theirs. Yet we continue to spend as if there were no tomorrow. We behave irresponsibly: As a nation and as individuals, we do not save, we do not invest, we live only for today.

A MORE DESIRABLE ALTERNATIVE

In the scenario just described, corporations play a passive, reactive role. This is probably unrealistic, for historically corporations have been activists, not ineffectual bystanders along the parade route of American history. While individual corporations acting singly can do little directly to increase national economic growth, create full employment in the economy, reduce inflation, or increase the value of the dollar, they *can* greatly influence the future of the work place. (Even if they choose a course of reaction over the more prudent course of proaction, this policy, too, will inadvertently shape the future.) Of course this does not mean that corporations are free to create any kind of future they desire. The American labor market is pluralistic; therefore workers, unions, and the government will all have a share of influence. Nonetheless corporations have the *opportunity* to shape the future of work in a way that meets the needs of the society and the economy—*if* they are able to link these needs to the self-interest of the other stakeholder groups. In short, it seems to me that only corporations have sufficient leverage to produce an alternative future to the one I've just described. This more just alternative would *not* be one in which workers would give up any rights they currently enjoy. In practical terms it seems impossible to rescind such rights; morally it is perhaps questionable to try to. A more positive and realistic future would be one in which corporations created working conditions *with the goal of infusing concomitant responsibilities* into the existing and inviolable arena of rights. In certain respects this would mean moving the United States in the direction of the industrial cooperation found in Scandinavia, Germany, and Japan, and away from the British/Italian-style confrontation where our inertia seems to be taking us. (Cultural and institutional differences forbid the wholesale borrowing of any foreign model; it will be necessary to create uniquely American policies that build on existing institutions and practices.) In addition to new national policies, this change would require nothing less than an entirely new philosophy and organization of work. It is to guidelines for the creation of such an alternative that I turn in the next chapter.

5

DESIGNING JOBS FOR THE 1980S:
FUSING RIGHTS
AND RESPONSIBILITIES

PARDOXICALLY most managers of large corporations are wedded to a philosophy and organization of work that encourages workers to constantly demand more rights and to constantly abandon more and more responsibilities. Managers counterproductively retain this philosophy because they accept the economic notion that there is only a single "optimal" route to efficiency. This has led to adherence to traditionally-designed organizations and jobs. In the managers' favor it must be said that this hierarchical, authoritarian, and monolithic structure has generally functioned well for over a dozen decades. At least it has been more efficient than the alternatives that have been tried (such as Maoist decentralization). Consequently managers are reluctant to fix a system that worked for so long.

As the previous chapters illustrate, however, many of the long-term trends of industrialism now appear to be unraveling. Because of the unprecedented events of the last decade—growing affluence, the educational explosion, resource scarcity, entitlementarianism, the new values of the Boom Babies, the shift to a services economy—the once-efficient traditional philosophy and organization of work appears to be becoming *in*efficient and *un*productive. The reason why American managers cannot see these facts and change the way they do business is that when individuals have been culturally conditioned to see reality in one way, it is incredibly difficult for them to change to an alternative perception. And it is doubly difficult for them to do so when the change appears to require that they give up considerable personal power. From the perspective of managers, advocates of work reform appear to be asking them to turn over their authority to a demonstrably irresponsible mob, to abandon, in effect, the marvelously efficient machine of industrialism that has created our smooth-running economy and democracy. Writing off this managerial perspective as unreasonable is likely to lead to little success at achieving reform at work.

It must be recognized that the traditional power of managers is threatened at the core by the prospect of workers assuming responsibility for greater productivity. So as not to offend domestic sensibilities on this score, let me support this assertion with an example from a country from which we have come to expect little of either its workers or managers:

CASE NO. 1: In January 1976 the twelve thousand employees of Britain's Lucas Aerospace—Europe's largest manufacturer of aircraft generators, engine control systems, and fuel systems—were faced with massive layoffs. But instead of rolling over and playing dead, the workers did something terribly un-British: They showed considerable enterprise in finding productive work for themselves. On their own, they developed a list of one-hundred-fifty products, most of which they could build *without* new capital expenditures—that is, using machines already owned by Lucas. They then prepared six volumes of two hundred pages each filled with technical drawings and economic calculations for their proposed products. The products all met the following criteria: (1) each was urgently needed by society; (2) each would conserve energy; (3) each would improve the quality of life; (4) each would be ecologically desirable; and (5) each would utilize the skills of the existing Lucas work force. The list of products included a small portable kidney machine and a highly efficient dual natural gas/petroleum car engine.

The company rejected all the ideas as "uneconomic" and went ahead with its original plans and laid off thousands of workers. Since the layoffs, other companies have started to develop the products created by the Lucas workers. And growing recognition of the social value of the products they invented caused the workers to be nominated for a Nobel Prize.[1]

While the Lucas experience is atypical in the unusual initiative demonstrated by the workers, unfortunately, it is typical in the response of the managers. In almost every instance where workers have assumed responsibility for the quantity and quality of their work, managers have responded to this "threat" to their prerogatives with the executive equivalent of work restriction. Time and again American managers—like their British counterparts—have killed off unusual efforts by workers. Apparently power and control are more important to many professional managers than profits and productivity.

CASE NO. 2: A classic instance of negative managerial reaction to unusually high worker initiative has been occurring in the General Foods Corporation. There threatened managers have nearly quashed what was one of the most interesting work-place experiments of the 1970s—the famous Gaines dog food plant in Topeka, Kansas. While the experiment may never have been as radical as it was once cracked up to be (Bob Schrank studied it closely and concluded that a lot less in the way of meaningful reform was occurring than met the eye of the popular press[2]), the plant was nonetheless opened nine years ago with the high hopes of many Americans that it heralded the dawn of a humanistic industrial age.

Productivity of the plant ran about 40 percent higher than in a traditionally designed and managed Gaines plant. It seemed that the source of the productivity at Topeka was the workers' assumption of responsibility for many things that were typically managerial prerogatives, such as choosing the methods of production, allocating tasks, recruiting new workers, electing leaders of work teams, deciding which additional tasks workers would take on, and setting work schedules. Because the workers took these responsibilities upon themselves, the need for middle managers in the plant was eliminated. In fact, seventy workers ran the entire Topeka operation with the help of only the plant manager, who acted as a kind of expert consultant and as a link to the rest of the corporation. But within five years after the plant had opened, the brass at General Foods headquarters had succeeded in getting Lyman Ketchum (the manager who had thought up the experiment) fired, in bringing the practices at Topeka into line with standard General Foods procedures, and in (no doubt their most satisfying act) introducing several layers of supervisors and managers into the Topeka operation. The responsibility, and ultimately the productivity, of the self-managing teams were thus gradually whittled away.[3] At about the same time, a highly productive experiment in a coal mine in Rushton, Pennsylvania, suffered a similar fate, in this case at the hands of threatened union officials.

It is a sad fact that almost all the well-publicized efforts of the 1970s to totally redesign work environments have failed to survive intact into the 1980s. In most documented cases of "socio-technical redesigns" (as these experiments were inelegantly called) the promising human and economic gains have eroded, the results of the experiments have not been diffused throughout the larger corporations in which they were housed, and the progressive managerial practices have regressed toward the organizational mean. In addition to the threat to managers, several other common

problems run through the reports of the dozen or so most famous
socio-technical experiments:

- The experimental designs were *monolithic.* The redesigners often fell
  into the industrial engineer's trap of trying to find "the one best way" to
  do a job. By substituting one inflexible design for another, the socio-
  technicians ignored the real differences in needs, desires, and abilities
  among workers.
- The experimental designs were *static.* Most social scientists believe that
  the productivity of workers improves whenever they are made the
  subjects of an experiment. It is not being viewed as guinea pigs that turns
  workers on, it is the sign that the boss cares enough about them to try to
  change their working conditions. This so-called Hawthorne Effect
  (named after the plant in which it was first observed) induces spurts in
  productivity for only about as long as the caring behavior of managers
  lasts. The trick, then, is to design an ongoing, dynamic work environment
  in which workers are continuously encouraged to participate in decisions
  affecting how they do their jobs. Sadly all the job-enrichment experiments of the 1970s (and most of the socio-technical redesigns) were
  one-shot, quick fixes. The redesigners ignored the fact that it is not
  merely a new design that makes a new job superior to the old. It is the
  ongoing involvement of workers in the process of change that is important.
- The workers had no stake in the experiments. The changes in work design
  were introduced by managers and outside consultants and not generated
  by the workers themselves.
- The redesigners succumbed to their own Maslovian *ideological belief* that
  intrinsic rewards are everything, and that workers are not interested in
  such nasty things as money. For example, workers at Topeka were
  expected to be more productive but not to share fairly in the fruits of their
  labors.

To generalize, the problem with the socio-technical approach is that, like
the Tayloristic system it sought to replace, it was based on a monolithic
view of human behavior (i.e., Maslovian) that led to a monolithic
organization of work (i.e., self-managing teams). While the socio-technical
approach was a clear improvement over Taylorism, it flew in the face of the
most important finding of the last decade: the diversity of worker needs
and values. That is, workers have different needs and values (some are
seeking Maslovian self-actualization at work, and some are not); moreover
what motivates each worker is likely to change over the course of his or her

life. For example, when Ted Kramer is right out of college he may want a demanding, highly exciting, seven-day-a-week, twelve-hour-a-day job —like managing a large advertising account. But ten years later Ted might find himself a divorced-single parent. Then he might well want to work six hours a day, five days a week in order to spend more time with his eight-year-old child. Neither Taylorism nor the socio-technical approach is responsive to such changes in worker needs and motivations—changes that are increasingly frequent in our brave new post industrial world.

GUIDELINES FOR SOCIAL POLICY

In the early 1970s social scientists claimed they knew how to create an enriched work environment that met the needs of modern workers, like Ted Kramer. They claimed they had the data to prove that American workers were bored and alienated. And they claimed that the desire of workers for "self-actualization" on the job was frustrated by the inhumane way that work tasks were designed. Underlying this argument was the purported existence of a universal "hierarchy of human needs," an idea postulated by the psychologist Abraham Maslow in the 1940s.

As Maslow saw it, all human beings have the same hierarchy of needs, and as each level of need is fulfilled, the next highest level becomes salient. These needs start with such basic physiological requirements as food and shelter, followed on subsequent rungs by safety, security, friendship, esteem, and—at the top of the ladder—the crowning human achievement, "self-actualization" (realizing one's full potential). Not unreasonably, social scientists in the 1970s argued that since American workers were in general safe, secure, and affluent, they must be searching for self-fulfillment through creative and challenging work. Once Maslow's assumptions about human nature were accepted—more by academics than by labor leaders or businessmen—the following litany of conclusions about work flowed as naturally as marbles off an uneven table:

Because work is organized in a stultifying assembly-line manner, job satisfaction is thwarted.

There is widespread discontent with working conditions, particularly among blue-collar workers.

America's affluent workers are more likely to be motivated by interesting jobs than by additional money or other benefits extrinsic to the work itself.

Workers are demanding jobs that offer such intrinsic benefits as challenge and the opportunity to learn and to grow.

Jobs can be readily redesigned (or "enriched") to reduce worker alienation and to increase productivity.

This was heady stuff and it inspired countless job-enrichment efforts and many socio-technical (job-redesign) experiments. But as the decade wore on, it became apparent that the social scientists could *not* produce data that supported the existence of the Maslow hierarchy. It became clear that money topped the hierarchy of a great many affluent workers (who in theory ought to have been seeking self-actualization), and that redesigned and enriched jobs seldom produced the predicted human and economic outcomes, at least not for a sustained period of time.

Today no analyst of sound mind would frame an argument for work reform on Maslovian assumptions about job satisfaction or on the quantitative findings about the changes in worker attitudes and productivity that are claimed to result from enriched jobs. These "hard" data have too often turned out to be social science fiction.[4]

What managers need today are some up-to-date guidelines for designing work to meet the problems of the 1980s. To be effective, such guidelines should build upon the positive characteristics of the young "nontraditional" workers, while at the same time providing disincentives to their negative characteristics (such as narcissism and selfishness). Moreover these guidelines must not fall into the trap of monolithic prescription that ensnared the socio-technicians; the guidelines must also account for the needs of workers with traditional values.

Guidelines for social policy are nothing more than rough indicators of future course of action—they should not be construed as inflexible laws derived from scientific experiment. With this important caveat, I suggest that the following performance criteria might be appropriate for the design of work in the 1980s:

Diversity. The work place should offer a wide range of tasks, each requiring different levels of skills, abilities, effort, degree of commitment, supervision, creativity, and length of time for completion. There should also be a spectrum of rewards and incentives.

Choice. The work place should make it possible for workers themselves to select jobs that meet their individual needs (since it is impossible for an organization to fairly identify and match individual needs with task requirements).

Flexibility. The work place should accommodate the differences in off-the-job commitments and interests of workers. To meet various levels of family responsibilities, working conditions and career paths should be individually tailored as far as practically possible.

Mobility. The work place should provide the opportunity for workers to move to other organizations, within limits, without penalty. Because worker needs, wants, and interests are constantly changing, and because few organizations can provide the full spectrum of diversity, choice, and flexibility necessary to accommodate these, a worker should have the unencumbered opportunity to move to find the conditions he or she seeks. Within organizations there should also be ample opportunity for lateral as well as noninvidious downward mobility.

Assuming that workers are paid a fair salary and retain all their current entitlements, it is hard to believe that they could ask much more from work than diversity, flexibility, choice, and mobility. But the purpose of work is not just to meet the needs of workers. (Unfortunately, for too long work was organized without any concern for their needs, but that is no excuse to compensate now by overreaction.) The other purposes of work are to provide the goods and services society needs and wants. Since the desires and requirements of American society are high, this means that productivity at work must also be high. And since worker productivity cannot be commanded, it must be elicited through *self-interest.* This suggests the need for two additional performance criteria:

Participation. The work place should provide workers with full information and authority to manage their own jobs. Workers should design their own jobs, set their own work schedules, decide their own salaries— indeed, be fully self-managing as far as their *own* work goes, to the extent that it does not affect anyone else's work. Workers should also participate in profits and ownership of stock in the companies in which they work.

Rights Tied to Responsibilities. As a necessary corollary to the participation criterion, every worker should be held responsible for all the decisions he makes or actions she takes.

Since many workers are unwilling to assume such responsibility, there is one final criterion:

Security. Managers should plan for full employment. This is not to say that workers should have academic-style tenure. Sadly, it is not recognized by either unions or management that workers can receive a real sense of job security through stock ownership, elaborate due process and grievance procedures, Lincoln Electric-type annual hour guarantees (see Case No. 4), and so forth, all without offering life-long sinecures.

Exemplary Cases

Stated generally, these criteria appear exceptionally radical, and I grant it is difficult to imagine a work place that would satisfy these factors and still be profitable and productive. It is therefore reasonable to ask what an organization that satisfies these criteria would look like. Because imperfection is the rule of life, no one organization could *perfectly* satisfy all these criteria. Remember, a central message of this book is that there are no monolithic solutions to the problems of work. There is, for example, no one way to "solve" a production function using these criteria. For not only is the work force diverse, but places of employment also vary in size, location, technology, the products they make and the services they provide, and many other significant variables. But for every organization there is a spectrum of appropriate conditions that would meet the established criteria.

Equally important, no such set of abstract guidelines is likely to induce managers to change the philosophy and organization of work in their companies. Realistically managers can be expected to demand evidence that the changes advocated will not only increase productivity, but will also not seriously compromise their authority. Managers, in short, will want to be assured that they would have a significant role to play in the new work places of the 1980s. In fact, they will change from authoritarians to authorities, as they come to act not as policemen but as expert consultants to workers. This should be a far more rewarding role to play.

The best way to respond to these legitimate concerns is to review the experiences of a handful of work places that meet at least some of the performance criteria set out above, all the while constantly reminding ourselves that—since there is a spectrum of appropriate designs for work—we are not searching for the "ideal" organization. Utopia is simply not to be found. Every example given below has its drawbacks and limitations, so nothing is to be gained by debating these examples. They are advanced not as solutions but as illustrations to make the guidelines appear less abstract. A convenient place to begin our tour of innovative work places is inside one of the nation's newest factories.

CASE NO. 3: ICI Americas, Inc., recently opened a chemical factory in Houston that, although it only employs about ninety workers, cost $85 million to build. This capital investment of nearly $1 million per worker makes the plant one of the world's most fully automated production facilities. In fact, machines do nearly all the basic work. When things are going right, there is so little for workers to do that they spend most of their time sitting around chatting or reading. Yet, surprisingly, the performance of each worker is more important to the productivity of this plant than it would be in a more labor-intensive factory. Since computers, robots, and other machines handle all the routine tasks, it is necessary for workers—who typically have a high school diploma plus a year of college—to assume responsibility for dealing with all *non*routine developments. Since machine down-time is incredibly costly, for the plant to operate profitably, workers must take the initiative in dealing with all unanticipated problems that arise. Says a company executive, "Workers here make bigger decisions, so they run the risk of making bigger mistakes." The company tries to encourage responsible behavior on the part of workers by entrusting them with degrees of responsibility far in excess of what similarly educated workers have in more typical plants. And the company has abandoned old-style industrial discipline, such as sending rule breakers home and docking them a day's pay. The company executive explains, "If somebody has broken a safety rule, we want him to think about his responsibility for the safety of others, not about how he got cheated out of a day's pay." In order to create a spirit of teamwork and cooperation, all workers are paid the same salary, and all share in all the tasks in the plant, from maintenance to construction.

The ICI plant is not advanced here as a paradigm of a progressive work place, although it seems better planned and managed than the average. There are two reasons for a stopover in Houston on a Cook's tour of informative work places: (1) The plant helps to erase the assembly-line stereotype that comes to mind whenever work is discussed. In fact, less than 1 percent of American workers are on assembly lines, and few new lines are likely to be built in the future. (2) ICI managers are attempting to deal with what might be called the "Three Mile Island mindset" that occurs in high-technology plants and in any other setting where workers must assume responsibility for their performance in the absence of constant and close supervision.[5] While the consequences of a failure by workers to assume such responsibility are seldom as potentially "explosive" as in a nuclear power facility, they *can* be dangerous in a chemical plant, and w*ill* have adverse effects on productivity in almost all work settings. This is one of the curious side effects of automation. Eventually almost all simple, repetitive industrial taks will be done by machines, or by workers in underdeveloped countries where labor is cheap. America will be left with industrial jobs that require problem-solving and analytical skills from workers who will have to *care* about their task and their co-workers. And moving out of the factory and into the more typical postindustrial American work settings (e.g., offices, stores, hospitals, restaurants, schools), it is clear that worker morale and attitude (e.g., showing genuine concern for customers, clients, patients, students) are already the prime source of productivity. One might add that they are also the prime source of *civility* in a service economy.

The managerial challenge of the next decade will be to find ways to tap more fully the natural abilities and acquired skills, training, and education of the 100 million American workers. This should not be interpreted as getting workers to labor harder. Rather, it entails organizing their work so they can work more effectively and help managers correct the small things that hinder efficiency. While this challenge of the next decade was accepted by the socio-technical school, either their Maslovian ideology led them to downplay the importance of pay and incentive schemes as sources of motivation, or they never asked the employees what they wanted.

In contrast to the socio-technical approach, several firms have for years successfully addressed the major problems of work by making participation in profits the keystone of their organizational philosophy, as the following case illustrates.

CASE NO. 4: Since 1934 the Lincoln Electric Company of Cleveland (the world's largest manufacturer of arc welding machines and electrodes) has operated on the principle of rewarding workers in cold cash for their efforts. It is not just "output" that is rewarded; indeed creativity and entrepreneurial behavior are especially prized. Highly paid to start with, workers receive an annual bonus based on four criteria—output, quality of work, cooperation, and ideas to improve productivity. This bonus effectively doubles the annual income of the average employee. (In 1975 the company's 2,421 employees received an average *bonus* of $11,608.) Workers at Lincoln are encouraged to find ways to eliminate their own jobs—and they get promoted if they do. Workers are willing to engage in this "abnormal" behavior (abnormal from the trade unionist perspective) because the firm has a job security agreement with its workers whereby it guarantees at least thirty-two hours of work fifty weeks a year for each employee with two or more years of service. (No specific rate of pay is guaranteed; the employee must be willing to accept transfer from one job to another, as well as overtime during periods of peak demand.) The company has not laid off a worker since 1951. Worker productivity at Lincoln is about 100 percent higher than in U.S. industry in general, and the cost of its products has not increased in several decades despite soaring material and labor costs. A great part of the cost reduction has resulted from eliminating supervisory personnel, who become redundant when workers assume responsibility for their own performance.[6]

(In general, American workers appear to be over-supervised. At the Honda car plants in Japan, the ratio of supervisor/inspectors to production workers is 1:200. In some U.S. car plants, the ratio is 1:10. Not only does such over-supervision discourage worker initiative, as the Lincoln case illustrates, there are potential savings in labor costs through the elimination of non-productive supervisors.)

Though highly successful, the Lincoln approach is not the only way to inspire workers to assume greater responsibility for their productivity. For example, there are several dozen worker-owned firms (described in the following chapter) in which employee-owners reap the full rewards of capitalists for their efforts. These companies—which include 16 plywood cooperatives in the Northwest—have records of productivity and worker commitment that, in terms of longevity, rival Lincoln's. Nevertheless profit and equity sharing alone have seldom been sufficient to generate worker initiative and responsibility. Workers at Lincoln, the plywood companies, and at nearly every other company with a truly outstanding human and economic record also have the rights and responsibilities of participation in the decisions that affect their performance.

Perhaps the clearest case of tying participation in decision making to participation in profits is the Donnelly Mirror Company of Holland, Michigan.

CASE NO. 5: All of Donnelly's five hundred employees participate in managerial decisions, and all participate in the firm's profits. The entire work force is organized into teams of eight to twelve workers. Each team has access to all the information it needs to be self-managing. Using this information, the teams have full rights and responsibility for making all decisions directly affecting their work: e.g., how fast to run the production line, when to shut it down for maintenance, when and how to implement a schedule increase, a product variation, or a method change. Decisions are made democratically, based on a consensus of the members of a team.

Each team elects a "linking pin," who then becomes a member of a team at the next level. This way, communication and participation flow in all directions throughout the firm. For example, ideas bubble up to an elected Suggestion Committee whose function it is to consider all suggestions that reach it, and to do something constructive about every suggestion. If the suggestion is deemed unfeasible, the committee ensures that the person who made it is promptly told why his idea is not being implemented. The committee has sweeping powers: For example, on the basis of workers' suggestions, the committee eliminated hourly wages and time clocks in favor of salaries.

There is also a company-wide representative committee that deals with grievances, pay policies, fringe benefits, promotions, and all other personnel policies and problems. Employees elect fellow workers to this committee, each represents six to eight teams, serves a two-year term, and is subject to recall by his or her constituents.

Every month a bonus is paid to the workers, based on all increases resulting from innovations, productivity gains, and savings in labor, materials, and operating supplies. Workers get special bonuses (and promotions) for finding ways to eliminate their own jobs. To provide the security needed to encourage this dedication to productivity, the company offers a guaranteed annual wage and a guarantee against technological layoffs. There is also widespread employee stock ownership in the company.

Although Case No. 5 sounds futuristic, if not utopian, it is based on a 1977 description from the *Harvard Business Review.*[7] As a result of adopting the system described above, Donnelly increased its sales from $3 million in 1965 to $18 million in 1975, and increased the size of its work force from under two hundred employees to over five hundred during the same ten-year period. Although labor and material costs escalated rapidly during this decade, the company succeeded in holding the line on prices for most of its products and actually *reduced* the prices of all the others. Donnelly now has one-tenth the U.S. national average rate of absenteeism and one-third the average turnover rate.

The policies developed at Donnelly are potentially acceptable to managers and shareholders because they lead to efficiency and profitability, acceptable to traditional workers because they allow plenty of security, acceptable to nontraditionalists because they provide unlimited opportunity to participate in decisions, and acceptable to unionists because the system is, after all, just a variation of their very own baby, the Scanlon Plan (see pp. 75–76). In a nutshell, the policies developed at Donnelly satisfy the needs of all major stakeholders in the work place, score high on the performance criteria outlined above, and offer a range of motivations that satisfies traditionalist and nontraditionalist workers alike.

Significantly entitlements are *not* a problem at Donnelly. The Donnelly experience illustrates the point underscored earlier: *Entitlements per se do not constitute a problem for American corporations or American society. The problem is entitlements that are demanded and awarded without the wherewithal to afford them.* That is, a highly productive company or nation can afford a high level of entitlements, while nonproductive companies and countries simply cannot. In this regard it is instructive to recall that the level of social and worker entitlements is higher in productive Germany than in nonproductive England, higher at productive Donnelly Mirrors than at hundreds of thousands of traditionally managed American firms. The crucial difference is that in countries like Germany and Japan, and in companies like Donnelly Mirrors and Lincoln Electric, workers don't demand or get entitlements that exceed the productive capacity to pay for them.

None of this is news to America's corporate leaders. They've recognized this fact of life for years. They've preached it to unions, to workers, to the government, and to the press. But while they've *said* all the right things, few of these corporate leaders have *acted* to make their corporate policies conform to their beliefs. In real life there is no way of reversing unsupportable levels of entitlements by bemoaning them. Preaching never got rid of sin. For example, industry analysts have been warning for years that American steel was being priced out of world markets because of low productivity, outmoded technology, and high labor costs. Recently it was estimated that labor costs at the Youngstown Sheet and Tube plant in Ohio could have been reduced by 21 percent by changing union seniority rules and by reducing plant manning levels that had been bargained into contracts.[8] Failure on the part of management and the union to make this and other practical changes led to the permanent closing of the plant. Now that it is too late, Youngstown workers are saying that they would gladly behave more responsibly if they were given the chance to try again. But they won't get the chance. Nor is there to be a second chance in the hundreds of other plants that have recently closed or will soon close because their low productivity makes foreign goods cheaper for American consumers.

Unfortunately, instead of taking proactive steps, most large corporations have been willing to alter their philosophy and organization of work only when there is no alternative to doing so. Some, like Youngstown Steel, wait until it is too late. Others, like the company in Case No. 6, change just in the nick of time.

CASE NO. 6: In 1973 the managers of Kaiser Steel decided to permanently close their mill in Fontana, California, because they were convinced that it could not compete with imported Japanese steel. Faced with the loss of their jobs, the workers at Fontana persuaded Kaiser to keep the plant open by agreeing to change their behavior. The hitherto adversary labor relations at the plant were quickly turned around, and workers started accepting the necessity for such things as limited layoffs and overtime work. The managers changed their behavior, too. Whereas they had previously been unwilling to listen to the advice of "dumb" workers, they now started listening. They followed the suggestion of the workers to improve the maintenance of machines, a simple act they had long resisted, but one that reduced the rate of rejects by 39 percent in the first instance it was tried. The managers had never believed the plant could run profitably, but it is still in operation in 1980. A union official identified the secret: "Nobody really knew what the workers could do if they cooperated."[9] (Ironically, the United Steelworkers of America union has recently applied the brakes to further worker efforts to cooperate with management to save jobs. In the midst of the 1981 steel slump, Fontana workers voted to accept a pay cut to prevent layoffs. The national leaders of the union voided the agreement on the grounds that it set a dangerous precedent.)

While Kaiser Steel is hardly a paradigm of progressive management —and the plant may still be closed for environmental and other reasons— the case is instructive nonetheless, for steel was one of the earliest industries to experience the conditions that all American industry is likely to experience during the 1980s. Case No. 6 also shows that it is possible— even in an industry with outmoded technology—to increase productivity by encouraging worker responsibilities. And, significantly, the Fontana workers gave up no rights of any consequence. If something positive can be done about the "worst case," then there is hope for the future.

In fact, it is pleasing to report that the 1970s witnessed limited but significant movement toward union-management cooperation. The most publicized example has been the formation of "labor/management councils" in several decaying northeastern cities, such as Jamestown, New York. The idea has been to call a truce to industrial warfare in order to halt the movement of industry to the sunbelt. In some instances, there have been dramatic increases in productivity. For example, by listening to the ideas of production workers—and rewarding them in cash for their increased productivity—output at the Jones and Laughlin steel plant in Louisville, Ohio increased by twelve hundred tons a month in 1980. Significantly, this occurred in an industry, a company, and a region known for poor industrial relations. "It's hard to change," says the Jones and Laughlin vice president for industrial relations. "It's a reorientation for management as well as the union."[10]

The most dramatic example of union/management reorientation was the election of UAW president Douglas Fraser to the board of the Chrysler Corporation (whether this was a wise move from the point of view of the company, the union, and the public interest, only time will tell) and the nomination of UAW vice president Ray Majerus to the board of American Motors. Other less dramatic, but perhaps more important, changes also occurred. For example, in August 1979 the United Steel Workers Union and the Dow Chemical Company reached agreement on a contract that contained the following provision:

The union agrees that it will use its best efforts to cause the employees to individually and collectively perform and render efficient work in order to keep the company competitive and thus improve the job security of the employees.[11]

In some quarters, cooperation moved from words to action.

CASE NO. 7: In 1977 the Uniroyal Company announced that it was closing its inner tube factory in Indianapolis. The plant was profitable, but it was plagued by chronic and worsening labor conflict. The company had constantly held the threat of plant closure over the workers' heads, and the workers responded by finding creative ways to reduce their output and make life miserable for the plant managers. When Uniroyal finally decided that it would concentrate its resources on its high-growth chemical business, the workers were forced to make sacrifices to save their jobs. Through their union, they found another owner for the plant, and agreed to give up such things as being paid for the time they spent at lunch and at union meetings. They agreed to assume responsibility for helping management find ways to make the plant profitable. In exchange for accepting these responsibilities, the new owner granted the workers the right to two seats on the board of directors and to 50 percent of all profits. Observers now say that workers deal with the new owner as a partner, not as an adversary.[12]

In the next chapter I cite cases in which workers have accepted far more responsibilities than did the workers in this example in exchange for actual shares in the ownership of the firms in which they worked. Unfortunately almost all these cases also resulted from the threat of plant closure, not from proactive steps on the part of union or management.

The most successful and lasting work-place reforms have not started as small-scale experiments that were then diffused throughout large organizations. Rather, the reforms that have taken hold and lasted have involved *systemic, total organizational change.* Not surprising, then, is the fact that work reform has succeeded in only a miniscule number of *large* organizations. In general, smallness appears to be a key element in increasing productivity. The Emerson Electric Company, for instance, consistently produces products at a lower cost than its prime competitor, General Electric. Whereas GE favors enormous production facilities, all of Emerson's plants have fewer than six hundred employees. Pratt and Whitney has what is probably the largest plant in the U.S. in Connecticut, but productivity is so much higher in a new, smaller plant recently built in

New England that the company vows never again to succumb to false interpretations of the notion of "economies of scale." Contrary to what economists and industrial engineers have claimed for decades, it is not necessary to build elephantine production facilities to obtain economies of scale. A few years ago, the chief executive officer of American Motors committed what amounted to industrial heresy when he demonstrated that his tiny company had the same economies of scale in production as giant General Motors. The real differences between the two companies, he said, were the economies of scale that GM enjoyed in distribution, research, advertising, marketing, finance and other staff operations. The upshot of all of this is that large organizations must find ways to reorganize themselves to achieve smallness of production, while maintaining the other advantages of large size.

The managerial challenge before the nation is to take the best from the experience of small, innovative firms like Donnelly, Lincoln Electric, and a few dozen others with at least some conditions that satisfy the micro-performance criteria and to *adapt these for application in large corporations.*

This adaptation has already begun in a few large companies, in particular General Motors (see Case No. 9) and Prudential.

CASE NO. 8: Without fanfare the Prudential Insurance Company has committed itself to redesign the jobs of all its employees. The word came down from the chief executive officer that all jobs at Prudential should be made as interesting as possible. While this fiat came from on high, the company correctly recognized that specific changes had to be designed below. Since no monolithic design was appropriate for the hundreds of separate operating units, each unit was charged with redesigning its own jobs according to the special requirements of its task, locale, and work force. While it might be possible to criticize the Prudential effort as simple job enrichment and not systemic organization change, the human results are nonetheless impressive. In the hundreds of units where jobs were redesigned:

57 percent of the units reported improvement in employee attitudes and morale; only 4 percent indicate a deterioration.

31 percent of the units report a decrease in turnover; only 5 percent report an increase.

55 percent of the units were independently evaluated as more participative in their managerial styles; none was reported to be less participative.

93 percent of the units indicated that the abilities of workers were being more fully utilized.

Increases in other performance measures were similarly impressive:

Service improved in 60 percent of the units.
Errors decreased in 50 percent of the units.[13]
Productivity increased in 43 percent of the units (down in only 3 percent).

Ironically, as the Prudential case illustrates, work reform—although democratic in nature—has worked best when top management has *ordered* it and has stood firm against the rearguard actions of threatened middle managers.

At few of the successful firms has the goal of reform been to improve job satisfaction or to reduce worker alienation. While the goals have varied, a common theme has been to find ways to better meet organizational goals (e.g., productivity and profits) *and at the same time* to improve the experience of workers on the job. It has usually been left to each particular group of workers to define this latter goal precisely for themselves. Workers have typically defined this goal in the following terms (using my language, not theirs):

To make better and more sensitive use of human resources.
To introduce greater democracy into the work place.
To alter the hierarchical power relationships in an organization.
To overcome the feeling of powerlessness in a big organization.
To turn the work place into a learning place.
To provide greater justice (equity, fairness) to workers.
To provide a setting where individuals can grow and find self-fulfillment (some workers have been reading Maslow, too).

While one might assume that these goals are consistent with the goals of the labor union movement, it is an unfortunate fact that most union leaders are uninterested in, or hostile to, work reform. Part of the unionists' skepticism is understandable (they've seen too many changes proposed by management that turned out to be worker exploitation disguised as Good Samaritanism). But part is illiberal (they are against change because they don't see how it can enhance their power). Nevertheless some unions are now making an honest and fair effort to deal with work reform as the case cited in Chapter 1 illustrates. The United Automobile Workers, under the leadership of Irving Bluestone (recently-retired vice president of the union's General Motors Department), has gone further than any other American union in embracing the quality-of-work-life concept. It is worth reviewing the UAW–GM experience along the long, hard road from Lordstown to Tarrytown.

CASE NO. 9: In 1972 a strike at the GM plant in Lordstown, Ohio, put the issue of the quality of work life on the front pages of American newspapers. What was newsworthy about this strike was that the majority of the six thousand workers at Lordstown were young (the average age on the assembly line was twenty-two), that many of them had engaged in sabotage, and that their grievance was not over money but over the kinds of working conditions that their fathers had accepted with resignation. Ironically, the Lordstown plant was not a dark, satanic mill. It was a new plant, with the latest technology and the world's most automated, fastest assembly line (which turned out 104 cars per hour, versus an industry average of 55). Nevertheless labor relations were Dickensian (workers had filed five thousand grievances in one six-month period).

What led to the cessation of production at Lordstown was the initiation of an old-fashioned speed-up on the line by GM's crack team of industrial engineers. Building on the very same techniques introduced by F. W. Taylor a half century earlier, these efficiency experts set out to make the fastest line run faster still.

In hindsight it appears that their biggest mistake was their failure to involve the union and the workers in the change (it is part of the culture of GM to be secretive about all managerial decisions, informing no one, not even its employees and stockholders, of its intentions).[14] But at Lordstown the workers responded to management's efforts to reengineer jobs on the line by redesigning their own jobs. Their favorite method was "doubling." Under this system, four workers might agree among themselves to become an informal team, and for a set period of time (say fifteen minutes to half an hour) two members of the team would work like the devil doing the work of all four, while the other two workers would rest, smoke, or chat. The workers claimed that this method improved the quality of their work by forcing them to concentrate on what would otherwise be a routine task, and improved their job satisfaction because it gave them a chance to schmooze with co-workers (schmoozing, which according to Robert Schrank is important to the quality of work life for blue-collar workers, is all but obviated on a fast and noisy auto line).[15] Doubling drove GM's efficiency experts up the wall. Nothing was more galling to them than to "have workers stand around chatting, while they are being paid to work!"

The managers responded by disciplining workers (sending them home for a day or more without pay). In turn, the workers responded by filing more grievances.

While it didn't get into the papers at the time, GM was having perhaps even more problems with its work force at its much older plant in Tarrytown, New York. For most of the late 1960s and early 1970s, Tarrytown was among the worst of all the GM plants in terms of absenteeism (about 7 percent on any given day), turnover, and grievances (typically, there were two thousand outstanding). Moreover, labor costs were extremely high and productivity was low (the plant's line turned out only fifty-six cars per hour). While the workers and the plant at Tarrytown were older than the workers and the plant at Lordstown, managerial philosophy was identical in both plants. According to Robert H. Guest, one Tarrytown manager admitted that "Management was always in a defensive posture. We were instructed to go by the book, and we played by the book. The way we solved problems was to use our authority and impose discipline."[16] But after numerous attempts the managers finally discovered that discipline cannot be *imposed*. Just when it looked as if it would be necessary to shut down the old plant at Tarrytown, the managers there hit on a novel idea: involving the workers in the process of developing solutions to the many production problems on the assembly line. In effect, this created an atmosphere in which the workers would impose discipline on themselves as responsible human beings. While the method worked each time it was tried, GM backed off this radical change in the philosophy and organization of work three times before finally committing itself to a joint quality-of-work-life project with the United Auto Workers in 1977. The most important aspect of this effort was the involvement of workers, supervisors, and union officials in lengthy and ongoing training sessions. At these sessions workers are given managerial information and some techniques for solving production problems. (Perhaps the most radical innovations are the involvement of *all* the plant's thirty-eight hundred workers in the project, and the *payment* of hourly workers to attend the training sessions—a practice almost unheard of in heavy industry.) According to Guest, the new participative approach has led to the solution of many production problems that seemed intractable under the former conditions of labor/management conflict. For example, workers found ways to reduce the percentage of "bad welds" from 35 percent to 1.5 percent. While the company still sticks to its self-defeating practice of secrecy and refuses to release figures for productivity, the union claims that work quality is up, absenteeism is down to 2.5 percent, and, most dramatically, grievances are down by 1000 percent.

Regrettably, GM seems not yet fully committed to authentic worker participation. At the opening of its new nonunion plant in Oklahoma City in 1978, GM divided the work force into 117 teams of from ten to seventeen workers, and gave them authority to police their own attendance and conduct, but no rights or responsibilities for self-management or participation in decision-making. The workers balked at this inauthentic participation and voted in the UAW.

It is worth noting in this regard that Chrysler had a quality-of-work program in name only at the time of its financial distress. But in June 1980 Chrysler and the UAW announced that workers would assume responsibility for quality control on the new K car, the model the company is banking on to make it solvent. (It is significant that in the past Chrysler workers were actually subject to reprisals by foremen if they called attention to shoddy workmanship.) Now that their backs are against the wall—and when it is probably too late—Chrysler managers are willing to borrow a page from Tarrytown in order to boost productivity. This pattern is typical of most of the cases cited in this chapter: Worker responsibility is encouraged only when the alternative is a plant closing or a company bankruptcy; unions and management have seldom taken proactive steps to prevent future crises.

The following foreword to a 1978 contract between Shell Canada and the Oil, Chemical and Atomic Workers International testifies how far at least one other union has come in making the quality of working life a union issue.

CASE NO. 10:

Both Management and the Union support and encourage policies and practices that will reflect their commitment to the following principles and values:

Employees are responsible and trustworthy, capable of working together effectively and making proper decisions related to their spheres of responsibilities and work arrangements—if given the necessary authorities, information and training.

Employees should be permitted to contribute and grow to their fullest capability and potential without constraints of artificial barriers, with compensation based on their demonstrated knowledge and skills rather than on tasks being performed at any specific time.

To achieve the most effective overall results, it is deemed necessary that a climate exist which will encourage initiative, experimentation, and generation of new ideas, supported by an open and meaningful two-way communication system.

It is worth noting that survey researchers have failed to identify much demand among workers for the kinds of conditions promised in this contract. Indeed it is "scientifically" found that workers only want to change such trivial things as lighting and the placement of water coolers. But experience—unlike survey research—shows that once workers get involved in decision making to the degree that they are at Donnelly, they quickly move from trivia to the tough underlying issues raised in the Shell Canada contract. Workers do not demand more initially because experience has taught them that they do not have the power to change anything that is important.

Another reason why there is not more overt demand for change is that there is a social presumption in favor of the status quo. At the extreme, it is assumed that the best work-place structure is the one that currently exists, that if there were a better way to organize work, it would have been found already. For example, there is a monolithic model to which almost all large law firms conform. Although few work places are less progressive, more inhumane—in fact, more medieval—than the typical corporate law office, the existing model is accepted without question "because that is the way things are done." But there are productive alternatives even to the tradition-bound organization of law firms, as Case No. 11 illustrates.

CASE NO. 11: Typically, large law firms hire young lawyers (associates) and condemn them to dog work for seven years. Young lawyers willingly submit in the hope of one day becoming partners and making "megabucks," as they say. The name of the game (it is literally a game) is "billable hours," in the service of which associates forgo vacations, weekends, and a good many lunches in order to impress partners with their twelve-hour-a-day dedication.

In contrast, the Los Angeles firm of Munger, Tolles and Rickerhauser was founded by a group of young lawyers (aged twenty-five to thirty-five) who decided to trade off the long-term possibility of hitting the megabuck jackpot for current satisfaction. Some of the policies they initiated are purely hedonistic: first-year lawyers get a month's vacation. But most of their radical policies affect the work itself. For example, new associates deal with real clients, not just footnotes on partner briefs. Right from the start associates are given full responsibility for entire cases. Promotions to partnership are made at the end of three years. This means that the firm is top-heavy (two partners for every associate, instead of the typical two associates for every partner). Consequently the difference in compensation between partners and associates is much smaller than in typical firms. But in lieu of Beverly Hills mansions, attorneys have the opportunity to take sabbaticals and to do extensive *pro bono* work on firm time. They also treat one another in civil, unlawyerly ways. For example, all the lawyers lunch together twice a week. At one lunch they hold seminars with outside experts, often on nonlegal topics. Significantly, the firm has the reputation of having the brightest lawyers in Southern California.

Flexibility, choice, participation, responsibility, and security—all the essential ingredients that are missing in a traditional corporate law firm are present at Munger et al. Yet in some ways it is unrealistic to compare this firm with the typical law firm. Since Munger and friends recruit only the top graduates from top law schools, it could be claimed that it is relatively easy to shove these young people out of the nest on day one, or that those top graduates are the only ones who would want to be given so much responsibility so soon. After all, the typical lawyer (or professional worker) is, by definition, *average*.

But one ought to be able to get the same results with *average* professionals that they get at Munger and company. For example, one could reinstitute the old apprentice notion that somehow got lost in the misguided rush to vocationalize the nation's schools and universities. For almost all professional tasks (and most other white-collar work in the fast-growing information industries), an excellent way to organize work is to put a young person under the wing of a much older one (so neither will be threatened by the other). The young person would be free to stay in the protégé status until he or she is ready to fly solo. But when he finally does go it alone, he would be held responsible *only for his final product.* That is, there would be no midcourse snooping or second guessing by "management." If the young person wanted to return to his or her old mentor for additional midflight tutelage, that would be his business.

I'm not too proud to admit that I'm average, at least in that I am reluctant to take full responsibility the first day on a new job. But I've been lucky; I've found myself in a protected situation three times in my checkered working career. Unhappily, the practice is quite rare at work today, simple and logical though it seems. (It may be coming back, however, under the with-it title of "mentoring.")

The work policies at the law firm described in Case No. 11 are remarkably consistent with the latest survey research finding about what is important to workers as they enter the 1980s. The much-maligned Michigan researchers have discovered that one-half of employed Americans report that they have problems with the inflexibility of their working schedules, and that the demands of work leave them with inadequate time for leisure activities.[17]

For what they are worth, such findings are at least in keeping with the only work-place revolution predicted in the early 1970s that is actually happening: flextime. Between 1974 and 1978 the number of Americans with flexible working schedules more than doubled. If the watchword of work in the 1980s is likely to be flexibility, then today's airline stewardess may in this regard be the prototype service worker of the next decade.

CASE NO. 12: The stewardess on TWA Flight 19 from IAD to LAX (check your airport IQ) is filling out her request for next month's flight assignment. She tells a nosy passenger that as long as she works the equivalent of sixteen days a month, she is free to schedule her flights in almost any pattern she chooses. Stewardesses who have children can schedule many short day flights so they can be home every night. Stewardesses who like to travel can schedule flights with long layovers in foreign cities. Stewardesses who are students can cluster their hours around their class schedules. The stewardess says, "The best part about this job is that it allows you to plan to enjoy the nonwork part of your life."

Admittedly stewardesses (and stewards, too—this *is* 1981) are untypical in that they have more flexibility and fewer hours of required work than the average worker. Nevertheless the general trend in the work force is toward more flexible patterns of work.

Along with the rapid increase in female participation in the labor force during the sixties and seventies came a complementary and parallel increase in the number of part-time workers. In 1960, 17.8 percent of American workers were part-timers; in 1978 the figure was up to 22.9 percent. Fully a third of all female workers are part-timers. And the demand for more part-time opportunities remains strong among women who are unemployed and those who are employed full time. Since nearly half of all American mothers with school-age children are in the work force, this unmet demand for flexible work schedules is easily explained. Moreover the issue is likely to get even hotter in the 1980s as inflation causes more retired people to supplement their incomes through part-time jobs, and as the desire to spend more time in family and leisure activities grows among workers in general.

Already there is evidence that the demand for part-time work far exceeds the supply of part-time jobs, which is kept artificially low by arbitrary government fringe-benefit regulations.

While flexibility has not yet arrived, a few progressive large corporations are engaged in an effort to provide individual workers with the choice among, and mobility between, a spectrum of different kinds of jobs. There is now some experimentation in firms like Polaroid with methods to assess the various rewards, demands, and challenges of jobs, to assess the interests, needs, and desires of workers, and to let workers select jobs that meet their needs. The company facilitates the process by providing training, placement, and other career services. Other innovative approaches in large corporations include Xerox's sabbatical program for workers who wish to spend a year doing public service. Below is a partial list of fringe benefits, incentive systems, and working conditions that have been tried in American work places and that would seem to score high on the performance criteria I outlined above.

Peer-Set Salaries and Raises. The seventy employees of Romac Industries in Seattle, Washington, vote on one another's raises.[18] If a worker wants a raise, he or she simply posts a pay-raise request, and five days later all the company's nonmanagerial employees vote on the raise on a one-worker/one-vote basis. While raises have been approved about 90 percent of the time, a few personally popular individuals with poor work habits have been denied raises on the grounds of equity. Edward Lawler has done considerable research that shows that there are many other ways in which workers can set their own salaries responsibly.[19]

Peer-Established Work Rules. In 1970 Arthur Friedman had a crazy idea. He decided not only to let the fifteen employees in his Oakland, California, appliance store set their own salaries, but also to decide what hours they would work, when they would take vacations (and for how long), and even to borrow money from petty cash without permission. During the five years he applied this philosophy he experienced no employee turnover, no losses from petty cash, no outrageous raise demands, and only a few rare cases of tardiness. In 1974 there were only three sick days for the *entire* work force. One of Friedman's employees told a reporter, "You have to use common sense; no one wins if you end up closing the business down. If you want more money, you have to produce more."[20] Overhead increased and volume decreased in Friedman's store during the experiment, but profits increased thanks to higher productivity. Entrepreneur Friedman is now applying his philosophy to a new and successful franchising business.

Opportunities for Learning at Work. The Dana Corporation of Toledo, Ohio, runs its own "Dana University," which is attended and taught by Dana employees—blue-collar as well as white-collar. While no workers are required to attend the school, there is great demand for admission because the company has a promote-from-within policy that is based on an employee's knowledge about his job and the company—that is, formal educational degrees don't count at promotion time. In addition to creating this learning environment, the company makes managerial information available to all workers as part of its Scanlon Plan (a system of

worker participation in productivity improvement in which workers receive
large shares of all productivity gains that result from the implementation of
their suggestions, à la Donnelly Mirrors). The company has also abolished
all corporate procedure manuals to encourage flexibility and employee
initiative.[21]

Task System. If one believes that workers are responsible, mature
adults, it follows that they should be paid for the work they complete, not
for the hours they spend on the job. That is, if a worker has done his job,
there is no reason why he should be forced to look busy until five o'clock
before he can go home. If someone has completed her task, she should be
free to leave. While this principle is impractical where a store, office, or
phone must be womanned from nine to five, that still leaves a lot of places
where it can be applied (manufacturing, mining, construction, and white-
collar work). One of the few places to do so is the Harman International
Industries plant in Bolivar, Tennessee. There productivity gains are shared
by allowing workers to go home when they have met the production
standard they negotiated with the company. If they don't want to go
home, workers can continue on their jobs and earn overtime bonuses.
But two hundred Harman workers opt for a third alternative: attending
the Harman School where courses are offered in everything from work-
related subject matter to piano playing, and are taught by managers
and blue-collar workers alike. The school has been accredited by the
county in which it is located, and many courses are open to the general
public.[22]

Salaries Instead of Wages. At Avon Products, Gillette, Black and
Decker, and Polaroid, workers who were formerly paid by the hour now
receive annual salaries. In general, this change has reduced absenteeism
and the need for supervisor policing, improved productivity and labor
relations, and increased the willingness of employees "to accept the
responsibility of reporting to work in situations where they formerly might
have stayed away."[23] The we/they attitude in business is one of the greatest
barriers to increased productivity because it is the source of the mistrust
that makes employees unwilling to assume responsibility for the quantity
and quality of their work. The we/they attitude is fostered by countless
"hidden injuries of class," such as the fact that all white-collar employees
have access to a free phone, while few blue-collar workers have such a right
(or privilege). One of the most effective ways to break down the blue-
collar/white-collar barrier is to abolish invidious distinctions in the way
people are paid. Robert Hulme and Richard Bevan have studied the issue
and conclude that there is a "presumption of irresponsibility applied to a
worker" that prevents employers from accepting "the fact that the

modern blue-collar worker performs the job not only for money but also for advancement, status and self-fulfillment, and these encourage responsibility."[24] Again, this reform seems so logical that one wonders why it hasn't been more fully implemented in U.S. businesses. At least part of the problem is that it runs against the need for worker flexibility. If people are not working full-time, paying them by the hour is the simplest—if not always the best—method of compensation. But a large part of the problem is that old devil inertia. Unions and management are *used* to paying people by the hour, and this tradition is too readily transmuted into the belief that this is the *only* way to pay people. One of the hundred largest firms in the U.S. still makes even its executives punch in on a time clock! Talk about encouraging responsibility.

Sick-Leave Banks. A great many employers have problems with worker abuse of the sick-leave privilege (which has come to be defined as a right). If an employee is "entitled" to fifteen days of sick leave a year, he or she will too often be inclined to take all of this time off to "recuperate" from job boredom on the beach, to do Christmas shopping, or to stretch out vacations with a timely illness. There is no way to "police" such abuses—employers can hardly ask for a note from a doctor (or from Mom) to justify an absence. But it is possible to encourage responsible behavior in this regard by creating a "sick-leave bank." Such a bank permits employees to pool their sick-leave days in a common fund available to workers who, because of extensive real illness, have used up all the time off to which they are entitled. While such a pool is an attractive benefit to workers, it also creates peer pressure not to abuse it. Where it has been tried, it has invariably cut down absenteeism. Worker committees approve all "loans" from the fund, and often require recuperated workers to pay back days before they become eligible for another "withdrawal."[25]

Well Pay/Safety Pay. Another novel way to reduce absenteeism is to provide "well pay." While several companies have tried out this idea successfully, it has been taken farthest at Parsons Pine Products in Oregon, where workers who are neither late nor absent for a full month receive an extra eight hours' wages. Parsons also has "retro pay," which is a sharing with workers of the savings in workers' compensation premiums resulting from reduced accidents. To support this effort, there is also "safety pay" which is a bonus for going a month without an accident.[26]

Quality Control Circles. In 1980, approximately fifty American companies had recently adopted the Japanese program of quality control circles. These circles are study groups of about ten workers each that meet regularly to solve quality and productivity problems related to their work. QCCs thus shift the responsibility for quality control from engineers to the workers themselves. They are led by workers, but receive staff assistance from management. Although financial incentives for problem solving tend to be downplayed—wrongly, I believe,—companies typically provide awards and other forms of recognition to successful circles. Worker participation in QCCs is strictly voluntary. Nonetheless in a typical Japanese company 90 percent of all workers participate, according to Robert Cole, who recently published a major comparative study of American and Japanese industry. The quality-of-working-life project at the General Motors Plant at Tarrytown (described in Case No. 9) is an American adaptation of the QCC approach. The process can be applied to nonmanufacturing companies as well. At the Chicago Title Insurance Company quality control circles have reduced the number of typist errors.

Cole notes that there are basically three alternative forms that an advanced, democratic industrial state can take: (1) *corporate paternalism,* in which corporations provide workers with entitlements; (2) *the welfare state,* in which entitlements come to workers from the government; and (3) *the Japanese system,* which is unlike the first two alternatives in that it does not create an unhealthy dependence of the individual on institutions. In contrast to the other two alternatives, Cole writes that in Japan the relationship of the individual to the organization is "one of reciprocal exchange of rights and obligations."[27]

Flexible Working Hours. In 1977 about 13 percent of all nongovernmental employers with over fifty workers offered flextime to at least some of their employees (but only 5.8 percent of all workers were actually on flextime). Here's how flextime is typically managed: All workers in an office are required to be at their jobs during specified "core" hours (say, 9–11:30 A.M.; 1–4 P.M.), but they can arrive at work anytime between 7 and 9 A.M., and go home anytime between 4 and 6 P.M. The only requirement is that they work at least 160 hours per month. If a worker works 170 or 150 hours, he or she carries a credit or debit of ten hours into the next month.

Usually not much greater variation from the forty-hour work week is permitted, but some companies do offer greater flexibility. At Equitable Life Insurance Company, for example, employees are free to choose from a smorgasbord of alternative schedules, including normal flextime, three four- and four-and-a-half day weeks, and nine- out of ten-day work stretches (with alternating two- and three-day weekends). Some German employers go so far as to offer individualized work year contracts in which employees negotiate any kind of arrangement or schedule that meets their personal interests, needs, or desires. A recent study indicates that flextime usually increases productivity and morale, while reducing tardiness, absenteeism, and turnover.[28]

Part-Time Work. Massachusetts Mutual Life Insurance offers jobs at "mothers' hours": 9:30 A.M. to 2:30 P.M. Control Data Corp. goes one step further: In a plant in St. Paul, it offers mothers jobs at similar hours, and makes a three-hour shift available to high school kids in the afternoon after the mothers have gone home. But such jobs are rare. Only 8 percent of the work force is on a *permanent* part-time basis (that is, in jobs that are regular and full-year rather than seasonal or occasional). One might expect that more permanent part-time jobs would be available, given the demand and the fact that most employers feel such jobs increase productivity while reducing labor costs and absenteeism. But as with flextime, employers report that part-time jobs increase administrative costs—that is, managers have to work harder. This fact probably explains more than a little of the resistance to the spread of a good idea. Also, as Fred Best has documented, the problem of fixed labor costs is a further disincentive.[29] Fixed labor costs include training, fringe benefits, record keeping, and payroll taxes that are identical whether an employee works full or part time. For example, because employers pay Unemployment Insurance tax only on the first $6,000 that a worker earns, it costs $222 more in such taxes to hire two workers part time at $7,500 each than it does to hire one at $15,000. Social Security taxes have a similar effect with higher-salaried employees.

Job Sharing. The deputy director of the California Employment Development Department in charge of legislative liaison is two people: Elizabeth Kersten and Mary Davies. Ms. Kersten owns two-fifths of the $29,880 job, while Ms. Davis holds down the other three-fifths, Ms. Kersten wants the reduced hours to spend more time with her family; Ms. Davies wants the reduced time because she lives two hours from her job on the California coast, where she finds the seclusion ideal for her avocation as a playwright. Pitney Bowes offers employment in which two women can share a production job, leaving one free to be with her children in the morning, and the other free to be with her children in the afternoon. As yet there are few examples of men sharing jobs. A striking exception is found in Santa Barbara, where seven men and women share five full-time medical technologist jobs. Not only does the scheme give everyone more leisure, it reduces their exposure to on-the-job radiation. In addition, there are several colleges and universities where husband/wife teams share a single academic appointment and home and child-care duties as well.

Leisure Sharing. In 1976 a severe cutback in the Santa Clara County budget in northern California led to a voluntary work- (or leisure-) sharing program. In order to save jobs, public employee union leaders reluctantly agreed to let the county offer workers the following options:

1. Giving up 5 percent of their annual income in exchange for ten and a half additional vacations days.
2. Giving up 10 percent of their annual income for twenty-one additional vacation days.
3. Giving up 20 percent of annual income for forty-two additional vacation days.

Layoffs were averted when 17 percent of the ten thousand county employees opted for one or the other of these leisure-sharing plans. In fact, the employees liked the program so much that when it came time to renegotiate contracts, their union bargained to retain these options. In Alameda County—across San Francisco Bay from Santa Clara—16 percent of the staff in the public defender's office annually choose to forgo 25 percent of their salaries in exchange for three-month "renewal sabbaticals." With the money saved, the office is able to hire four additional attorneys. So taken is the state of California with the job-creation possibilities of leisure sharing that in 1979 the legislature passed two bills, one facilitating reduced work time for state employees, the other offering subsidies to private employers to recoup the fixed labor costs that result from work-time reductions.[30]

Employment Security. One of the basic tenets of American industry is that corporations require the ability to lay workers off during periods of economic downturn. In industry in general—and autos and steel in particular—the country has grown accustomed to the spectacle of cyclical redundancies. Tens, sometimes hundreds, of thousands of workers are frequently sent home for periods lasting from a few weeks to many months. The blow of these layoffs has been softened in recent times by generous state unemployment insurance and by employer-provided supplementary unemployment benefits. Nonetheless, blue-collar workers (unlike most white-collar and almost all professional and managerial workers) face frequent periods of reduced income. Unlike the rest of the work-force, they cannot plan on being employed the next month.

This system generates understandable worker antagonism towards their industrial employers. From the perspective of blue-collar workers, employers treat them as the expendable factor of production, much less important than capital or real property, and certainly less important than the comfort of executives who will throw thousands of people out of work before they will take even minor cuts in their own six-figure salaries. Unions play on this unfortunate situation, exacerbating class differences and demanding exorbitant wages and benefits as compensation for cyclical layoffs (significantly, workers in the auto and steel industries demand and receive increases in compensation that far out-pace increases in their productivity and the average increases in wages of American workers in general). Thus, the price industry pays for the ability to lay-off employees is unrealistically high pay and a lack of employee loyalty.

In Japan the system works differently. For example, the New Japan Steel Corporation operates a ranch and fish hatchery as subsidiaries, a major purpose of which is to provide jobs for steel workers during periods of economic downturn. When demand for steel slackens, the company doesn't lay off its workers; instead, it transfers them to the ranch or hatchery (or "loans" them to other companies in counter-cyclical industries). The Japanese cannot understand our system. The Chairman of Sony, Akio Morita, has said that American management "hires other people at their own risk and when they (the managers) create a problem, they fire these people. The fault is with the management."[31] The Japanese credit their lifetime employment system with generating workers' loyalty and confidence in management that leads to identification with company productivity goals.

It is far from obvious, however, that the U.S. can or should adopt the Japanese system, many aspects of which run deeply against the grain of our culture, not the least "un-American" of which is the availability of a large pool of part-time workers—early retireds, students, mothers of young children—who are willing to be moved in and out of the work force in order to keep primary earners employed. Without going as far as the Japanese, American industry still can do a better job of planning for full employment. While it's not always easy, work can be scheduled to smooth out the effects of the business cycle. For example, while successfully competing in the highly unpredictable women's fashion industry, the Olga Company has managed to avoid significant layoffs even when the economy turns down and inventories rise, as in 1980. Olga's competitors—many of whom operate what are no better than sweatshops—continue to say that it is impossible to do for even a year what Olga has done for decades. In the highly cyclical auto-parts industry, Fel Pro Incorporated has never laid a worker off in sixty-two years. The secret at Olga and Fel Pro is dedication on the part of top management to planning for full employment. Nonetheless, dedication isn't always enough. Dana Corporation, which had gone as far in this regard as any American company, was forced to lay off workers in 1980 because it was too reliant on one industry—the depressed U.S. automakers—for all its business. Thus, in some industries, successful planning for full employment would entail diversification of customers and products and, perhaps, agreements with nearby counter-cyclical industries for the temporary transfer of workers. While it may be impossible to achieve absolute employment security in this country, there is no doubt that American companies could do a better job than they do at present.

Not all the conditions discussed here are appropriate in all work places in all times. Nor is the list rigorously all-inclusive; it is merely *suggestive* of the kinds of conditions that have the characteristics of diversity, choice, flexibility, mobility, participation, rights tied to responsibilities, and security. It is significant that few traditional fringe benefits appear on the list, nor do such new fringes as group legal and auto insurance. Because American workers in large corporations are "benefited up," fringes do not offer much in the way of motivation, productivity, or enhanced responsibility. Contrarily, several incentive systems are on the list. This runs counter to the Maslovian wisdom of the 1970s, the crux of which was that money no longer mattered much to workers. Finally, conspicuously absent from the list are job enrichment, which is merely the replacement of one monolithic job design with another, and *traditional* profit-sharing plans and ESOPs (employee stock ownership plans), which because they typically offer *in*authentic levels of participation, fail also to tie rights with responsibilities. (See Chapter 6 for examples of authentic profit and equity sharing.)

The implications of the above list for large corporations are enormous, for what it suggests runs counter to most trends in compensation and benefits. Between 1967 and 1977 the dollar value of company-provided benefits increased at an annual rate of 17 percent, while salaries and wages increased only 10 percent per year. During this era forms of compensation were dictated *not* by their effects on motivation, but rather by the results of compensation and benefit surveys. Unfortunately few companies are heeding the warning of benefit consultant David McLaughlin that "merit increases are basically a fiction in today's corporation."[32] While I agree that companies must again provide incentives and rewards for performance, my suggestions go even further: The performance criteria I propose may be necessary to create worker motivation, loyalty, commitment, and responsibility in the next decade when there may be no growth to finance new fringe benefits, new entitlements, or higher salaries.

The best way to change a company's or a nation's productivity/labor cost ratio is to alter the congeries of fringe benefits/incentive schemes/working conditions. These conditions have to be such that workers can clearly see that it is in their *self-interest* to improve the productivity/labor cost ratio. Jawboning won't do it. Systems like the one developed at Donnelly Mirrors will.

In Chapter 4 I concluded that the inevitable outcome of current entitlement trends is undesirable. Here I am arguing that the only positive and realistic way to avoid such a future is for companies to infuse concomitant responsibilities into the existing and probably inviolable arena of rights.

In other countries the notion of employee responsibility has been taken further than it has in the United States: In Japan the vast majority of workers in large firms have organized themselves into quality control circles to take responsibility for improving the quality of their work; in Germany workers have won the right to membership on all corporate boards of directors; and in Yugoslavia workers are now learning to manage the firms that they own cooperatively. While none of these examples is without its negative side effects, it is nonetheless true that Japanese workers have increased the quantity and quality of their output through assuming responsibility to do so; that German workers have moderated their wage demands and have created a climate of labor cooperation on a continent characterized by class conflict; and that the Yugoslav manager-workers outproduce the workers who have little responsibility (and few rights, for that matter) in the centrally planned industrial systems of Eastern Europe. I am not suggesting that the United States should or could adopt any of these models, because it is culturally, economically, and politically different from Japan, Germany, and Yugoslavia. But we can learn from these nations that it is possible to increase worker responsibilities *without* reducing worker rights. Their experience teaches us that there may be an alternative to the tragic trade-off between security and responsibility. The key to realizing this alternative will be the willingness of managers to create organizational structures and incentives that permit and encourage workers to take responsibility. Since the power to change organizations is in the hands of managers, workers cannot be expected to rise up and assume responsibility on their own initiative.

In conclusion, it seems neither unduly radical (nor unduly conservative) to assume that workers will behave more responsibly if they assume the risks that go with their own freely chosen behavior. They might also become more satisfied and productive in the bargain.

Concomitant with assuming such risks is the need for workers to receive a fair share of the financial gains that result from increases in productivity. Long-term motivation and commitment are not likely to be elicited when workers perceive that the fruits of their greater efforts go exclusively to managers and shareholders. Many mechanisms are available for providing employees with participation in the gains that result from working and producing more, ranging from the simple act at Harman International giving workers more time off the job, through the complex systems of productivity sharing at Donnelly Mirrors and profit sharing at Lincoln Electric, to the fundamental structural changes in ownership described in Chapter 6.

6

THE UNREALIZED
OPPORTUNITIES OF WORKER
CAPITALISM

CASE NO. 1: The scene is the loading dock of a medium-sized manufacturing firm in southern California. The president of the firm is addressing several hundred of his employees gathered below in a parking lot. It is the firm's "Harvest Day," the annual meting-out to employees of their shares of the bounty produced during the last year. The wealth is distributed in the form of stock in the company, which is held in a nonvoting trust. It has been a good year; with this "harvest," the employee trust will contain 7 percent of all the shares in the company. In his brief speech the president explains that workers are as entitled as investors to reap shares of the surplus produced by the company. He tells the workers that they, too, are investors, for they invest their time, energy, and creative efforts in the firm.

As the president speaks, many workers are fidgeting and some are grousing audibly. A Spanish-speaking woman says to her companions, "I need a new refrigerator, and he gives me a piece of paper."

CASE NO. 2: The scene is a meeting of the Personal Justice Committee of International Group Plans (IGP), a Washington, D.C.–based insurance company in which workers have been given half the shares of the company and half the seats on the board. The committee is considering a complaint lodged by one of the firm's "work groups" (self-managing teams of six workers each) against a member of the group. The worker in question has a chronic record of absenteeism and tardiness. The other members of his group are complaining that they have to pick up his share of the work. The committee meeting degenerates into bickering and shouting. The committee members, all workers themselves, eventually drift back to their own jobs with nothing settled. Such chaotic meetings are said to be common at IGP. The company tries, says one worker, "to make *every* decision democratically."[1]

CASE NO. 3: The scene is the *last* stockholder meeting of the 178 worker-owners of the Vermont Asbestos Group. The date is May 1, 1978. Two years earlier these asbestos miners had put up $100,000 of their own money as collateral to buy the mine from the GAF Corporation, which had decided to close it rather than spend $1.5 million to meet environmental and worker safety standards. In the first year of worker ownership the mine had made a pretax profit of $1 million, and from March 1976 to December 1977 it had made a profit of $3 million. Reviewing what they had accomplished in less than three years, the worker-owners found that they had satisfied all EPA requirements, had met all payments on their debts, and had accumulated $1 million in new assets. Between 1975 and 1978 wages had jumped from $3.26 per hour to $4.96, and a common share of the firm that a worker had bought for $50 now had a book value of $2,103. At the meeting the workers discuss the action of the company's top managers in investing in a new subsidiary against the express wishes of the workers, who had overwhelmingly voted against the plan. An observer describes the scene: "Now, this was a real slap in the face of the workers-shareholders. . . . They most decidedly expected that as share-holders they would have a say. When they realized that they didn't even have a say as shareholders, that was just the end."[2] Feeling betrayed, the workers vote to turn management of the firm over to a local contractor, to whom they sell controlling interest.

While sketchy and impressionistic, all three of these cases illustrate some of the major human problems that beset what has become known as "worker capitalism," or employee ownership of stock in the companies for which they work. While much has been written about the legal and financial technicalities of employee stock ownership, relatively little attention has been directed to the human issues raised by this radical departure from traditional modes of ownership. Yet business leaders, trade unionists, scholars, and workers themselves are likely to be as interested in the human as in the financial side of this intriguing social experiment. In response to this interest, my aim in this chapter is to summarize and evaluate the limited American experience with worker capitalism; identify where the movement has failed and where it has succeeded; analyze the various causes of success and failure; and synthesize out of all this a pair of general principles to guide those who would join the movement.

If forced to summarize the available cases, studies, and data on worker ownership, my generalizations would read as disappointing news:

1. There has been little increase in job satisfaction, morale, or company loyalty among worker-owners.
2. There has been little increase in motivation on the part of employee stockholders. That is, few companies have found a measurable effect on worker performance or productivity resulting directly from stock ownership.
3. Workers have generally displayed indifference toward stock ownership. This lack of interest has been manifested in several dramatic instances when workers have sold off their shares to the first attractive bidder.

But these are merely generalizations about the experiences of perhaps three thousand American companies that have formal policies encouraging employee stock ownership. In fact, there are easily three dozen worker-owned firms that are clearly exceptions to these generalizations. These are firms in which records of high profitability, productivity, and worker morale are *directly attributable* to worker ownership. That encouraging economic *and* human results have been obtained only in a miniscule percentage of cases is explainable, in large part, by the fact that one is comparing not only apples and oranges, but avocados as well, when generalizing about "employee stock ownership." This loosely used concept embraces a conglomeration of not fully commensurable organizational forms. For instance, each of the three distinct forms of worker stock ownership described below has a quite different track record.

Cooperatives. These are firms in which worker-capitalists own equal shares, are paid equally, and have equal voices in matters of company governance. While in a given cooperative some workers might hold slightly larger ownership shares than others and some might be paid slightly more for undertaking more difficult or onerous tasks, and in another the worker-owners might hire a professional manager to serve as the chief administrative officer, these exceptions notwithstanding, *equality and democratic self-management* are the prime characteristics of cooperatives. Examples include sixteen plywood companies in Oregon and Washington and two garbage-collection companies in San Francisco.

Joint Partnerships. Included in this category are firms in which a founder of a company shares ownership with his employees. In other instances, employees own a large block of shares, and the remainder are owned by the community in which the company is located, or are traded on a market. Examples include: IGP, half owned by its founder and half owned by its employees, and the Mohawk Valley Community Corporation (described below), owned in partnership with the employees by citizens of Herkimer, New York, where it is located.

Trusts. These are companies that use the increasingly popular employee stock ownership plans (ESOPs). In such firms a fixed amount of stock is typically placed in a trust as collateral for a loan drawn on a bank. As the loan is paid off, the stock held in trust is conveyed to the employees. While ESOPs come in many sizes and permutations, there is usually a restriction on the voting rights of stock held in trust, the proceeds generated by the trust usually serve as a deferred compensation plan (a pension fund is the closest analogy), and the stock is distributed unequally to employees in proportion to their wages. Companies with ESOPs include AT&T, Atlantic Richfield, and Mobil.

On the basis of measures of worker productivity and morale, cooperatives appear to be the most successful form of worker capitalism. The record of joint partnerships is mixed. And while many companies with ESOPs have truly outstanding records, there is no convincing evidence to suggest that worker stock ownership is in any way responsible for producing these high levels of economic and human performance.

These general conclusions must be hedged, however. Much of what I am reporting is, by necessity, anecdotal. Moreover some of it is unavoidably dated: The dynamics of worker-owned firms are such that today's facts are tomorrow's inaccuracies. Nevertheless my conclusions are buttressed by the only rigorous quantitative study of employee-owned firms, which was recently undertaken for the Department of Commerce by Michael Conte and Arnold Tannenbaum. In this study of ninety-eight U.S. and Canadian firms (median sales = $25 million; median number of employees = 350) the authors found that "the more equity the workers own, the more profitable the company, other things being equal."[3] Moreover they found a positive correlation between the percentage of employee equity on the one hand, and worker attitudes and productivity on the other: The more equity the workers owned, the better their morale and performance. For this reason conventional ESOPs—that is, the 90 percent of Kelso plans without substantial employee ownership—are *not* the main subject of attention in this chapter. Rather the primary focus is on firms in which at least one-quarter of the shares are owned by employees.

While the amount of equity is clearly a key success factor, some subtle organizational variables that separate successful from unsuccessful examples of worker capitalism are also analyzed in these pages. But before one company can be called successful and another one not, it is necessary to define success. That is, what are worker-owned firms trying to achieve?

GOALS OF WORKER CAPITALISM

It would be an error to evaluate all employee-owned firms solely by the standard financial yardsticks applied to the Fortune 500. In many instances the goals of worker-capitalists are not identical to the goals of executives at Exxon or General Motors. Some worker-owned firms, for instance, have consciously chosen *not* to grow. While most employee-owned firms strive for high profitability like any capitalist enterprise, they also frequently try to achieve goals that are foreign to large, publicly held firms. Below are five common goals of worker-owned firms, some of which are unlikely to be of prime concern to America's corporate giants.

Goal 1: Save Jobs. One of the most common objectives of forming a worker-owned business has been to rescue a plant from closing or a small company from bankruptcy. Most cooperatives, many joint partnerships, and a few trusts have been formed when a large corporation has announced that it intends to close a plant or division that is no longer economically viable. Particularly in one-industry towns where a plant or company closing would lead to economic ruin for the entire community, workers have been willing to pool their own savings and to borrow from local banks and investors in order to purchase a failing enterprise. For example, in 1975 Sperry Rand announced plans to close its library-furniture manufacturing facility in Herkimer, New York. Although the plant was profitable, the corporation said that it didn't fit with Sperry Rand's overall product strategy, and moreover was unlikely ever to earn the 22 percent return on invested capital that the corporation had reportedly set as the minimal profit standard for all its divisions. While closing the plant was a reasonable financial decision on the part of Sperry Rand, the 270 Herkimer workers concluded that *it was unreasonable for them.* So they banded together with community leaders and raised $4 million to buy the plant (including a $2 million loan from the federal government). In the first year of worker ownership as the Mohawk Valley Community Corporation the company earned $875,000 on $13 million in sales (helped along by a savings of $600,000 in overhead that was formerly paid to Sperry Rand).

Goal 2: Save Capitalism by Reforming It. In 1958 the philosopher Mortimer Adler teamed with a lawyer named Louis Kelso to produce a remarkable book, *The Capitalist Manifesto,* which attempted to dislodge the cornerstone of Marxist doctrine that "property is theft."[4] Not so, wrote Adler and Kelso, for even a careful reading of *Das Kapital* reveals no evidence to support the claim that private property rights are inherently unjust. All that can be demonstrated is that the *concentration* of ownership in the hands of a few individuals gives them the political power to reduce the freedom of others. Moreover it is specifically the *control* of the means of production—rather than holding actual legal title to it—that affords such power. Therefore the concentration of ownership of the means of production in the state gives Russian Communist Party bosses totalitarian powers that far surpass those of the wealthiest capitalists in the United States.

Kelso and Adler thus reasoned that justice would *not* be served by abolishing private property, but by *diffusing* its ownership. In effect, a lot of capitalism would be better than a little capitalism. The genius of worker capitalism, according to Adler and Kelso, is that it permits the continued existence of a market economy, property rights, and political freedom, while at the same time addressing the problem of inequality by making "every man a capitalist."

That a reformed type of capitalism could be more just than state socialism has become an exciting idea to many liberals and conservatives alike. Populists like Russell Long and George McGovern now find themselves joined with the conservatives who head Hallmark Cards and *U.S. News and World Report* in singing the praises of a new system that would allow the nation to have its cake of freedom, while distributing its slices more equally.

Goal 3: Bring Democracy into the Work Place. In the labor relations arena there are currently three major and overlapping reform efforts operating at full gear: (1) the "quality-of-working-life" movement, which seeks to redesign working conditions to allow employees to develop their full potentials on the job; (2) the "industrial democracy" movement, which seeks to introduce the democratic values and processes of the broader society into work organizations; and (3) the "employee rights" movement, which seeks to inject constitutionally guaranteed civil rights into work settings. Advocates of all three of these movements see worker capitalism as a vehicle for the realization of their aims. Their argument is that it is wrong for managers to *prescribe* working conditions for employees. Only through *self*-management can workers establish the conditions that meet *their* needs, as opposed to the needs of management. Employee ownership is seen not only as a direct path to self-management, but also as a long-term guarantee of workers' rights.

Goal 4: Increase Employee Motivation. While all companies are concerned with the issue of employee motivation, very few subscribe to the theory that stock ownership has a positive effect on worker performance. Corporations have usually operated under assumptions that employee motivators range from money to interesting work to loving supervisors.

Ownership has been largely overlooked as a motivator, both in practice and in the literature of organizational behavior. Indeed even Adler and Kelso fail to develop the effects of ownership on motivation, other than to say that an equity position is likely to reduce wage demands that are not matched by productivity gains. Most economists and business leaders seem tacitly to agree with John Kenneth Galbraith's theory of managerial motivation: Ownership is irrelevant; what counts is personal power, prestige, security, and comfort.[5]

As Galbraith is well aware, there is considerable irony in the fact that the dominant assumptions of motivation in American industry are out of synch with the dominant assumptions of our economic system. For one of the most basic assumptions of capitalism is that the ownership of property is a prime motivator of human behavior. For example, it is often remarked that the owners of a Mom and Pop grocery store will work twelve hours a day, six days a week; but if Mom and Pop go to work for someone else, they will demand a forty-hour week, even at a reduced income. Equally common-place is the observation that people will treat their own homes—no matter how humble—with "the pride of ownership"; but let them rent a house and they will treat it as if "it belongs to somebody else." The introduction of ESOPs on a broad scale has led some companies to evaluate the attitudes of their employees to see if stock ownership has the motivational effects it is reputed to have in the more purely capitalistic conditions of grocery store ownership. For the first time since the Depression ruined the last significant effort to establish worker capitalism, a few companies now claim that they are establishing stock ownership plans with the express purpose of improving employee morale and performance.

Goal 5: Economic Advantages. For all the idealistic and humanistic hoopla that surrounds the issue of worker capitalism, most of its practical manifestations have been pragmatic and unabashedly crass. Thanks in large part to recent changes in the tax code, creation of ESOPs has tremendous economic advantages, particularly for small- and medium-sized firms. Among the fabled advantages are tax deductions for payments on the principal as well as on the interest on loans obtained through an employee trust, and the opportunity for an owner to obtain significant savings in estate taxes while passing on a firm to his heirs without the necessity of a public stock offering. Workers cooperate in such tax prestidigitation because they are promised increases in their retirement incomes as a result of the formation of ESOP trusts.

Significantly these diverse goals of worker capitalism often come into conflict. For example, if a company uses an ESOP to reduce estate taxes, this goal could conflict with the goal of increasing work-place democracy. The heirs to a company may wish to put stock into an employee trust for tax reasons, but they may also wish to restrict the voting rights of employee stock to maintain their personal power and influence in the firm. Such conflicts are often at the heart of the poor performance of the worker-owned firms evaluated below.

WHERE WORKER CAPITALISM FAILS TO MEET EXPECTATIONS

Goal conflicts have frequently prevented realization of the opportunities of worker capitalism *even in companies that are otherwise successful.* This is most often the case in companies that have ESOPs, for the goal that usually lies behind the creation of such plans is *not* employee motivation but the desire of the existing management group to retain control of the firm. To achieve this goal, they contrive a plan that ensures a highly disproportionate share of the total stock will pass into the hands of top management. While most workers receive some shares (the earnings on which will create an attractive pension plan), they do *not* receive a sense of ownership of the firm. Technically they can vote their shares through the stock trustees, but practically there are great inconveniences in doing so. Thus stock ownership through an ESOP typically offers all the incentive to greater productivity of a decent pension plan—which is to say, very little.

In this vein, the company described in Case 1 is an impressive economic success. It was successful before it started placing stock in trust for its employees, and has continued as roughly the same healthy, historical growth rate by most financial indicators since creating the trust. Untypically the founder of this firm created the employee stock ownership plan with the publicly stated goal of reforming capitalism. But this goal has come into conflict with the goal of transferring ownership to the founder's heirs, and with the fears of other shareholders that their stock will be diluted. Additionally stockholders and managers fear that employee ownership will proceed to the logical conclusion of *employee control* of the firm. From the point of view of the workers, the stock plan doesn't go far enough. Several employees of the firm have told me that they view the plan as paternalism at best, as a sop to forestall union activity at worst. These employees said that their limited equity position had no discernible effect on their own motivation or, as far as they could tell, on the motivation of their fellow workers.

Hallmark is an example of a firm where the potential tension between the goals of the Hall family heirs and the goals of the new class of capitalists being created in the firm is being successfully resolved: The Hall family has agreed to sell, on their deaths, 65 percent of their stock (controlling interest) to the employees. Some small ESOPs have been extremely well-designed and managed. Within two years, the owners of Quinn & Company, a New Mexico-based member of the New York Stock Exchange, transferred 100 percent of their stock and complete voting rights, to all of the company's 130 employees. Such corporate giants as Mobil, AT&T, and Atlantic Richfield belong in a different category altogether. Although each has recently introduced an ESOP, such an insignificant portion of outstanding shares is being transferred to their trusts that any potential for conflict (or employee motivation) won't arise for decades.

Moving as far from the affluent, antiseptic world of Hallmark as one can go in the United States, one ventures to McCaysville, Georgia, in southern Appalachia. In this impoverished setting sixty brave and entrepreneurial women attempted to start their own clothing factory in 1968 after an unsuccessful year-long strike against Levi-Strauss. With economic support from such unlikely sources as the Southern Christian Leadership Conference, the women attempted to run their cooperative according to the "participative democracy" ideology of the 1960s. Journalist Daniel Zwerdling has documented the pathetic efforts of McCaysville industries to make worker capitalism conform to their counterculture ideology:

> But the co-op structure soon began to fall apart. The members simply did not know how to make a democracy work. For instance, the women did not know when the entire membership should make a decision or when the elected manager could better make the decision on their behalf. Sometimes the co-op tried to be *too* democratic, to a fault.[6]

In addition to suffering the perils of ideology, the co-op was harassed into reconstituting itself as a conventional partnership by Georgia state officials who wanted no truck with the unconventional. Today the company is a partnership owned and run by four of the original members of the co-op. Worker ownership and self-management linger only as memories.

Like the good ladies of McCaysville, Jim Gibbons, founder and president of IGP, is a graduate of the civil rights and antiwar protests of the 1960s (see Case 2). After having made a small fortune through the innovation of selling group health insurance by computerized mailings, Gibbons put his money behind his principles and in 1972 transferred half of IGP's stock to his employees in a nonsalable trust. He then told the employees to elect half the members of the board of directors (he appointed the other half).

From Zwerdling's account, it would seem that Gibbons issued philosophical manifestos to his workers with a frequency that would make Hugh Heffner's head spin. During a transitional period that presumably approximated the "dictatorship of the proletariat," Gibbons guided the company with these philosophical statements. He established a Worker's Congress and a system of committees to run the company. After that, Gibbons was as good as his word: He let the "state" wither away. Under self-management, the workers several years ago voted themselves a $9.60 per hour minimum wage for the lowest paid employees (plus profit sharing). They then voted out several experienced department heads in favor of people who "had their heads straight." They also voted themselves three months' paid sick and maternity leave, paid vacations of up to a month for clerical workers, and banned the keeping of all attendance records.

According to the latest written reports, IGP was in trouble. High turnover, absenteeism, tardiness, and sloppy work had driven up costs, and profits had leveled off. Democracy had degenerated into anarchy, and Gibbons was said to have taken back some control of the firm.[7]

Unfortunately the initial high hopes for worker-owned and managed firms have often ended in such disappointment—particularly when the firms were started for ideological reasons. Other examples: In Britain left-wing Labour Party backbenchers in 1975 provided government help to save Meridian Motorcycles (makers of Triumph) from bankruptcy, and to turn it into a cooperative. At about the same time a left-wing coalition formed the *Scottish Daily News* as a cooperative. Within a year both had folded.

In America even the successes have seemed to sour. On more than one occasion the goal of financial security has come into conflict with the goal of self-management, and workers have decided to take their profits, even if it meant having to go to work for someone else after the satisfying stint of working for themselves. For example, the worker-owners of the *Kansas City Star* recently sold their company to Capital Cities Corporation for $125 million, a sum apparently too tempting to resist.

Thus outrageous misfortune seems to dog the heels of the advocates of worker capitalism: When a success story finally comes along, the workers fink out and peddle their shares. Certainly by any quantitative measure of human results there are countless more disappointments than successes among worker-owned firms.

But a few (a *very* few) cases illustrate that when goal conflict is removed or successfully managed, worker-owned firms have been able to outperform their competition in the public and private sectors on standard economic measures, while at the same time achieving the special social and human goals of worker capitalism.

WHERE WORKER CAPITALISM MEETS EXPECTATIONS

If longevity is a measure of success, sixteen plywood factories in Oregon and Washington are the best examples of worker capitalism. For approximately forty years the oldest of the plywood cooperatives have survived and thrived in a highly competitive, highly cyclical industry. While no 1970s data are available, Paul Bernstein writes that output per man-hour in the worker-owned mills ran 30 percent ahead of conventionally owned firms during the previous two decades.[8] That the companies are still financially successful is evidenced by the fact that they have become targets for conglomerate acquisition. Within the last few years ITT and the Times-Mirror Corporation have purchased two worker-owned mills. That the firms are efficient is evidenced by the fact that when one of the mills was so purchased, its conglomerate owner had to add eight new foremen to get the work done. Once the workers were no longer self-managing, they were apparently less efficient. The main sources of higher productivity in the mills are: lower overhead (e.g., there are no high-salaried executives); elimination of middle management (e.g., there are no first-line supervisors); greater manpower flexibility (e.g., all workers learn many jobs and are willing to shift when and where they are needed); and quality control (e.g., through responsible handling, the worker-owners can make productive use out of cheaper materials that hired hands in conventional plants break through carelessness).

According to Paul Bernstein, the mills operate under strict egalitarian principles: one worker, one share, one vote, and equal salaries. In some respects it is harder to become a member of one of these co-ops than it is to acquire a seat on the New York stock exchange. Shares (costing up to $60,000) are not cheap for blue-collar workers who have little capital. Although shares can be purchased with a small down payment and paid for over time through monthly payroll deductions, money alone won't get a worker a share and a job. There is a required trial period in most mills in which prospective worker-owners are tested to see if they have the attitudes and willingness to work required of all co-op members.

Although mill owners do not retire rich, the benefits of ownership are many: free lunches (the workers know there "ain't no such thing," but they prefer this tax-free benefit to larger shares of taxed profit), gas from company pumps purchased at wholesale prices, and one- to three-month sabbaticals (a rare fringe benefit outside academia). But the psychic benefits of ownership are the most remarkable. Independent observers all comment on the pride and "rugged individualism" of the millers. These people take guff from no master, and this is apparently worth a great deal to the millers, many of whom could earn more working for someone else.

It is curious how this individualism mixes with egalitarianism in the plywood mills. While these values might seem to conflict, the millers manage the two quite nicely by not treating their egalitarianism as an ideological fetish. Equality is the rule in the mills simply because equality is fair and because it works. There is no socialistic rejection of the broader system: "We're capitalists," the workers have told more than one reporter. And Bernstein reports that self-management is taken seriously by the millers. For the sake of efficiency, day-to-day decisions are made by an elected board or by a hired professional manager—but every important nonroutine decision is taken by a vote of *all* the worker-owners.

Although these are generalizations about sixteen companies, each with a unique constitution, it seems that workers are highly motivated in all of them. As one co-op member told Bernstein, "When the mill is your own, you really work hard to make a go of it."[9]

There are also a few instances where worker-owned companies have been successful alternatives to *government* ownership. In San Francisco, which is not exactly a hotbed of free-enterprise ideology, garbage collection has for decades been provided by two worker cooperatives. There have been few calls to "nationalize" this service because of its manifest benefits to the city. Unlike New York, Los Angeles, and other large cities that provide municipal trash collection, San Francisco is a kind of refuse utopia. Where municipal governments provide trash collection, it is often necessary to buy off garbagemen with high salaries and unconscionably generous pensions—yet the service often remains poor. San Francisco, in contrast, enjoys relatively low cost and excellent service. In 1969 Carter Bales came from the New York office of McKinsey and Company to compare San Francisco's scavenger system with that of the Big Apple's. No comparison, he told a group of young consultants at the time: "In San Francisco, garbagemen *run* from trash can to trash can."[10] They don't go on strike either.

The source of the different behavior of New York and San Francisco garbagemen may be the self-images of the two groups. In New York garbagemen are seen as, and see themselves as, people who have to be bribed to do dirty work. As one who grew up in San Francisco, I was surprised to find this attitude in other cities; for while going to school in San Francisco, I never recall hearing the children of garbagemen teased about their fathers' line of work. To us, garbagemen were owners of a small business, and not much different from plumbers in status. Once a month we even saw the trash collector at our door in jacket and tie collecting the bill for the service he provided. The whole system was thus geared—

without forethought, of course—to build the self-respect of, and respect of others for, those who provided an essential public service.

In addition to these examples of thriving co-ops, there are several joint partnerships that also seem to be economically successful. One of these is the Saratoga Knitting Mill, which was purchased in 1975 from the Cluett, Peabody Company by forty of the seventy workers in the mill. The employees now own about 60 percent of the stock; the rest is held by outside investors. The company is an exception to the others described in this section in that stock ownership is unevenly held (sixteen plant managers hold about half of the stock) and there is little or no democratic self-management. Nevertheless the company is a financial success: While production in the mill dropped below $4 million during the last year of conventional ownership, the company expects the total for 1979 to top $10 million.

The nation's only trust in which there is 100 percent employee ownership is also an economic success. In 1975 five hundred employees of the South Bend Lathe Company bought their failing enterprise from Amsted Industries for $10 million. The entire amount was borrowed (with federal help), and financed through placing ten thousand shares of stock in an ESOP trust as collateral. The company will pay off the loan over twenty-five years, during which period the shares will be paid out to the employees. Currently the shares are voted by a committee of five employees, including both managers and "workers."

In the first year of employee ownership, after meeting loan repayments, the company was profitable enough to give every worker a raise, a $50 Christmas bonus, an extra week of paid vacation, and a turkey at Thanksgiving. Before the end of the second year the company had paid off $4.5 million in debt. At the end of three years the company had accumulated $2.3 million in cash and other assets, raised employee salaries by 45 percent, and increased earnings per share from $20 to $45. According to a *post hoc* study of the company by researchers from the University of Michigan, both workers and managers felt that the change in ownership had "contributed substantially to the satisfaction of all employees, to the motivation of workers and, ultimately, to the productivity and profitability of the company."[11] After studying company records the Michigan researchers concluded that the rate of grievances had dropped, waste had declined, and productivity had increased in the period immediately following the worker takeover. The researchers note that communications in the plant improved, and they suggest that this could be the reason for the increases in the other human and economic measures. But a more direct reason may be peer pressure, which is probably the most effective form of "industrial discipline." At South Bend Lathe, and at most other successful worker-owned firms, there appears to be little need for authoritarian supervision or Taylorism. Workers care not only about their own work; equally important, they care about the efforts of their co-workers. As one South Bend Lathe worker-capitalist told a *Time* reporter, "It's, 'Hey, you've got your hand in my pocket if you don't do your job.' "[12] Nevertheless Zwerdling reported growing dissatisfaction at South Bend Lathe over the fact that allocation of shares of stock is based on salary, and thus managers receive a disproportionate number of the shares paid out of the trust. Another indicator of ferment was that 180 employees signed a petition asking that half of the seats on the board of directors be allocated to workers. Finally, in 1980, the worker-owners hit the bricks in an eight-week strike against management when their request for a cost-of-living adjustment was rejected. John Deak, president of the union representing the workers, explains the situation: "It seems unusual, but the workers and I quickly found out that we aren't the owners at all. . . . Some pickets went on company property—and the company got an injunction to keep us off. We maintained that, since we were the owners, we had a right to be on that property. But the judge said we were shareholders, not owners—and ordered us off."[13]

It will be instructive to monitor how these conflicts are resolved at South Bend Lathe and at other worker-owned firms (such as Saratoga Knitting) where there are invidious distinctions in the ownership of stock between workers and managers, even though people in both categories are technically employee-owners. William Foote Whyte has firsthand experience at such worker-owned firms as the ones in Saratoga and Herkimer, New York. He has noticed that after a brief honeymoon, old conflicts rearise between managers and workers. Whyte says that managers are

> likely to assume that workers, now becoming co-owners of the firm, will appreciate the wisdom of management decisions and will comply more effectively with managerial orders. . . . Such failure on both sides to recognize the social requirements of the new form of ownership leads . . . [to] the deterioration of hopes, trust and mutual confidence as labor and management slide back into the same old frictions and misunderstandings that prevailed before the change in ownership.[14]

EVALUATION OF SUCCESSES AND FAILURES

What is striking about both the successful and unsuccessful cases reported above is the workers' total lack of preparation for their new rights and responsibilities as owners. Consequently they often see ownership as "just a piece of paper" or as "just another deferred compensation plan." With this attitude, workers are unlikely to behave much differently from the way they did before they received their shares. If improved employee attitudes and productivity are to be the goals of worker capitalism, workers will have to be taught that there is a difference between being an employee and being an owner. Some of what must be taught is economic: Even at the successful plywood cooperatives, hired professional managers complain that worker-capitalists do not understand the economic necessity of reinvestment. Some of what must be taught is social: Workers are often unaware that ownership entitles them to a say in the running of their firms. The need for education is usually recognized only after it is too late. For example, 86 percent of the miners recently polled at Vermont Asbestos said that the situation there might have developed differently had there been an education program to prepare them for independent self-management.[15]

Another problem is that most former owners and professional managers have been unwilling to surrender the rights and responsibilities of ownership to worker-capitalists. This is not necessarily a sign of authoritarianism or manipulation on the part of those in power. The fear that worker control will degenerate into license and anarchy will occur to even the least paranoid managers when they read Zwerdling's account of IGP! All that can be said to allay this legitimate fear is that chaos seems only to have ensued when worker capitalism was pursued for purely ideological reasons. (Even so, one wonders if proper educational preparation of the managers and workers of IGP and McCaysville might have led to different outcomes.)

But, as Whyte notes, most managers and owners, for whatever reasons, have been unwilling to change the power relationships in their organizations to make them congruent with the altered patterns of ownership. And in the case of most ESOPs, this problem has been compounded by the frequent limitation on the voting rights of stock held in employee trusts. In a recent telephone survey of forty-five companies with ESOPs a researcher found that only one-third of the managers interviewed believed that ESOPs had any positive effect on employee attitudes.[16] Only in the twenty-two companies where voting rights *had* been passed on to employees was there any positive correlation between the introduction of an ESOP and the managers' perception of improved employee attitudes (fifteen of the twenty-two firms with voting rights reported an improvement in employee attitudes).

While this telephone survey is far from methodologically convincing, it nevertheless gives added weight to the Conte and Tannenbaum study and to the generalizations I have drawn from my review of the available cases: that is, a little bit of worker capitalism is of little or no use to the workers or to their firms. The bottom line is this: If a firm wishes to achieve improved human results from worker ownership, it will probably have to adhere closely to two principles.

The Principle of Ownership

If the owner of a single share of General Motors stock were to describe GM as "my company," this petty investor would be greeted with gales of derisive laughter. For everyone knows that this "owner" of General Motors could not even set foot on "his" company's property without the permission of management. But if the owner of one of the five hundred shares of an Oregon plywood cooperative were to describe that firm as "my company," this worker-owner would be viewed as speaking with some authority. There is a difference between owning a few shares in a company and actually *owning* a company. Workers who participate in the ESOP at Mobil are no more owners of that company than participants in pension funds are owners of the companies in which these funds have investments, or holders of life insurance policies are owners of the mutual company issuing their policies. One might well have "a piece of the rock," but that piece is more analogous to a taxpayer's piece of a U.S. Navy aircraft carrier than it is to Mom's half interest in the corner grocery store. John Deak, the shop steward at South Bend Lathe, makes the point this way: "You take a working man who says, you own something, and that is exactly what he [means], I own it and I have a key to it, But an ESOP doesn't give you a key to the plant"[17]

Peter Drucker has contributed to the misconceptions about the nature of corporate ownership.[18] His exaggerated claim that "pension fund social- ism" is revolutionizing the American corporation totally ignores the fact that professional managers have nearly complete *control* over almost all giant, publicly held U.S. corporations. And as Adler and Kelso point out, it is *control*—not ownership—that ultimately counts. It doesn't matter a whit to professional managers if the shares of *their* companies are owned by ESOPs, pension funds, Arab sheiks, or little old ladies from Pasadena. For the managers recognize a fact of life: Even if Thomas Aquinas Murphy didn't own a single share of General Motors, no one would laugh if *he* referred to GM as *his* company. For Murphy and his fellow top executives exercise more of the rights of ownership than do GM's shareholders. They have the "key."

Title to a few shares in a large company does not fool anyone into thinking that he or she owns it. People will act like owners only when their equity is significant. And there is evidence that when people are actual owners of a company, they act with impressive productivity. A study undertaken by two of my colleagues at USC shows that privately held firms have three times the average net income as a percentage of sales as publicly held firms, and their return on assets is 12 percent greater.[19] Thus we should not be surprised that Tannenbaum and Conte found that employee-owned firms are one and a half times more profitable than comparable, conventionally owned firms in their respective industries. To repeat: The more equity the workers have, the greater the profitability of the company. John Lupien, while acting as worker-chairman of Vermont Asbestos, offered an explanation that might help us to understand how a significant equity position affects worker productivity:

> Everybody feels that they can do a little extra, not just to save the jobs but to make it better for themselves for the future—and they won't do it now for a big company. They feel, "Well, they're making the money, why should I work any harder?" We can create an incentive that a big company cannot, because everybody will be a shareholder.[20]

It is little wonder then that the ballyhooed "worker ownership" at the Chicago and North Western Railroad has failed to achieve the results that Lupien describes at Vermont Asbestos. At North Western only four hundred of the company's more than twelve thousand blue-collar workers invested in the company when it shifted from conventional ownership. This means that six hundred of the original one thousand "employee-owners" were managerial personnel, and the lion's share of stock was purchased by a handful of top executives. This was no way to run a "worker-owned" railroad.

In sum, the effects on employee morale, motivation, and productivity appear to be the most positive when:

· Ownership is *direct* (that is, not through a trust).
· Ownership is *widespread* (that is, almost all workers are shareholders, not just managers or those workers who are sophisticated enough to take the initiative to invest).
· Ownership is *broadly held* (that is, when all workers have significant, not just nominal, equity).

The ownership principle thus can be stated: *The more worker ownership in a company, the better.*

The Principle of Responsibility

In several cases the performance criteria described in Chapter 5 have been incorporated into the philosophy and organization of work in employee-owned companies. In particular, ownership seems to tie rights to responsibilities. Worker-owners see more clearly than any other category of workers the need to take full responsibility for the quantity and quality of their work.

Significantly it has been where management has withheld full responsibility from workers that the rights of ownership have had no positive effects on behavior, morale, or productivity. For example, while John Lupien of Vermont Asbestos saw clearly the need to adhere to the principle of ownership, his personal downfall—and the ultimate demise of worker ownership of the mine—can be traced to his failure to share managerial responsibility with his co-owners (see Case No. 3).

While workers are likely to reject responsibilities without accompanying rights, they are also likely to see rights without responsibilities as no less of a sham. (In this vein, the failure of ESOPs to act as motivators may be due to the fact that shares come free to employees. It may be that they don't appreciate something they haven't paid for, as they don't appreciate stocks that are held in nonvoting trust. In both instances there is a disjunction between rights and responsibilities.)

The second principle of worker ownership thus may be stated: *Worker-owners need to assume all the responsibilities of self-management that the right of ownership entails, including all the positive and negative consequences of success or failure of the enterprise.*

THE RISKS OF OWNERSHIP

Inherent in these two principles is an unambiguous message to American managers: Worker capitalism is not for those who are uncomfortable with wide-scale and authentic employee participation in ownership and management. Since no one is forcing managers to adopt worker capitalism, they probably should attempt it only if they can make a full and unstinting commitment to the two principles stated above: genuine ownership and full responsibility. Of course, if managers do not wish to use worker ownership to achieve greater worker motivation, job satisfaction, loyalty, or productivity, they can still go ahead with it for purposes of establishing a deferred compensation plan or of taking advantage of various tax breaks. But if these are their aims, they should not be surprised to find *no* positive human effects. Moreover, if they enter worker ownership with *limited* economic aims, managers are in no position to criticize the entire movement for failure to achieve the wider human aims to which they had no real commitment in the first place.

Even those managers and business owners who are committed to the broader human goals of worker capitalism have reason to raise doubts about how practical the system is for achieving these goals. For example, it is in opposition to the two principles stated above that the critics of worker capitalism make their most convincing stand. They argue that it is unconscionable to permit workers to invest their life savings in the stock in the companies for which they work. As Peter Drucker and most labor leaders argue, putting all of one's eggs in a single basket is a suicidal investment strategy for workers. For as surely as there is a Sears, Roebuck, the value of stock can fall as well as rise. Moreover small- and medium-sized companies have an undeniable tendency toward bankruptcy. Therefore, the critics contend, the risk of stock ownership is simply too great for workers to assume.

There is much merit to this argument. It implies that worker capitalism isn't for every worker (as, I have suggested, it is not for every manager). Some workers are risk takers and some are risk averse; it seems reasonable that the former ought to have the opportunity to become worker-capitalists, while the latter should not be forced to make the investment. Still, it is rank paternalism to say that workers should not have the *right* to assume the risks of ownership open to the middle classes. Moreover it is not only insulting but unfactual as well to say that risk-taking or entrepreneurial behavior is class-linked. Indeed most of America's successful "self-made men" had their origins in the social classes that the paternalists seek to protect from the excitement of worker capitalism. More to the point, employee-owned firms may be less likely to go under than firms in which there is little employee motivation to keep them going. Hard work and commitment are major factors in the success of small- and medium-sized firms, as the plywood cooperatives proved by surviving the Depression while conventional plywood firms were going belly up. At any rate, the fear of worker bankruptcy is hypothetical. Instead of going broke, the record thus far shows that worker-capitalists have made out like—well, capitalists—by selling their shares to conglomerates at handsome profits.

The fear of bankruptcy seems most justified when applied to companies in which stock is traded on markets. I see no reason to quarrel with Keynes' notion that the stock market is a casino. The price of stock traded on a market can rise or fall without regard to how successful a company is or how hard its employees work. One need only look at the stock listings in the morning paper to find examples of profitable companies with shares selling at depressed prices. This is reason enough not to subject workers to

Wall Street roulette. Sears discovered this the hard way. For years it has been the largest company in the United States with significant employee stock ownership (25 percent). While Sears stock was going up, the employees were quite satisfied with stock ownership. But when the price of a share of Sears dipped from $62 to $20—due largely to the vagaries of the stock market—employees' alarm at seeing half the value of their defered compensation plan disappear forced the company to retrench on stock ownership and to institute a standard pension plan.

There are many other reasons why employee stock ownership is impractical for large corporations. It is significant that only one successful cooperative or joint partnership in America has ever had as many as one thousand employees. (Worker-owned Graybar Electric Company has more than five thousand employees, but it appears to be a traditionally managed firm.) While there is no optimum number, the maximum seems to be in the five hundred to six hundred range; beyond that, it may be impossible to achieve the camaraderie and community spirit needed for success. Even if this size problem can be solved through decentralization, as it has in large worker-owned firms in Spain and Yugoslavia, large U.S. corporations would still lack an appropriate mechanism to finance the transition from public to employee ownership. Even by milking the ESOP tax breaks for all they are worth, it would take several generations before all the employees of General Motors had enough equity to allow them realistically to think of themselves as "owners" of the corporation. Even with 25 percent equity, it is not clear that Sears employees have ever thought of themselves as "owners" of anything but a decent pension plan. And no non-ESOP financing mechanisms are currently available other than government loan guarantees, which are available only when a plant closing will have a devastating impact on a community. Even when this qualification is satisfied, technical, political, and economic problems remain. This was demonstrated in a recent unsuccessful year-long attempt to pry a $250 million loan guarantee out of the Carter administration to buy the closed forty-one-hundred-employee mill of the Youngstown Sheet and Tube Company.

THE FUTURE OF WORKER CAPITALISM

· A 1975 survey by pollster Gary Hart found that 66 percent of all Americans favored "employees owning most of the stock of the companies in which they work."[21]

· A 1978 Harris poll found that 64 percent of all American office workers felt that they would be more productive if their companies "let all employees share equally in the profits of the company."[22]

· In June 1979 the Third International Conference on Self-Management attracted over five hundred conferees to discuss reports from worker-owned and managed companies.

· On July 24, 1978, the San Francisco *Examiner* reported on that city's New School for Democratic Management, which was founded to train managers of the "5,000 food and housing cooperatives operating in the United States and perhaps 10,000 other alternative enterprises," including producer cooperatives and worker-managed firms.

Despite the enthusiasm for worker capitalism demonstrated by these items, unless there are radical changes in U.S. tax laws, it seems highly unlikely that the movement will make significant inroads among the two thousand largest U.S. corporations during this century. In 1978 I polled twenty-one of the nation's leading experts on work-place reform (see Chapter 7) and they estimated that there is only a 30 percent probability that even five percent of large American businesses will be worker-owned (that is, the workers will own a *majority* of stock in companies in which they work) in 1990. But this group of experts (and another group of forty top corporate executives, trade unionists, and scholars that I polled in 1979) gave a much higher probability to the passage of federal legislation in the coming decade that would facilitate worker ownership of plants about to be closed by large corporations. What no doubt lay behind this forecast is the fact that the Commerce Department's Economic Development Administration had already supported the employee purchase of the South Bend Lathe and eight other companies threatened by closure.

Moreover three members of the U.S. House of Representatives introduced the Voluntary Job Preservation and Community Stabilization Act in 1978—a bill designed to allow workers and communities to assume ownership of firms and plants faced with termination. If passed, the legislation would make $100 million in federal loans available for this purpose. A key provision in the bill is federal support for technical assistance to worker capitalists. In recognition of the lack of preparation of workers and manager for their new roles, rights, responsibilities, and risks, the bill would provide funds for consulting and training in finance, marketing, and other technical areas, as well as in organizational development.

A prime mover behind the bill is Representative Stanley N. Lundine, who as a mayor of Jamestown, New York, had personal experience rescuing failing industries by transferring them to worker ownership. Testifying in behalf of the bill, Lundine said:

> Our experience shows that local people—both workers and managers —often have better ideas than executives from remote conglomerates about how to run their businesses. Conglomerate owners may abandon plants because they see more profitable opportunities elsewhere. Conglomerate owners may react too hurriedly to temporary losses, and pull out before making much effort to turn the business around. But employee and local community owners have too much to lose from such choices, and because of their personal stake in the firms, have every reason to try and make them viable.[23]

Not everyone who has studied the issue of rescuing failing enterprises is as sanguine as Lundine. Economists in particular question the wisdom of propping up firms that would, without government assistance, die natural deaths. For capitalism to work, inefficient firms must be allowed to fold so that capital and energy can be directed to enterprises that are more responsive to the needs of the market. The economies of Britain, Italy, and France are in trouble in no small part because of governmental decisions to subsidize firms that would never survive on their own. Lundine is no doubt correct in stating that many divisions and plants of conglomerates are closed, not because they are inherently inefficient, but because they are mismanaged. Nevertheless economists ask if mismanagement is the cause of 5 percent or 50 percent of such closings. The answer to that question will confirm or deny the wisdom of the Lundine approach. Economists also wonder how government is to identify which firms can be saved by worker capitalism and which are so basically rotten that all the employee effort in the world couldn't make them profitable.

The need for the Voluntary Job Preservation and Community Stabilization Act may have been mooted by the creation of the National Consumer Cooperative Bank in 1980. Funded with $300 million from the U.S. Treasury, the bank will be able to borrow up to $3 billion from private sources and lend this to nonprofit cooperatives. Although it seems that housing and consumer cooperatives will get the lion's share of the available funds, producer cooperatives are also eligible. The Bank's future is uncertain, because the Reagan administration has opposed its funding.

Little noted in the passage of the Chrysler bailout bill was the requirement that the company establish an ESOP with $162.5 million of its stock. The stock must be distributed on a per capita basis to all employees, union and nonunion, with full and immediate voting rights. Depending on the price of the stock and several other variables, in four years the employees should have something in the area of 10 to 20 percent of the outstanding shares—theoretically enough to give them controlling interest. To keep creditors from panicking, the company and the union are playing this point down.

As with the Chrysler bankruptcy, worker capitalism should find its most fertile field for growth in plant closings and in the spinoffs that are inevitable by-products of the hyper-conglomeration of the late 1960s and late 1970s. In addition, a few new firms might be started as cooperatives, and a few paternalistic owners of firms, such as the Halls of Hallmark and the late David Lawrence of *U.S. News and World Report,* will no doubt deed their companies to their employees on their death. Another likely area for expansion of worker ownership is the mutually owned company. Since these savings and loans and insurance companies currently operate under the fiction that they are owned by their depositors and policy holders, the transition to worker ownership would require no more than a simple change in their federal charters. In fact, one can imagine interesting forms of joint partnership between worker-owners and customer-owners arising in the *distant* future. (Worker ownership may even take totally unexpected forms. Already Eastern Airline has announced a plan in which its pilots will own the planes they fly and lease them to the airline.)

The greatest immediate restraint on the growth of worker capitalism is the inability to solve the problem of the termination of worker ownership. While ESOPs and other mechanisms have been invented to put shares in the hands of workers, no such mechanism has been invented to take them back. Currently, for employee ownership to work, it is usually necessary to hold employee stock in trust or, in the case of co-ops and joint partnerships, to forbid the sale of the stock while the employee is still working for the firm. This means that worker capitalists are often owners of second-class stock. Frequently the only market for their stock is the firm itself, and the stock can only be sold back to the firm when the employee dies, retires, or quits. A secondary problem that arises from this situation is that cooperatives have the deuce of a time ensuring their perpetuation from one generation to another. For instance, the entire work force in some of the plywood companies has grown old together without ever selling stock to new blood. The value of the stock has appreciated so greatly that few young blue-collar workers can afford to buy in. At the other extreme, where employees are perfectly free to sell their stock on the open market, managers question the motivation value of such plans if workers can treat their shares like speculators. Such complex practical problems will no doubt retard the spread of worker capitalism.

Finally, an ideological issue continues to confound the spread of worker ownership. The movement has been given a bad name: socialism. The critics of worker ownership—whether they be Peter Drucker, labor union leaders, or the editors of the *Wall Street Journal*—have learned that the most damaging thing to say about the movement is that it is socialistic. Since Americans would foreswear apple pies and Chevrolets if they had the socialist label on them, this tactic is clearly dirty pool. While worker capitalism has many problems that will keep it from spreading in the near future, these problems do not stem from its being socialistic. Worker capitalism ought to be accepted or rejected for what it is, and it is not socialism. Socialism is the ownership of the means of production by the state, not by individuals. It is hard to understand the logic of calling a system in which managers exercise stock options and take equity positions in their firms capitalism, while calling one in which workers do the same thing, socialism. In other countries, ideological terminology is far less important. As the following examples illustrate, what counts is that worker ownership by any name leads to greater justice and productivity.

Worker "Capitalism" Abroad

In late 1979 the Chinese government officially sanctioned collectively owned (as opposed to state-owned) enterprises. During the Cultural Revolution these cooperatives—employing about twenty million workers —were condemned as "vestiges of capitalism." Now more progressive Chinese leaders favor forming collectives as a fast and efficient way of responding to the nation's growing problem of youth unemployment. One of the most fascinating developments in this regard is occuring at the #17 Textile Mill in Shanghai, where the sons and daughters of several hundred workers recently were having trouble gaining admission to the overcrowded university system, and even more trouble getting a job in a labor force where unemployment is probably as high as it is in the U.S. The workers' solution was to each invest about $35 to create a "subsidiary" textile plant that would be manned by their sons and daughters. The workers now own all the shares in the new plant, and will reap any profits that might be earned (or absorb any losses from their investment).

At the other end of the Eurasian landmass the European Economic Community announced in 1976 that it was adopting the principle of profit sharing and recommending the practice to all its member states. In a report prepared specially for the Common Market, profit sharing was said to lead to a more equitable distribution of income, a slower rate of wage inflation, and increased worker satisfaction.[24]

Perhaps even more significant is the thriving condition of the European cooperative movement.

Spain. In 1941 a Catholic priest went to Mondragon in the Basque region of Spain to found a worker cooperative that eventually created eighty-two spinoff cooperatives that employed over ten thousand workers in 1975. Over 90 percent of these cooperatives are involved in manufacturing (others are engaged in construction, agriculture, and fishing). All the cooperatives are closely linked in a confederation and all participate financially in a common bank. In order to keep all units small, when a cooperative reaches a certain size, the bank finances the creation of a spinoff cooperative to produce new product lines. Half of all profits are ploughed back into the cooperatives to encourage overall growth in the Mondragon community (sales = $334 million in 1974–1975).

Although all workers must buy into a Mondragon cooperative in order to get a job, no worker is allowed to own more than 5 percent of the particular unit in which he works. Equality is also encouraged by a rule that permits only a maximum 3:1 salary differential among all worker-owners. While Mondragon has not yet evolved a system of complete worker self-management, it is moving in that direction: The ultimate body of authority in Mondragon is the General Assembly, composed of all workers.

Britain. The cooperative movement was born in Great Britain. Unfortunately, it almost died there: In 1900 there were over two hundred British cooperatives; today there are only twenty-six. Socialist ideologues have recently tranished the cooperative movement in Britain. Anthony Wedgwood Benn pushed the Labour government to form three cooperatives in 1976, each of which went bankrupt before the year was out. Significantly cooperatives with pragmatic philosophies have not only survived but thrived in Britain's beleaguered economy. Worker-owned Scott Bader, a chemical firm, has been advanced by E. F. Schumacher as a model for industrial firms in advanced nations. And the John Lewis Partnership—a department and food store chain—has been owned by its twenty-three thousand employees for over fifty years. This "partnership" is actually a trust held entirely on behalf of the employees—but ownership is collective, not individual (that is, workers cannot take their "shares" and sell them on the stock market). In 1978 the partnership did £ 400 million in sales. After about half of the profits were reinvested for future expansion, £ 9 million was shared among the "partners" as a cash bonus (at the rate of 18 percent of each worker's salary). The firm is governed by a written constitution that provides not only for the contractual division of all profits among worker-owners but also for governance by a series of Partner's Councils —democratically elected committees at several levels of the firm to which managers are held accountable.

Yugoslavia. This country is communist with a difference: Instead of the *state* owning productive enterprises, *workers* own them as cooperatives. In 1950 Marshall Tito broke with the Soviet centrally-planned economic model and created a greatly decentralized economy. The guiding ideological principle in Yugoslavia is "From each according to his abilities, to each according to his *labor*," a significant departure from the Soviet Marxist maxim: ". . . to each according to his *needs*." In Yugoslavia workers have the right of self-management in the firms they own. They decide their own work hours and pay scales and elect firm officers and managers. Through their elected officials they have the final say on everything from budgets to pricing policy to mergers. Because such self-management would be unwieldy in a very large firm, workers are organized into groups of no more than six hundred. Unhappily democracy at work has not spilled over to the political system—Yugoslavia is still an authoritarian state. Nonetheless on a purely economic measure the system works: GNP growth in Yugoslavia was the highest in Europe in the 1970s and advanced at three times the U.S. annual rate during the same period.

France. There are 537 companies in France associated with the Confédération des Sociétés Coopératives Ouvriéres de Production. These cooperatives employed over thirty thousand workers and had sales of over $600 million in 1975. While these companies are all independent and are in industries as diverse as construction, printing, and metals, they are all united in the Confédération for purposes of raising capital and sharing information.

Italy. Like so much else in Italy, the cooperative movement is dominated by Communist unions. Over 11,000 cooperatives are members of the Communist Lega (League), which employed 170,000 workers and had a combined sales of $4.6 billion in 1977.[25] Profits from Lega affiliates are not distributed to members, but are all reinvested in order to create jobs. The Lega—authoritarian, highly centralized, and hierarchical—is organized somewhat like a large multinational corporation. Thus, ironically, cooperatives in democratic Italy are far less democratic than are cooperatives in communist Yugoslavia. It would seem that the Italians are capable of bollixing up the best of systems!

7

HOW TO CHANGE THE ORGANIZATION

ALTHOUGH the work-place reforms I advocate have been successfully demonstrated, they have not been adopted in many organizations. Why not? One reason managers have not changed the philosophy and organization of work in their companies may be that they do not know what to do. The purpose of the cases presented in chapters 5 and 6 is to inform managers of the many options they have for organizational change. Another reason why managers have not acted may be that they know what to do but not how to do it. For help on this score, I polled twenty-one of the nation's leading experts on work-place reform and asked them—on the basis of their personal experiences as consultants, evaluators, sponsors, and observers of several hundred efforts at work-place reform—to identify what works.[1] The method I used to garner and collate the experiences of these experts was a simple one. We all met together at the Ford Foundation for a day and a half to discuss the characteristics of successful and unsuccessful efforts to change work places. At that meeting I recorded all the specific comments made with regard to the implementation of change and then fed these back to the participants a few weeks later with the request that they indicate the degree to which they agreed or disagreed with what had been said. What follows is the numerical breakdown of the degree of agreement among the participants with one another's statements. (Because all participants did not respond to all the questions, the replies do not always add up to twenty-one.)

THE EXPERIENCE OF TWENTY-ONE EXPERTS WITH THE IMPLEMENTATION OF WORK-PLACE REFORMS

1. Ironically, work-place reform is often successful when top management "orders" it to be done as a matter of policy.

	Agree Strongly	Agree	Undecided or Neutral	Disagree	Disagree Strongly
Number of Replies	2½	14½	0	2	1

2. Experience shows that when workers are powerless, they see only the trivial things they have the power to change: e.g., lighting, placing of water coolers. But once they get involved in making decisions, these trivial issues disappear and they start to address the tough underlying problems.

	Agree Strongly	Agree	Undecided or Neutral	Disagree	Disagree Strongly
Number of Replies	3	12½	2½	1	1

3. The two major problems that have been encountered in all work-place reforms are *decay* of enthusiasm and lack of diffusion.

	Agree Strongly	Agree	Undecided or Neutral	Disagree	Disagree Strongly
Number of Replies	3	12½	1½	2	0

4. One way to deal with decay is to establish a kind of organizational "flywheel" to keep things going when enthusiasm flags. The flywheel can be an outside consultant, a union, a committed top manager, a contract, or any other kind of *institutionalized* device.

	Agree Strongly	Agree	Undecided or Neutral	Disagree	Disagree Strongly
Number of Replies	3	12	1	1	0

5. The problem with diffusion is that there is no *thing* to diffuse. There is only the *process* of working together. That is very hard to package and to sell to those who haven't experienced it.

	Agree Strongly	Agree	Undecided or Neutral	Disagree	Disagree Strongly
Number of Replies	6	7	2	5	0

6. It is a mistake to insist on perfection. Since it is impossible to design a job change that will satisfy everyone, get on with the job for the majority who will be satisfied, and give the others the opportunity to transfer to the kind of situation they want.

	Agree Strongly	Agree	Undecided or Neutral	Disagree	Disagree Strongly
Number of Replies	2	12	2	1	0

7. A problem with social scientist-led intervention is that such individuals are interested in the fun of experimentation and not in the nitty-gritty of institutional life. Unless social scientists alter their goals, interests, and focus, they are not likely to be fully effective in changing the long, tough, boring facts of institutional life.

	Agree Strongly	Agree	Undecided or Neutral	Disagree	Disagree Strongly
Number of Replies	3	9½	4½	2	1

8. The main thing unions can bring to successful reforms is assurance of long-term commitment to work-quality efforts. In nonunion shops employers can renege on projects at any time because they are noncontractual.

	Agree Strongly	Agree	Undecided or Neutral	Disagree	Disagree Strongly
Number of Replies	3	10	4	3	0

9. What seems to work when implementing work-quality interventions? Which of the following factors were most often present in successful work-quality projects?

	Agree Strongly	Agree	Undecided or Neutral	Disagree	Disagree Strongly
a. Top management commitment.	14	7	0	0	0
b. Systemic, total organizational change.	8	5	4	2	2
c. Active participation of a union.	6	10	4	1	0
d. No invidious distinction created between "experimental groups" and others.	7	9	3½	1½	0
e. Worker participation in *all* phases of project.	8	8	3	1	1
f. No time pressures to show early success.	10	6	1½	3½	0
g. Guarantee of job security.	12	8	1	0	0
h. Equal commitment to both economic *and* human goals.	10	9	1	1	0
i. Project structured in such a way that *all* workers see benefits.	7	10	2	2	0
j. Gains (profit) sharing.	7	13	1	0	0

	Agree Strongly	Agree	Undecided or Neutral	Disagree	Disagree Strongly
k. Managers retrained to act as consultants, negotiators, trainers, and counsellors.	5	10	3	3	0
l. Workers early on given management information (and training on how to use available data).	7	12	2	0	0
m. Presence of a skilled outside consultant.	2	10	5	2	0
n. Workers organized as teams.	2	6	9	4	0
o. Project starts with diagnostic study of how to do better work.	2	9	4	5	0

As interesting and as useful as this how-to information is, I would be less than candid were I to claim that it has been the absence of such information that has prevented managers from changing the philosophy and organization of work. For it must be recognized that such information has been readily available for nearly half a decade. Thus there must be some other reason why managers have not put this knowledge into practice. This reason, I believe, was clearly identified by the experts at the Ford Foundation conference:

10. Many good work-reform projects have been killed by managers who feared they would lose power and control. In many cases control and power are more important to managers than profits or productivity.

	Agree Strongly	Agree	Undecided or Neutral	Disagree	Disagree Strongly
Number of Replies	9	11	0	0	0

The Ford Foundation conferees suggested that, in addition to feeling threatened by changes that appear to lead to the abridgement of their power, managers have also been conditioned to believe that the way they do things now is not only the best way, but the only way. That the conferees should arrive at these conclusions is not at all startling. After all, it was in recognition of these facts of life that industrial psychologists and other practitioners of "organizational development" had sought for years to alter the personal behavior, values, and even personalities of individual managers in order to promote productive organizational change.

For nearly two decades the corporation executive has been laid out on the head shrinker's couch. His fears have been probed by Freudians, his world-view analyzed by Jungians, and his id (et cetera) massaged at Esalen and other centers of "humanistic psychology." He has suffered through scores of encounter groups to (1) find his Human Potential, (2) develop a hearty and healthy Primal Scream, and (3) pursue, *ad seriatim,* BFT, EST, TA, and TM. In an applied vein, organizational psychologists have dissected the manager's power needs, motivations, and leadership style with such quaintly named tools as the Managerial Grid (as opposed to the rack?), the Minnesota Multiphasic Personality Inventory (developed at the Mayo Clinic?), and the Leadership Behavior Description Questionnaire. In a different intellectual tradition psychoanalyst Michael Maccoby[2] recently analyzed how William H. Whyte's[3] Organization Man has become the "heartless" Corporate Gamesman of the 1970s.

What is the purpose of all this psychological probing of the corporate executive? One implication is that the characters and personalities of individual executives are in large part responsible for corporate performance. From Abraham Maslow to Douglas McGregor to David McClelland and now to Michael Maccoby, it has been assumed that individual managerial behavior is at the core of such problems as institutional inflexibility, bureaucracy, resistance to innovation, insensitivity to employee needs, and social irresponsibility.

This is truth, by half.

THE MISSING HALF OF THE ANALYSIS
OF ORGANIZATIONAL BEHAVIOR

The study of behavioral problems in organizations has been dominated by psychologists. They have provided many invaluable insights into the processes of management, not the least of which is the now undeniable fact that human factors are singularly important determinants of success or failure in most organizations. But this finding is, alas, inadequate as a guide for corrective action. If individuals are defined as the cause of poor performance in the firm, one is often left with the near-impossible task of changing personalities or behavior to achieve effective organizational change. Many psychologists are not at all daunted by this imposing task. They assure all who will listen that personalities can be changed (or at least behavior can be modified). But lay folks seldom are willing to swallow this line. They know only too well that the state of the pedagogical art precludes teaching new routines to superannuated canines. Observation teaches that few fifty-year-old authoritarian managers ever become open and democratic, and that few aggressive Type A's ever become calm and introspective Type B's. Although psychological civilians have witnessed heroic efforts on the part of friends to alter their behavior patterns, they've also seen the devastating onrush of recidivism ("when his real personality finally reemerged, it was with a vengeance").

Certainly the personalities of corporate executives are of critical importance to the performance of most firms. But psychological analysis of organizational behavior is as *threatening* as it is important because it places the burden of change squarely on the individual: There is something right or wrong, healthy or unhealthy, nurturing or destructive about *you*. In addition to the understandable reluctance on the part of managers to accept such a burden, the psychological focus can also be rejected as an incomplete and inadequate explanation of organizationl behavior. The missing element is *the organization context* in which managers find themselves. This is the half of the analysis concerned with the institutionalized social relationships that maintain the functioning of the corporation. This is the organization structure and ideology that compose the *culture* of the firm.

A focus on culture rather than on personality permits the manager to get off the couch. A cultural/structural approach to the study of organizational behavior can be rooted in the discipline of social anthropology. While psychologists are interested in *individual* differences in character and personality, social anthropologists focus on the *aggregate* behavior of whatever group (tribe, nation, or firm) they are studying. An example helps to clarify the difference in levels of analysis: While the psychologist would be concerned with the difference in behavior between the personalities of, say, Stalin and Solzhenitsyn, the anthropologist would look for what the two Russians had in common. He might then find that the "national character" of Russians contained elements of authoritarianism, mysticism, and gloominess.

Stereotype is not the purpose of such analysis (although it can degenerate to that level). Rather, the goal is to (1) identify the shared beliefs, ideas, customs, expectations, and symbols of a group; and (2) identify the principles of social organization that underlie the structure and functioning of that group. In brief, the anthropologist attempts to discover the *system of beliefs* and the *system of actions* that characterize the group.[4] These two mutually supporting systems constitute a group's culture. Thus when one speaks of the culture of Firm Z, one refers to the complexly interrelated whole of standardized, institutionalized, and habitual behavior that characterizes that firm only. The culture of the firm, then, is the unique behavior that binds its members together and differentiates them from other groups. There is nothing normative about this definition. The culture might be good or bad, functional or dysfunctional, effective or ineffective, pleasurable or painful, all depending upon the criteria by which we choose to evaluate it. One of the major precepts of social anthropology is so-called cultural relativism—that is, there is no single normative standard applicable to all cultures. What is good for the Mangbettu (for whom cannibalism apparently was once a cultural practice) is, simply, whatever the Mangbettu say is good for them. Although anthropological practice thus precludes the normative evaluation of the culture of any particular firm by outsiders, the corporate equivalents of the Mangbettu might want to evaluate their *own* behavior from time to time!

This is what industrialist John Z. De Lorean has done for (some might say *to*) General Motors.[5] In 1973, after seventeen years of service, De Lorean reluctantly quit GM when he was earning a salary of $650,000 per annum. The source of his *reluctance* to quit is not terribly difficult to identify, but his reasons for are more difficult. As head of GM's Car and Truck Group, De Lorean was in charge of Chevrolet, Buick, Olds, Pontiac, Cadillac, the GMC Truck and Coach Division, as well as the corporation's Canadian car and truck operations. De Lorean says that he resigned from this lofty power post for (1) personal reasons (he liked the company of glamorous women, and to wear fancy Italian suits and modishly long hair: all no-no's in conservative Detroit); (2) social reasons (he felt that GM was not providing safe, environmentally sound, fuel-efficient cars, enough opportunities for blacks, or enough participation for workers); and (3) business reasons (he felt that GM was noninnovative, unwilling to take risks, bureaucratic, overcentralized, and inefficient). To be fair to GM, a disgruntled executive could make the same kinds of sweeping charges against almost any of the nation's two hundred largest firms. Nonetheless De Lorean documents each of his charges with a scholar's eye for precision and detail. Unlike Robert Townsend, who brought the same caliber of charges against his former employer, Avis (a division of ITT),[6] De Lorean names names, gives dates, and cites documentary evidence.

But De Lorean is not interested in making a legal case against General Motors. His is a cautionary tale of how the culture of a firm can induce moral men to behave immorally. GM's central failing, he argues, was that its top executives *failed to recognize the existence of any of the problems he documents*. Because of this blindness, it was impossible for GM executives to act to correct the problems that had its customers, suppliers, and dealers (as well as environmentalists and energy conservationists) infuriated with the company. For example, the culture of GM was such that the company failed to see that it was behaving not only socially irresponsibly but also against its own long-term interests by not providing an energy-efficient line of cars to compete with Japanese and German imports. Moreover the culture of the company was such that "General Motors management thinks that what it is doing is right, because it is GM that is doing it and the outside world is wrong. It is always 'they' versus 'us.' "[7]

Such attitudes, according to De Lorean, led the corporation to market a car they knew was unsafe (the Corvair), and to engage in the subsequent seamy episode of trying to prove that Ralph Nader was a homosexual when he called the public's attention to the Corvair's safety problems. The myopic and self-deceiving culture of GM also led to enormous wasted investments in the Wankel engine, the catalytic convertor, and air bags. Finally, De Lorean documents how mismanagement led to the problem at Lordstown.

Again, let us be fair to GM. The company is one of America's best managed, most enlightened, and most deservedly envied corporations. As I described in Chapter 5, GM has of its own volition become a corporate leader in the quality-of-working-life movement. Thus if things at GM were only half as bad as De Lorean claims, one wonders what the managerial culture is like at such backward companies as Chrysler, Mobil, and Union Oil. And one begins to see how difficult it will be to change the philosophy and organization of work in large U.S. Corporations.

THE CULTURE OF MANAGEMENT

Generalizing across the corporate community, it seems reasonable to assert that there is a common culture of management that most executives in large U.S. companies share to at least some degree. Of course we must be careful not to be too sweeping. After all, the personal differences among corporate executives are manifest. On one extreme there are the

"Eastern Establishment" political liberals who manage the entertainment and news industries of the nation; at the other end of the spectrum there are the conservative middlebrows who manage the auto and steel industries. And political leanings, life-styles, and industry type do not begin to exhaust the ways in which managers might be differentiated: Levels of educational attainment, race, sex, age, cognitive styles, and performance records are just a few of the many other attributes that might be used. In short, managers in Exxon, IBM, and CBS might be as different from one another as Spaniards, Englishmen, and Italians are.

Yet executives in large American corporations also have certain similarities—just as Spaniards, Englishmen, and Italians all share in a common Western European civilization. Executives have these cultural similarities in part because most large corporations have certain *structural* similarities. They are almost all complex, hierarchical organizations run by professional managers who are the employees of absentee owners. Most executives also share common life histories: Data from a 1974 *Forbes* study indicate that the typical corporate executive is a middle-aged man (a midwesterner) who has spent most of his working life in one corporation, to which he came almost directly after graduating from Princeton or Yale.[8]

In the late 1950s William H. Whyte described how these similarities in background and organization environments conspired to produce a "modal type"—the security-seeking, bureaucratic, other-directed Organization Man who eschewed innovation and risk and played it safe, "the company way." This submissive, conformist attitude was rewarded with warmth and security, high income, and promotions. Having grown up during the terribly insecure days of the Depression, the Organization Man took to the comfort of the corporation like a six-month fetus takes to the womb.

When Whyte first published his study, his characterization was vehemently denied by spokesmen for the corporate world. Curiously corporate spokesmen today admit that the characterization was accurate *at the time,* but argue that organizations in the 1970s have "sent the grey flannel suit into mothballs."[9] Today even Whyte's harshest critics concede that there was, and is, a dominant managerial culture. The debate is over the characteristics of that culture.

Change in the Structure

Maccoby now claims that Whyte's Organization Man has given way to a new breed of corporate cat, the Gamesman, whose

> character is a collection of near paradoxes understood in terms of its adaptation to organizational requirements. He is cooperative but competi-

tive; detached and playful but compulsively driven to succeed; a team player but a would-be superstar; a team leader but often a rebel against bureaucratic hierarchy; fair and unprejudicial but contemptuous of weakness; tough and dominating but not destructive.[10]

Most of all, this puzzling fellow (who may even be a woman in the liberated 1980s) views business as a game. The Gamesman's vocabulary is drawn from professional sports. He speaks of "the game plan," "making the big play," and "punting" when in trouble—all while trying to win the "money game," the "marketing game," or whatever game he happens to be playing. And that is the significant point: It does not matter what game he is playing, Maccoby tells us, for the Gamesman lacks all conviction. He is amoral, selfish, heartless, and uncommitted. The Gamesman is concerned only with his career. He will move anywhere and do anything, as long as he is progressing up the corporate ladder. Making or marketing Kepone is no different from making or marketing baby food. This amorality seems to derive from viewing his work as a game. A game, of course, is less significant than "real life." If work is only a game, then it is permissible to bluff ("only a fool would show his hole card") and even to cheat ("the best basketball and football players know that 'holding' is part of the game"). Finally, the Gamesman is arrogant. He feels that he can run any organization, including the government (which is, after all, just another game—albeit with slightly different rules).

Where have we met this character? He is the recent Harvard M.B.A., the dynamic manager of the high-technology corporation of the late 1960s. We met him at the Watergate hearings: the young wet-behind-the-ears functionary who "managed" the White House for President Nixon. (I recall meeting one of these young men shortly before the Watergate incident reached epic proportions. I asked him if he planned to stay in Washington. "Of course," he replied, "where else could a twenty-six-year-old M.B.A. have so much power?" Where else, indeed.)

No doubt Maccoby has identified a real type. But has this Gamesman become the "typical" American manager? I suspect not. The high-technology boom has abated a bit, and many of the small companies in this industry that were the Gamesman's stomping grounds have been swallowed up by big corporate bureaucracies. And the phenomenal growth that protected and nurtured the Gamesman in a few large companies is now a thing of the past. The go-go companies that would once tolerate the fierce competitiveness of the Gamesman have now started to develop the middle-age paunch and slower pace befitting those who now, too, are part of the Establishment. Indeed one suspects that Maccoby's data (based on a sample of two companies, and some of the information over ten years old) might not be all that reliable given the recent, rather rapid organizational changes in the high-technology companies he studied. Today the Gamesman may be out of step with the larger, slower-growing companies in which he now finds himself. Most Gamesmen now probably have two options: conform to the norms of mature firms, or get out and go solo.

Here is the ultimate weakness of Maccoby's model: It is not personality that is the crucial variable in organizational behavior; it is the organization, both its structure and its culture. The systems of belief and action of giant corporations will usually wear down the maverick; even the toughest, like De Lorean, eventually succumb to playing it the company way, or they exit to the independent world of the land developer or venture capitalist.

One of the most important findings of American anthropologists has been that certain cultures are not conducive to certain personality types. Although all societies probably contain a random cross section of personalities, only certain behaviors are *rewarded*. Introspective and morose individuals do not flourish in societies that stress openness and gregariousness. Culture may not determine personality, but it greatly *influences* it. It is not so important, then, whether or not the Gamesman has overtaken the Organization Man. The crucial difference is how the *organization* has changed. Regardless of what kind of behavior is being rewarded, it is still the organization that sets the cultural norms to which young executives must adapt if they wish to succeed.

But why this insistence on stereotype? The probable truth is that today's corporate managers are a diverse lot, with different personalities and characters. They are just people—liberal and conservative, intelligent and dull, aggressive and shy, authoritarian and caring. There is little analytical value in stereotyping them. Probably we would find (if we cared to make the effort) that corporate executives conform to the same personality types as a random cross section of the population. More important, to categorize is to run the risk of caricature. The temptation is to seize upon the modal personalities identified by psychologists and to see all executives as "Jungle Fighters" or "Gamesmen," and consciously or subconsciously try to fit everyone into the archetype. When we say of someone, "He's the typical bureaucrat," we close our eyes to the complexity of personality. Is anyone really the "typical" bureaucrat?

Individual managers, then, are all different, but they share a managerial culture. That is, corporate executives share a common—albeit limited —belief system about corporate life. As a participant-observer in several large organizations, I have attempted to identify some of the cultural characteristics (values, ideas, norms, symbols) common to corporate settings. From my informal anthropological inquiry, I would claim that the managerial culture is characterized by a congeries of mutually supporting and complementary values.

Economic Efficiency. A content analysis of speeches by business leaders will reveal a high use of such terms as "productivity," "consumer (market) sovereignty," "optimization," "least cost," and "the most efficient allocation of goods and resources." If one can believe what businessmen say, they value economic efficiency very highly. When I recently undertook to informally measure the values of executives from thirteen major corporations, I learned that efficiency was, in this small sample at least, valued higher than nine other social objectives including liberty, equality of opportunity, environmental quality, and full employment.[11]

Growth. The behavior of executives indicates that growth is a significant goal in most large organizations. Indeed it is probably their prime indicator of success, even more important than profit maximization. Of course these two goals often are achieved simultaneously, but if a trade-off is necessary, the managerial culture often dictates the primacy of growth over profit. This is a quite logical ordering of preferences; after all, the primary beneficiary of profit is the stockholder, while most of the benefits of growth accrue to managers. Growth gives managers bigger empires, bigger pensions (through increases in stock value), and higher status (it is "better" to work for General Motors than for American Motors). Growth can be measured in terms of larger sales volume, more items produced, more employees, more branches, bigger market shares, and more operations in more countries.

Short-term Profitability. When corporate executives talk about "performance," they mean how their profits fared in a quarter or in a year. Unlike Japanese executives whose goal it is to build long-term business relationships (and full employment for their nation), American managers are driven by short-term considerations. These are not traditional American business values. Edwin Land of Polaroid contrasts how traditional entrepreneurs like himself view business from how modern American managers view their role: "My view of business and the ordinary business world's view of business are quite antithetical. [My essential concept is] that the role of industry is to sense a deep human need, then bring science and technology to bear on filling that need." Land is considered a maverick by most corporate leaders who are in the camp of Alfred Sloan, past chief of General Motors. Sloan wrote: "The business of GM is making money, not making cars." But not just making money; more to the point, U.S.

corporate executives agree that their prime role is to provide profits for their shareholders—specifically, short-term profits to keep Wall Street off their back, thus giving them the antonomy of operation that they prize.

Loyalty to the System. Although there is a great deal of personal freedom in the corporate world (even executives of steel and oil companies openly belong to the environmentalist Sierra Club), certain types of behavior are nevertheless taboo. Most important, the manager must never question the appropriateness of the current corporate system. The properly socialized manager simply does not express criticism of the prevailing forms of ownership and governance of the firm, of the competitive structure of his industry, or of the role of the corporation in society. In the same exercise that I refer to above, I found that corporate executives uniformly rejected *all* major alternatives to the status quo: greater free market competition, economic decentralization, greater government-corporate cooperation, and greater government regulation in the public interest. Significantly the executives gave lip service to the values of free market competition, but resisted all suggested steps that would lead to its realization. (For this reason I do not list "free enterprise competition" as a major value of the managerial culture.)

Loyalty to the organization is also prized. The worst charge that can be brought against a manager, according to De Lorean, is that "he is not a team player":

> And being a member of the management team meant that you supported your boss' decisions, and the corporate decisions, even if you thought they were wrong. When you opposed your superiors, you were accused of "not being on the team." Charlie Chayne, vice-president of Engineering, along with his staff, took a very strong stand against the Corvair as an unsafe car long before it went on sale in 1959. He was not listened to but instead told, in effect, "You're not a member of the team. Shut up or go looking for another job."[12]

Managerial Authority. Within the walls of the corporation the military model of the relationship between superior and subordinate is often sacrosanct. In most large corporations one simply doesn't question the boss. On a higher plane, the culture of management dictates that the most important things to preserve are the "prerogatives" that make managers accountable to no one on matters of corporate strategy, policy, planning, marketing, production, finance, technology choice, and on all matters relating to the structure of the organization and the structure of work tasks. Managers firmly believe that, while they do not own their corporations, they have the moral and legal right to govern them as if they were their own private property. (Consequently a change in the organization and structure of work is not seen as a routine decision but as a direct challenge to one of the most important managerial prerogatives.)

Camaraderie. There is a code of behavior that dictates that all interpersonal relations within the firm must be friendly and courteous, but not intimate. Everyone is called by his or her first name in American business (as the lowliest cub reporter at Time Incorporated, I was once told to call Henry Luce "Harry" should I ever run into him). One must always show concern about the health, family, hobbies, and interests of one's co-workers. All meetings must be conducted in a climate of near-Victorian politeness and cordiality. Anger, hostility, and signs of weakness, fear, compassion, or love are taboo. A sense of humor is prized, so long as it is not cynical. Openness is valued, but it is always improper to question the appropriateness of the basic values of efficiency, growth, authority, and loyalty. In short, this code of interpersonal behavior serves to shield the other, more basic aspects of the system of belief from attack from within. It supports the efforts to create a coherent "team."

This is far from an all-inclusive list of important corporate values (one might, for instance, reasonably include such values as security, power, and stability), nor is the list rigorously taxonomic or scientific "truth." It is merely suggestive. It serves only to shift the focus of analysis from individual to collective behavior. Its logical justification is that the values identified are consistent with, and complementary to, the structures of large American corporations. That is, it would appear that the values of efficiency, growth, short-term profitability, loyalty, authority, and camaraderie are *functional* for large, complex, hierarchical, manager-run firms.

More precisely, they *were* functional. While the ascendant managerial values were functional as recently as ten years ago (though De Lorean argues that they had become outmoded by the mid-1960s), they clearly are inappropriate today. In fact, they are *dys*functional. The values of economic efficiency and growth put the corporation squarely in opposition to the values of environmentalists, consumerists, and the majority of young people who are concerned with the quality of life. The values of loyalty and managerial authority put the corporation squarely in opposition not only to organized labor (a traditional foe) but also to young people and to the majority of citizens who, in the wake of Watergate, are concerned about the morality of the leaders of powerful social institutions. As De Lorean documents, the tyranny of organizational culture can be complete. Such

cultural imperatives as order, efficiency, and loyalty will often be adhered
to beyond the point of rationality, morality, or legality (for example, those
involved in the Watergate scandal and the recent cases of corporate bribery
succumbed to organizational pressures that encouraged and rewarded the
kind of unethical behavior these individuals probably would have abhorred
in their private lives). Moreover, the culture of an organization may grow
dysfunctional over time and prevent an organization from effectively
pursuing its own goals—for example, when it leads to hostility to innovation or to rejection of individuals or groups who could make a contribution
to the firm. Counterproductively, a firm will often select people who are
compatible with its outmoded culture or reject people and ideas that could
bring needed vitality to the organization. Consider the following cases:

· At an executive conference in a large organization (100,000 employees)
a top planner suggested that the basic strategy of the organization was
based on some faulty assumptions. He suggested that the organization had
not really defined its basic mission and that it should redo some crucial
analyses before continuing to commit enormous resources to a major
program. Within a year he had lost his staff, his title, and was given a
smaller office. Shortly thereafter he left the organization. The organization
floundered for three years while pursuing the strategy the planner had
questioned. Finally a new top management team came in and adopted the
planner's suggestions, which ultimately proved successful.

· One of the nation's largest metal-manufacturing firms chose as its chief
executive a man with forty years experience in the firm. Starting on the
shop floor, he had worked his way to the top of the company while earning
a graduate degree in engineering. The man was chosen by his fellow
executives (who had a working majority of the board of directors) because
of (1) his familiarity with all aspects of the company and (2) his reputation
for being a "team player." Within five years Japanese firms had won a
major share of the company's market.

· A leading manufacturing firm was highly centralized and most important decisions were made at the top of the hierarchy. All the top executives
belonged to the same golf club where they often discussed important
business while playing or dining. The club excluded Jews, Catholics,
blacks, and women from membership. As the end of the 1970s approached, the company found it harder to recruit and retain top young
managers. Top management could not understand why the quality of its
younger executives was not up to the standards of its competitors.

These cases are based on actual incidents that I have witnessed personally in large American organizations. They exemplify some ways in
which a prevailing culture in a firm can become dysfunctional. Rigid

adherence to a culture that may once have been appropriate for a given era or stage in development can limit the firm's ability to:

Adapt to changing market conditions.
Develop or accept new technologies.
Tolerate new ideas.
Respond sensitively to societal shifts.
Create an appropriate philosophy and organization of work to meet the
    expectations and needs of younger workers.

Anthropologists have documented dozens of cases of once-successful cultures that literally fell apart when their environments changed. Because these tribes could not adapt to such influences as Christianity, a market economy, modern technology, urbanization, or an external (national) political authority, they disintegrated and left their people in chaos and anomie, a state sometimes called "culture shock."

Business organizations also have trouble adapting to environmental changes. For example, rigid adherence to economic efficiency may become socially dysfunctional in an era when society will no longer permit corporations to behave solely as industrial institutions. Businesses are becoming social institutions, with many constituencies and many goals. In addition to pressures from stockholders to use capital efficiently, there are now pressures from consumerists, environmentalists, labor unions, and the government to produce safe and durable goods without damaging the environment and without wasting energy. Moreover all these things must be accomplished while providing plentiful and satisfying jobs. Most corporations have not been sensitive to these societal changes, and have seen their public acceptance sink to an all-time low in public opinion polls. Corporations have responded to changes in public sentiment with an "economic education" campaign designed to dismiss consumerist and environmentalist demands and to discredit as "disloyal to capitalism" those who advance them. This misreading of the public interest stems in large part from the defensive rigidity of the managerial culture, and has perversely led to even greater public mistrust of corporations.

Internally the dictates of the culture of industrial efficiency can be equally counterproductive. Until recently the prime task of management has been to use capital and natural resources as efficiently as possible. But the energy shortage and the attitudinal change about the quality of work and the environment seem to have foreclosed many of the once limitless options for the uses of capital and natural resources. In the future the prime task of management will probably be the development of human resources—if only because less than 20 percent of all workers in the United States are still engaged in the direct production of goods. Service and knowledge industries have only one resource—people. Unfortunately the culture of economic efficiency often views people as the factor of production that should be traded off (that is, eliminated). No American corporation has yet approached the development of human resources with the same commitment that almost all have to the development of capital and natural resources. This rigid adherence to the managerial culture could, perversely, lead to a lowering of efficiency in the very corporations where efficiency is a leading goal.

Institutional inflexibility is a difficult problem to counteract because patterns of behavior are rooted in past success and in observable truths. Economic or industrial efficiency was once an appropriate single goal for large corporations, and even today it is a reliable guideline for action in the vast preponderance of instances. But few guidelines, no matter how honorable and long their lineages, are *always* applicable. "Honor they father" is almost always a worthy precept, but not when Dad is beating Mom with a baseball bat.

Sadly corporations often respond to an external change by accentuating the very behavior that puts them out of phase with the environment. For example, when a company experiences problems assimilating the first woman or black manager it hires, it will often respond by recruiting white males who quintessentially embody the traits that are most in conflict with those of the group that requires assimilation. It seems logical to recruit one's twins because "we all get along so well; we never have important disagreements." The process of twinning[13] accentuates the difficulty of change. Furthermore selecting only people who are already compatible with the prevailing culture can be counterproductive when what is needed is a different perspective to give validity to the organization. Twinning may be tolerable in small companies, but in large corporations it runs against the pluralistic grain of the nation to whose needs the company is attempting to be responsive. Twinning does reduce conflict, but a certain amount of healthy conflict is the source of innovation and change in an organization.

Identifying the Culture of a Firm

If a firm wants to alter its culture to cope with changes in the environment, it must first identify the prime characteristics of that culture. Through some kind of analytical process it could then be determined which aspects of the culture are functional and should be retained, and which are dysfunctional and should be changed. One way of analyzing the culture would be to introduce a social anthropologist into the firm for six months or so, and ask him or her to write an enthnography of the corporation, much as the anthropologist would do as a participant-observer in a primitive culture. As far as I know, this has never been done in a major American corporation. An alternative course would be to undertake a self-analysis of the culture for some unthreatening purpose.

Warren Bennis once suggested a tool that might be appropriate to this end.[14] He argued that companies should prepare "institutional resumés" for recruiting purposes. He noted that a prospective employee usually knows very little about the firm that is interviewing him or her (significantly in England they turn this phrase around: a prospective British employee "interviews a firm"). Bennis posited that a great deal of job dissatisfaction among young managers might result from a poor "person/environment fit." In short, many people choose the wrong place to work because of a lack of information or misperceptions they develop during the recruiting process. Consequently Bennis argued for greater "truth in recruiting." This might begin with the preparation of an institutional biography that would be the basis for writing a firm's resumé. Such an exercise could be a tool for identifying the managerial culture as well. Either or both processes could start by distributing a questionnaire to key managers in an organization.

To be successful, such an exercise would have to be anonymous and, in particular, nonthreatening to the key managers who took part in it. Below, for purposes of illustration only, I've adapted Bennis's lighthearted questionnaire for preparing the institutional biography of Corporation Z. While the informal tone of this questionnaire might be appropriate for an advertising agency or a San Francisco head shop, it might be inappropriate for most large corporations. Therefore it should be viewed not as a model to be copied but as a checklist of the kinds of structural and cultural traits that corporations might want to identify as the first step in changing their philosophy and organization of work.

INSTITUTIONAL BIOGRAPHY OF CORPORATION Z

1. *Age*

   Apart from the actual chronological age of the company, would you characterize Z as:

(1) Infant	(5) Suspended adolescent	(8) Middle-Aged
(2) Toddler	(6) Young adult	(9) Old
(3) Prepubescent	(7) Adult	(10) Senile?
(4) Adolescent		

2. *Health*
Apart from the financial health of the organization, would you characterize the state of health at Z as:

(1) Robust	Z's age	(7) Declining
(2) Sound	(4) Improving	(8) Infirm
(3) Better than can	(5) Convalescing	(9) Paralyzed
be expected given	(6) Remittently feverish	(10) Virtually bankrupt?

3. *Key Events*

   a. Describe the three most pivotal events that have occurred since the founding of Z:
      (1)   (2)   (3)

   b. What is the *best* thing that has occurred at Z during the past two years? Why?

   c. What is the *worst* thing that has occurred at Z during the past two years? Why?

4. *Qualifications*

   a. What distinctive competencies does Z possess?

   b. What competencies does it need to develop? Why?

5. *Characteristics*

   a. What five short, descriptive phrases or adjectives best describe Z?
      1.
      2.
      3.
      4.
      5.

   b. Circle the phrase/word you'd most like to change.

   c. Underscore the phrase/word you'd most like to preserve.

6. *Norms of the Organization*

   a. How much contact and interaction is required among people at Z?

1	2	3	4	5	6	7
A great deal						Virtually none

   b. What amount of intimacy is appropriate at Z?

1	2	3	4	5	6	7
Intimate, informal						Distant, formal

c. To what extent are people encouraged to be collaborative and mutually supportive?

1	2	3	4	5	6	7

Environment is   Environment is
collaborative, supportive   individualistic, unhelpful

d. How would you describe the decision-making climate at Z?

1	2	3	4	5	6	7

Participative   Authoritarian

e. To what extent is Z a place where people are happy with their work?

1	2	3	4	5	6	7

Happy   Unhappy

f. To what extent does ability count at Z, or is it *whom* you know that is the key to rewards and promotions?

1	2	3	4	5	6	7

What you know   *Whom* you know

g. To what extent is Z open to new ideas?

1	2	3	4	5	6	7

Open   Closed

h. To what extent does Z accept employees with nontraditional life-styles or views?

1	2	3	4	5	6	7

Open   Closed

i. To what extent is the organizational climate characterized by rumor, gossip, pettiness, and role playing?

1	2	3	4	5	6	7

Frankness is   Back-stabbing
the norm   is the norm

j. To what extent is there a preoccupation with the appearance of working?

1	2	3	4	5	6	7

Can relax when   Must always
there is no work   look busy

k. How are employees rated for raises and promotions?

1	2	3	4	5	6	7

Judged on   Judged on "fitting in
performance   on the team"

l. To what extent is clear and definite responsibility fixed at each level of
the organization?

1	2	3	4	5	6	7

Clear   Unclear
responsibilities   responsibilities

m. To what extent are all workers treated like mature adults?

1	2	3	4	5	6	7

Treated like   Treated like
adults   children

n. To what extent is Z concerned with planning for the future?

1	2	3	4	5	6	7

Proactive, long-   Reactive, crisis
range planning   management

o. To what extent do all employees participate in any gains that come about
from their increased productivity?

1	2	3	4	5	6	7

Employees receive   Employees receive
all gains   nothing from gains

p. To what extent are people encouraged to take risks?

1	2	3	4	5	6	7

Risk taking rewarded   Playing it safe rewarded

q. To what extent does the person at the top set a good example?

1	2	3	4	5	6	7

Practices what he preaches   Preaches but doesn't practice

r. To what extent is the company self-satisfied?

1	2	3	4	5	6	7

Willing to engage in   Complacent, unwilling
introspection, self-analytical   to question basic assumptions

s. How is company performance measured?

1	2	3	4	5	6	7

By quality or effectiveness   Management-by-the-numbers
of product or service   (30 different profit ratios)

t. What happens to new ideas?

1	2	3	4	5	6	7

Carefully considered and   Killed off quickly by
tried whenever practical   staffs or committees

u. To what kinds of outside organizations do most managers at Z belong (circle no more than three)?

(1) Country club   (5) Church groups
(2) Rotary club   (6) Sierra Club
(3) Exclusive downtown men's club   (7) Common Cause
(4) The Y   (8) None

v. Who gets promoted at Z? (See Maccoby for description of types.)

(1) The Craftsman   (4) The Gamesman
(2) The Jungle Fighter   (5) The Entrepreneur
(3) The Company Man   (6) Other (describe)

7. *Nature of Work*

a. What is the rhythm of life at Z? (Circle one)

(1) A six-day, twelve-hour grind   pressure and relaxation
(2) Typical five-day-week, eight-   (4) Seasonal
    hour days   (5) Relaxed
(3) Intermittent periods of   (6) Slow and dull

b. To what extent is there attention to work *quantity*?

1	2	3	4	5	6	7

None   A great deal

c. To what extent is there attention to work *quality*?

1	2	3	4	5	6	7

None   A great deal

d. To what extent is *process* (bureaucratic, administrative processes) more important than the final *product*?

1	2	3	4	5	6	7

Product oriented   Process oriented

e. To what extent are there opportunities to learn on the job?

1	2	3	4	5	6	7

Learning-oriented   Must have all skills
organization   before you start

f. To what extent is there job mobility in the firm?

1	2	3	4	5	6	7

High mobility   No mobility

g. To what extent is there flexibility in the choice of working hours and other
    working conditions?

1	2	3	4	5	6	7

Great flexibility   Great rigidity

h. To what extent is there reliance on a standardized, detailed work manual
    or code?

1	2	3	4	5	6	7

Individualized approach to   Monolithic
people and to problems   work rules

i. To what extent is there adequate job security?

1	2	3	4	5	6	7

If you do your job, it's   Can be out on
yours for as long as you like   your ear tomorrow

j. How are jobs designed?

1	2	3	4	5	6	7

Designed to encourage   Reduced to simplest, routine
individual initiative   level for purposes of control

k. To what extent do people know where they stand?

1	2	3	4	5	6	7

Quick and clear feedback   Never sure how you
on performance   are perceived

8. *External Affairs*

a. How concerned is Z with the welfare of the local community?

1	2	3	4	5	6	7

Great involvement   No interaction

b. How concerned is Z with the welfare of its consumers?

1	2	3	4	5	6	7

Consumer oriented   "Let the buyer beware"

c. To what extent is the company defensive about outside criticism?

1	2	3	4	5	6	7

Candid and open to   "Them" vs.
outside critics   "us" mentality

d. To what extent will Z lie to increase profits?

1	2	3	4	5	6	7

Always ethical   Unethical behavior is the norm

e. What is the typical image that outsiders have of Z?

1	2	3	4	5	6	7

Good guys   Bad guys

9. What is the current company joke (the gag about the company that no one would dare tell the boss)?

10. What do you think Z wants to be when it grows up?

Changing the Culture

From time to time all firms should stand back and take a long look at themselves in a mirror. It is unimportant whether the mirror is an ethnographic description of the firm's culture undertaken by a participant-observer, an institutional questionnaire, or some other tool. What counts is that there be an open exploration of the culture of the group, followed by an open discussion of the results that were found. Benefits of such an analysis might well accrue to the individual, the firm, and the society.

One of the fastest growing companies in the U.S. recently analyzed some of its basic managerial assumptions and found that they led to the sacrifice of long-term employee motivation and productivity in order to satisfy short-term stock speculators. The company had decided to institute a profit-sharing plan, but at the last moment the idea was nixed because funding the plan would have prevented the achievement of certain return-on-investment goals that had been set earlier. These goals were measured by arcane ratios that are fully understood only by accountants and stock analysts. At the last minute, the company's top managers asked themselves, "Who are we running this company for anyway, Wall Street analysts and finance consultants?" The managers then went back and developed a new set of performance measures and corporate goals—ones that were appropriate for what *they* wanted to achieve for themselves, their employees, and their long-term investors.

It is interesting to note that the characteristics of risk taking, entrepreneurship, innovation, ethical behavior, worker participation in decision making and profits, and openness to new and divergent opinions tend to appear as a *common cluster* in many organizations. For example, Levi-Strauss, Atlantic Richfield, and Cummins Engines display these positive characteristics in spades. At the other extreme there are a great many companies that have *none* of these characteristics. Chrysler, U.S. Steel, and Union Oil, I would guess, display the exact opposite cluster of characteristics. Moreover I suspect that executives in this latter group of firms would recoil at the thought of distributing any form of institutional questionnaire to their managers (let alone their workers), while the former group of companies might well go along with some version of such a questionnaire. The rule might be: If a company is willing to distribute an institutional questionnaire, it does not need to do so!

The culture of an organization is a product of both the ecology (or environment) in which it has grown, and the "tone" established by its leaders. Some top managers establish a successful culture through good example. At the Atlantic Richfield Company, Robert O. Anderson and Thornton Bradshaw actively participate in political discussions at the Aspen Institute where a variety of ideas—many of them anti-business—are aired and analyzed. Their willingness to examine business' dirty linen in public not only gives their company great credibility with a public and media grown accustomed to secretiveness and defensiveness on the part of business leaders, it also sets the stage for openness and candor on all levels of Atlantic Richfield. Some executives convey their companies' values by written statements of their philosophies. James Cash Penney wrote that every policy, method and act at J.C. Penney must meet this test: "Does it square with what is right and just?" What may have been more important is that Mr. Penney practiced what he preached. He exuded integrity—and this signaled an important behavioral message to his employees.

While integrity is a value that never goes out of date, it is nevertheless important for companies to continually check the degree to which even the most successful culture remains in tune with the changing environment. In the final analysis, a truly successful culture is one that institutionalizes change. In this respect, the eleventh commandment at the 3M Company is, "Never be responsible for killing an idea"—a rule of thumb that paves the way for innovation.

Any rule or codified set of behavior can be carried to the extreme. Henry Ford saw himself as the guardian of the personal virtues of his employees. In this role, he saw fit to send spies into his workers' homes to insure that they were living up to proper standards of morality and cleanliness—that is, *his* standards. No doubt, there is a fine line between moral authority and paternalism, but most corporate leaders today err so far on the side of cultural and ethical laissez-faire that there is little danger that they will follow Ford and overstep the line. In fact, not only do most corporate leaders not take the effort to consciously identify the kind of behavioral example they wish to set for their firms, they are not even aware when they are *un*consciously setting a negative one. Most corporate executives seem blissfully unaware that their cultures might be too oriented to the short-term, too concerned with management-by-the-numbers (at the expense of establishing a long-term reputation for quality and service), too defensive with criticisms from government, the media and academia (when candor would carry the day), and too complacent about past successes (when the world is changing about them). These are common cultural pitfalls that only a few innovative top managers seem to be aware of, and even fewer are actively seeking to evaluate the basic managerial assumptions of their firms to see if they are appropriate for the future.

The entire purpose of this chapter is to stress the need for corporations to look honestly at themselves if they want to learn to cope with the changing environment. Organizations, as De Lorean illustrates, can create tyrannical cultures. At Philip Morris, for example, every top executive I met on a recent visit there constantly had a cigarette in his hand. The culture of that firm is such that it causes otherwise intelligent people to risk their lives in order to prove that they are "team players." Significantly I was told time and time again that "there is no pressure put on Philip Morris managers to smoke." Here, then, is another example of the corporation's blindness to its own behavior that De Lorean spotted at GM. While in most companies such inability to see the effects of culture on individual behavior is not as dramatic as it is as Philip Morris, I would argue that cultural pressures to conform are to be found in all organizations, public or private. What separates growing and adaptive organizations from dinosaurs is that the former accept the necessity of constantly working to overcome the inevitable temptations to play it the company way, and steadily work to create a culture that encourages positive and productive behavior.

There is no denying that the process of analysis of institutional culture can be threatening ("Why don't we hire any Jews [Gentiles]?" "Why do we all wear flags in our lapels?" "Why do we all smoke?" "Why don't we encourage entrepreneurial risk taking?"). But such questions are probably *less* threatening than the related probing that the psychologist would direct at an individual, or that would come out in a T-group.

Of course *people* are the problem. But some problems must be addressed *indirectly* to be successfully resolved. It is hard to imagine a policy change more frustrating or futile than one that is based on changing people, since there are only two ways to change people in an organization: fire them or alter their personalities. From time to time one reads of studies that conclude that "the schools could be improved if only there were better teachers" or "local governments would be more effective if they had more talented administrators" (one would like to add that "the world would be a better place if there were fewer sinners"). The fact is that most organizations are stuck with the people they have. In most instances wholesale firing is not in the cards. Moreover there is no guarantee that there is a sufficient supply of "better people out there" to serve as replacements. Certainly a company *can* make personnel changes at the margin. The trick is to alter the systems of action and belief in the firm so that these new people can be effective when they join the firm. This doesn't mean trying to make the old-timers into people they aren't. It means altering the rewards and norms to tolerate the old behavior while at the same time encouraging the new behavior. That way, no one is unduly threatened.

An anthropological approach to organization change would thus begin with an analysis of the structures and sanctions that encourage and discourage certain kinds of behavior. If adherence to the traditional philosophy and organization of work is rewarded at Company Z, then it is such a system that Z is likely to get in response. But if it is decided that a new system is needed, the reward system at Z could then be altered. This is not easy to do, but it is much less threatening than singling out traditional managers and trying to change their personalities. Culture (or structure) is simply easier to change than personality. One hopes that in the long run behavior will change to meet the new structure of the organization. The assumption is that few people are born with, for example, bureaucratic personalities. If bureaucratic behavior is no longer sanctioned, then other aspects of the individual's personality might emerge. This approach is not foolproof. All I am suggesting is that an attempt to train people to become less bureaucratic that leaves the structural rewards for bureaucratic behavior untouched is not likely to be effective. Moreover any approach that singles out *people* for change when it is the *institution* that is determining their behavior is patently unjust.

Such a process of cultural change should not be confused with Skinnerian conditioning. Culture change is an open and participative process, not a manipulative one. It is a pluralistic process, not a monolithic one (that is, it is not necessary for all individuals to go along with all the changes in the culture). Ultimately cultural change attempts only to alter the *way* things are done. The individuals involved may well remain nasty or loving, selfish or generous, hostile or kind. They are free to go to a shrink on their own time if they don't like who or what they are. They (and we) may even find that they really aren't so crazy after all.

8

NATIONAL POLICIES TO FOSTER FULLER UTILIZATION OF THE HUMAN RESOURCE

How small of all that human hearts endure,
That part which laws or kings can cause or cure.
—SAMUEL JOHNSON

THE previous chapters explore some of the potential human and economic consequences that might result from an alternative philosophy and organization of work in America. Those chapters dealt only with practices and policies internal to a firm or a plant (what economists call the "micro" level of consideration). But there is, in addition, a range of "macro" or national considerations that are the concern of public policy. While the list of such considerations could be kept extremely short by proactive and responsible behavior by private employers (the most effective way to keep government out of business is for business to keep its own house in order), there are nevertheless a few work-related issues that would require national action no matter how diligent and public-spirited business might become. Foremost among these macro-level work concerns is the persistent and expensive problem of unemployment, which causes human resources to be underutilized and leads to the ruin of many lives. This is a problem that labor economists find impossible not only to solve but even to define.

DEFINING UNEMPLOYMENT

When more and more people are thrown out of work,
unemployment results.
—CALVIN COOLIDGE

To THE uninitiated, President Coolidge's definition of unemployment looks like double-talk. But labor economists will recognize that their own definitions are as unhelpful as Old Cal's. Stanley Moses has compiled sixteen different definitions of unemployment, all of which have been put forward by legitimate labor economists. Significantly these different definitions yield sixteen different rates of unemployment—ranging from 2.7 percent to 61.2 percent—even though each is based on the same U.S. government figures.[1] This range of opinion is extreme—even among economists.

Like the rich, the unemployed have always been with us. Only the percentages change: from a twentieth-century low of 1.2 percent in 1944 to a high of 25.2 percent in 1933.[2] Unfortunately most years of low unemployment have been during war-time. Only in the Roaring Twenties did America have a prolonged period of both peace and low unemployment. With the exception of the Depression and a few years of severe recession, peacetime unemployment hovered in the 4–5 percent range for the first seventy years of this century. Then something happened during the last decade: Average unemployment rose to 6.2 percent. The reason for the rise, it seems, is demography. In the past unemployment rates were determined by the rate of job creation and job loss; the rising rate of unemployment in the 1970s, in contradistinction, was created by the unprecedented percentages of Americans looking for work. This is not to slip into Coolidgian tautology. In 1974, for example, 2.2 million new jobs were created; nonetheless the unemployment rate *rose* from 4.9 percent to 5.6 percent! In fact each year in the 1970s greater and greater percentages of the total population became employed than ever before in peacetime. But unemployment rates also rose because of the entry of the Boom Babies into the labor force, and because of the choice of millions of middle-class women to seek paid employment rather than work in the home (or in addition to work in the home). The entry of the Boom Babies was a one-time phenomenon. But the entry of women into the paid labor force is a continuing trend. The rate of female participation in the labor force grew from 33.9 percent in 1950 to 50.9 percent in 1979. Since the male rate of employment is about 77 percent, it is possible that even more women will seek paid employment in the 1980s.

Because the official unemployment rate fails to distinguish between such changes in demographics and changes in job opportunities, some labor economists advocate a new employment barometer: the Employment-Population ratio (E-P). The E-P is the ratio of employed people to the total working-age (sixteen and over) population. The ratio stood at 59.4 percent in early 1979, up from 55 percent in 1974.[3] While the E-P corrects some of the misleading aspects of the official unemployment rate, it still fails to account for the following kinds of problems with the *quality* of jobs:

Subemployment. Working less than full time, full year (and often for less than the minimum wage) is a chronic problem for many workers. It has serious consequences for the life-styles and life chances of families when it afflicts heads of households.

Low-Level Unemployment. Many disadvantaged and minority workers are trapped in jobs that offer them little in the way of dignity and self-esteem. These jobs are characterized by harsh and arbitrary discipline, unhealthy, unsafe, or inhumane working conditions, and the absence of a career path.

Involuntary Employment. Many older people are forced to take jobs because they cannot live on their retirement incomes; many heads of households are forced to moonlight because they cannot attain a decent standard of family living on wages from primary jobs. (In 1978, 4.5 million Americans held two or more jobs, representing about 4.8 percent of the total work force. Perhaps if all Americans could live on the income of one job, unemployment rates would be somewhat reduced.) And many women who would prefer to stay home and raise their children are forced to take paid jobs because of government eligibility requirements for social services.

Underemployment. The under-utilization of the skills, training, and education of workers is fast becoming a major source of work-place problems in society. As the levels of educational attainment of the work force rise, discontent and low productivity spread among more qualified workers who are forced to take jobs that were previously performed by those with lower qualifications.[4]

Even if the official rate of unemployment would fall to 4 percent, such problems with job quality would persist. There is unfortunately no adequate measure of these employment problems.

Unemployment, in short, is a complex, multifaceted issue that defies simple definition. But because we insist on using simple definitions, public policy often is misdirected and the underlying problems are seldom addressed. Programs designed to combat the full range of unemployment problems must be sensitive to the complexity of the phenomenon if they are to be successful.

CREATING ENOUGH JOBS/
CREATING THE RIGHT KINDS OF JOBS

Since Keynes, America periodically has tried to combat unemployment by manipulating macroeconomic policy (principally through increasing the money supply and government spending, and through tax cuts). Each of these methods, when pursued long enough to actually create a significant number of jobs, appears also to create inflation. Moreover the Keynesian approach does not address the problem of the "structurally" unemployed (the poor, uneducated, and minority workers who never seem to find jobs even at times of "full" employment); nor does it address the problems of job quality or underutilization defined above. What is needed are *non*macroeconomic policies that address the problems of job quality and structural unemployment while being noninflationary in the process. In fact, for many decades the federal government has taken some *uni*maginative steps in this direction. It has attempted to:

1. Improve Labor Market Information. The idea here is that markets work better when there is more information available to both buyers and sellers. But successfully generating employment forecasts, collecting current data, and disseminating both in a timely fashion to the people who need them has proved as elusive as the creation of antigravity.

2. Reduce Racial Discrimination. Here the government's record is mixed. Affirmative action has been quite successful for women and middle-class blacks, but it seems to have had little effect on the employment opportunities of the truly disadvantaged.

3. Control Immigration. This is a policy in name only. Ambivalence about immigration has prevented both liberal and conservative administrations from steering a clear course. While conservative presidents feel the push from their constituents to limit immigration to reduce welfare costs, businessmen say they need immigrants to do the jobs that native Americans won't do. Moreover libertarians oppose, on ideological grounds, issuing the identity cards that would be needed to halt the flow of illegal aliens.

While liberal presidents feel the push from labor unions to reduce immigration, they also hear from humanitarians who claim that it is the special mission of America to keep its shores open to "the wretched and huddled masses." And recently many upper-middle-class professional women—particularly in the Sun Belt—have advocated open borders because they see that their liberation depends on an adequate supply of Spanish-speaking maids to do the housework they no longer have the time to do. Even those who aren't driven by ideology or self-interest are of two minds on the subject. While worrying about the very real danger of creating another Quebec in the American Southwest, these people also recognize that Spanish-speaking immigrants tend to be law-abiding and that they increase the standard of living of native Americans by working extremely hard at such essential tasks as harvesting crops, fixing roads, and other forms of back-breaking labor.

4. Provide Public Service Employment. While some might argue that this is a form of macroeconomic policy (i.e., government spending), it probably should *not* be considered in that category because it is specifically targeted at the structurally unemployed, while macroeconomic policies are a shotgun approach aimed at unemployment in general. The main problem with this approach is that the government is a lousy shot. For example, when my university applied for a CETA worker, we were sent the daughter of a Beverly Hills doctor. Not only did this woman have an M.B.A. degree, but she was domiciled in her parent's $300,000 house. Taxpayers across the country have grown irate about similar (if not so blatant) abuses.

Between 1968 and 1978 the federal government spent nearly $36 billion on CETA and other so-called manpower programs. In 1978 alone it spent $8.4 billion on 1.4 million public service jobs. While these programs no doubt reduce the unemployment rate somewhat, they seem not to touch the structural problems to which they should be targeted. The reasons for this failure appear to be that:

· State and local governments often use CETA funds to hire people they would have hired anyway.
· When these governments do hire from the pool of chronically unemployed, they don't prepare these people for nonsheltered employment in the future. The nature of most CETA jobs (and training) is such that workers don't acquire the discipline needed to hold a regular job.
· The jobs created are temporary. Even when a hardcore unemployable finds his way into a CETA job, he or she remains employed only for as long as funding lasts. (Forty percent of all CETA "graduates" are unemployed a year after leaving the program.)[5]

One would be hard pressed to make a convincing argument that the inherent weaknesses of these programs could be overcome by either better management or more money. Like the Keynesian approach, they are simply ineffective. While I would not advocate scrapping them all in the absence of good alternatives, I would argue that as a first step it is necessary to develop some imaginative alternatives. Unfortunately it is in the realm of imagination and innovation that traditional manpower economics fails. The assumptions of economists—which they take to be laws—constrain their imaginations so that they constantly reinvent the same old trickle-down policies of macro-stimulation and the same old targeted manpower programs. For some unfathomable reason economists of all ideological stripes believe that the way to make a failed approach work is to do more of it! What is really needed is a new set of assumptions for labor economics in the upcoming era of slow growth.

ALTERNATIVE ASSUMPTIONS FOR A NEW LABOR ECONOMICS

Economists are right about at least one thing: The trick is always to "optimize" a set of conflicting factors. Unfortunately the set of factors traditional economists have been intrepidly optimizing for two centuries is today incomplete, insufficient and inappropriate. While traditional economists could content themselves with optimizing production functions that include only three variables—land, labor, and capital—the New Economist of the 1980s will undoubtedly have a more complex task. In the emerging resource-scarce, highly industrialized, highly polluted, highly populated, highly interdependent, and highly contentious world, it is increasingly anachronistic to make policy choices solely and simply by trading off more expensive factors of production for cheaper ones (or *apparently* cheaper ones, for what is cheap today may be rare tomorrow).

Traditional economics as it is practiced in America today is concerned only with *efficiency*—that is, with optimizing the three traditional factors of production. Unfortunately, as Arthur Okun has demonstrated, efficiency is gained by trading off equality.[6] Unfortunately, as E. F. Schumacher has shown, efficiency is gained by trading off the quality of life.[7] Unfortunately, as J. K. Galbraith has shown, efficiency is gained by trading off certain freedoms—particularly consumer sovereignty and competitive markets.[8] In effect, the scope of traditional economics is simply too narrow. For by excluding liberty, equality, and the quality of life from the scope of its concerns, the discipline of economics excludes the highest values of the majority of the population. Optimizing land, labor, and capital the way economists do with their production functions leads to unemployment, inequality, pollution, and social alienation—outcomes that may be acceptable to some economists, but are unacceptable to most other Americans. There is thus a misfit between the operating philosophy of the economy and the new goals of the pluralistic polity.

While it is not useful here to offer a thorough critique of the discipline of economics, it is nevertheless important to at least call attention to its manifest shortcomings. For it is this discipline that informs—even dictates —the prevailing philosophy and organization of work. Following willy-nilly the dictates of economics: People are replaced by machines; interesting craftwork is replaced by dull machine tending; organizations are structured hierarchically; workers are abruptly laid off when the economy turns down; and maximization, optimization, least cost, and all the other notions of industrial efficiency are applied indiscriminately to the organization of work and to the treatment of workers. This is not to argue that machines should never replace workers or that workers should never be laid off. But the problem with economics is that it does not indicate when it is inappropriate to do such things. Economic assumptions, because they are misconstrued as laws, dictate that machines *always* should replace workers when this leads to greater efficiency.

Sometimes, however, it is *inappropriate* to replace people with machines —particularly if one is trying to achieve liberty and equality and to improve the quality of life, *in addition to* increasing efficiency. But the old economics is single-minded. It can maximize the factors of production *only* to achieve efficiency. Thus the New Economics would have to be more inclusive than the old variety. It would have to pursue all four of the prime goals of political economics (liberty, equality, efficiency, and the quality of life) *simultaneously*.[9] Such a New Economics does not yet exist (below I argue that not even Schumacher's Buddhist economics fills the bill). But whatever form it ultimately takes, the concerns of the New Economics must transcend the simple optimization of the traditional factors of production. What is needed is a new, complex calculus for satisfying many extremely broad factors of production *and consumption*. These disparate, nonequatable, noncommensurate, and nonfungible factors might include: employment, energy, ecology, efficiency, equality, excellence, enfranchisement, education (and enjoyment?).

My argument is that in choosing appropriate national work policies, the New Labor Economist will have to satisfy simultaneously all these E Factors. These E Factors are, in effect, performance criteria for national work policies in a new slow-growth economy. America will not be considered a *just society* unless it satisfies nearly all the following performance criteria.

Employment: America will have to provide a job for every citizen who wants one.
Energy: America will have to provide an adequate long-term supply of energy.

Environment: America will have to provide a safe environment with clean air and water.

Ecology: America will have to husband its natural resources so these will be available to future generations.

Efficiency: America will have to provide an adequate standard of living, on the average no lower than what is enjoyed today. This requires improved productivity and technological innovation so the country can remain competitive in the world economy.

Equality: America will have to provide greater economic security for the poor, reducing the gap between the poor and the middle class by bringing the poor up to a decent standard of living, *without* reducing the standard of the middle class.

Excellence: America will have to encourage and recognize individual merit, rewarding those who contribute to the satisfaction of the other factors on this list.

Enfranchisement: America will have to provide every citizen with a voice in the affairs that determine his or her daily life. This will mean increasing individual freedom of choice in all aspects of life, particularly work.

Education: America will have to provide equal access to a form of education that is adequate preparation for the work conditions that are emerging.

Enjoyment: Here I am uncertain. Must America provide conditions for its citizens in which they are happy and satisfied and where they find transcendent reward? Or will satisfying the other factors on this list bring all the enjoyment that a society is expected to provide its citizens?

This is quite some list. I wish to make clear that it is *not* my personal wish list. Rather it is designed to reflect the goals of the major interest groups in America: unions, corporations, minorities, the professions, environmentalists, journalists, educators, the "new class" of bureaucrats—*even* economists! Because I assume that America will continue to be a pluralistic democracy, I suggest that any new national work policies will have to score high across the board on the above performance criteria. Failure to do so is likely to lead to rejection by one or more of the powerful groups that have the power of nullification in the delicately balanced American political system. This list thus provides a "reality test" for alternatives to current work policies.

I am sad to say that it is this test that Schumacher's Buddhist economics flunks. While I personally share many of Schumacher's values, I have no illusion that his values are shared by the groups that have power in America. Buddhist economics satisfies a set of performance criteria appropriate for Asia and Africa, but it will be rejected in America because it does not satisfy the requirements of efficiency, enfranchisement, or excellence.

When applied to America, Schumacher's "small is beautiful" philosophy is nostalgically appealing, but it is an unrealistic guide to changing American work policies. For the philosophy would require the dismantling of at least the five thousand largest U.S. corporations—an impractical idea. The country could not afford to write off what surely amounts to over three-fourths of its total investment capital, particularly since these very same corporations provide many good, secure jobs because they are the most effective competitors in world markets. For example, if the United States tried to compete with Japan, Inc., using an economy composed of the equivalent of lemonade stands, its markets would be swamped with foreign goods and millions of jobs would be exported. As Galbraith points out, the giant corporations are the showcases of the modern economy, providing most of the productivity and wealth to pay for the social entitlements of the welfare state.

The challenge, then, is *not* to dismantle the large corporations, but to *reform* them so they meet the humanistic and environmental goals that Schumacher wished to achieve—without scuttling the efficiency that is the bulwark of the nation's standard of living. On this task Schumacher and his followers are silent. Before his death Schumacher's only reply was that Americans should reduce their standard of living. Such an argument strikes a discordant note with perhaps 90 percent of the American public. In addition, Schumacher's notion that technology is the demon does not sit well with the American citizenry. For example, his damning of the 1969 moon landing might have gone down well with the folks at the British Soil Association, but to most Americans the lunar program was the best thing the country did collectively since it saved Europe from the Nazis. Schumacher talked about appropriate technology. But more important if one *really* wants to change things is *appropriate ideology*. When it comes to convincing Americans to mend their ways, Schumacher's inappropriate Buddhist connection mars his otherwise brilliant contribution.

Above I argue that the traditional *discipline* of economics has considerable shortcomings as a guide to a more appropriate organization of work. But as this review of Schumacher suggests, economics is not just a discipline, it is also a collection of *ideologies*. And each of the major economic ideologies addresses itself directly or indirectly to the issues of work. Moreover, like Schumacher's Buddhist economics, each of the other standard economic ideologies is an inappropriate guide because each also requires a consensus of values—that is, a national willingness to coalesce around a single goal. This flies in the face of political reality. As Schumacher was willing to forsake a great deal of liberty, equality, and efficiency to maximize the quality of life, Milton Friedman and other Libertarians will sacrifice equality, efficiency, and the quality of life to maximize liberty. Marxists and other Egalitarians will sacrifice all other values to maximize equality, and Corporatism (an inelegant term that describes the prevalent ideology among American economists and businessmen) will sacrifice all other values to achieve efficiency. While of the four ideologies Schumacher's has the saving grace of being the only one not dependent on growth, all four are nonetheless equally out of phase with the exigencies of a complex, modern democracy. All are equally inappropriate in a society where policies must deliver on liberty *and* equality *and* efficiency *and* the quality of life. None of these ideologies, then, can cope with the complexity of the E factors.

Therefore I suggest that the search for just national work policies should proceed without the discipline or the standard ideologies of economics as guides, but with the E factors as tentative criteria against which to evaluate alternative work policies.

As an illustration of what this would mean in practice, consider the major public policy issue of providing "full employment." The classic economic answer to this problem is "growth." The assumption of the ascendant economic ideology is that full employment flows as naturally from growth as pure water from mountain springs. *If* this assumption were valid, it would take something like nine years of uninterrupted 5 percent real growth in GNP to reduce unemployment from 7 percent to 4 percent.[10] Realistically the odds against the nation achieving that kind of growth are about a thousand to one. But even if it were possible, the environment E factor would not be satisfied because all the stops on pollution would have to be removed, and the equality factor would not be satisfied because, as I argue above, growth does not provide jobs for the "structurally" unemployed at the foot of the employment hierarchy.

Egalitarian economists, as we have seen, offer a different answer to the problem: "government jobs." But when the government acts as the employer of last resort, bureaucratic social overhead is enormous. Thus the factor of efficiency is sacrificed.

New Economists would look at the problem still differently. They would seek to satisfy the demands for equality *and* efficiency simultaneously. For example, one could turn the egalitarian argument on its head and *make the private sector the employer of last resort*. One way to accomplish this would be to borrow the insurance notion of "assigned risk" and make every large and medium-sized corporation responsible for providing minimum-wage jobs for people from a pool of chronically unemployable workers (the number of slots assigned would depend on the size of the corporation). The advantages of this approach to the society as a whole would be tremendous. Social overhead would be greatly reduced by getting the government out of the entitlements business almost completely (welfare, unemployment insurance, public service jobs, public housing, food stamps, and the like could be cut back almost entirely). Crime, poor health, child abuse, and other by-products of poverty would be brought down to the levels found in northern Europe. Although corporations would object at the outset, they would have a tremendous incentive to find productive ways to use the workers assigned to their payrolls. And since corporations are far better at manpower training than the government is, the chances are that they would find creative ways of making use of this currently untapped human resource. This will be especially true if Ivar Berg is right that the characteristics of employed and many unemployed ghetto residents —perhaps as many as half—are identical.[11] He posits that if some ghetto residents are demonstrably productive, employers might find that many more can be employed productively than they currently assume.[12] Indeed Berg suggests that since most economic growth seems to be occurring off the books in the underground economy where ghetto youths are overrepresented, these "workers" may be among the most productive members of the society!

Certainly employers would benefit from an economy in which everyone was working. Because the costs of social entitlements would decrease, everyone would be paying less tax. This would create demand for goods and services. Eventually the less productive workers would pay for themselves through their increased demand for goods and services. America could have full employment in the broadest sense.

While one does not expect easy acceptance of this idea, diminishing financial resources and growing social unrest may drive the nation to it. Because the system has been able to produce such abundance in the past, the employed majority has assumed that it could afford to buy off the jobless minority with welfare, food stamps, guaranteed incomes, and unemployment insurance (which is often another form of income transfer). Indeed economists claim that it is more efficient to pay the price of such programs than to provide jobs for the chronically (or structurally) unemployed. But in reality the price demanded by the jobless for being bought off in this manner is proving too high. Through crime and a host of other assorted social ills, the jobless are driving up the price of their complicity to intolerable levels.

At a certain point—a point long since reached in such cities as Chicago, New York, Los Angeles, St. Louis, Atlanta, Washington, and San Francisco—the affluence of the majority becomes insufficient compensation for the costs of the misbehavior of the chronically unemployed underclass. In some of the nation's largest cities members of the middle and working classes who have not found ways to escape to the suburbs feel as if they are prisoners in their own homes at night. The nation's cities—once the seat of civility and civilization—are being abandoned to lawlessness and other uncivilized behavior.

None of the traditional solutions to this problem—welfare reform, a guaranteed income, repressive police measures—has worked. While economists claim that such policies can be made to work through better management, higher levels of funding, or stronger commitment, in truth it is the policies themselves that are bankrupt. None of them can provide the only measure that will alter the behavior of the underclass: a job. These people need jobs to break the frightful cycle of dependence that creates generation after generation of people who not only make no productive contribution to society but who are actually counterproductive. Only a job can turn these people into independent, responsible, and productive citizens. Neither macroeconomic policies nor government make-work programs can produce real jobs in the numbers needed for those who seldom work even when the official rates of unemployment are low. Desperate problems require innovative solutions.[13]

The approach I suggest has many practical problems, but they are fewer and less significant than the problems involved in the Schumacher approach to full employment (return to small-scale, labor-intensive cottage industries) or the classical economic approach (grow at full tilt and wait for the jobs to trickle down). And I would not claim that the approach I have offered here is the most or the only appropriate response to the problem of unemployment. In reality, since there are many problems of unemployment, there probably is no single solution. The problems of unemployment might thus require not one action but a series of discrete yet compatible private and public programs, many of which could be initiated at the state, community, or plant level. Such programs might do one or more of the following: facilitate the withdrawal from the paid labor force of reluctant workers; help those who need and want jobs to acquire them; increase the mobility of workers; and make the job market more flexible. In doing so, the following kinds of strategies would be noninflationary and more

effective in meeting the macro- and micro-performance criteria laid out
above than are either the current Keynesian or "manpower" programs:

· Reduce *institutional rigidities* in the labor market, such as seniority
rules.

· Reduce the minimum-wage requirements for those under twenty years
of age and unmarried, and *raise them* for persons over twenty and for
persons under twenty who are married with children (to make work more
competitive with welfare).

· Provide a program of *midcareer worker retraining* or sabbaticals that
covers school tuition and a substantial part of the foregone income.

· Provide programs that allow workers to *taper off before retirement.* For
example, fifty-five-year-olds could work four days and sixty-year-olds three
days a week.

· Establish a system of *domestic "Fulbrights"* for people who would like
to take a year or two away from their regular jobs to engage in some kind
of public service. (Xerox has such a program for its employees.)

· Provide for *transfer payment reinvestment.* Money now spent on
welfare, food stamps, and so forth could be made available to businesses
that agree to hire a chronically unemployed person.

· Reform *unemployment insurance practices* to provide incentives for
employers to plan for full employment and for the unemployed to look for
work.

· Restrict *overtime employment.* While it is not clear to what extent
reduced work time *creates* new jobs, almost all European countries have
provisions for *avoiding* layoffs through shortening the length of the work
week. Furthermore these countries have pursued active policies to restrict
overtime employment and to increase vacation time under the assumption
that at some point this will inevitably lead to job creation.

· Use *alternatives to layoffs* during periods of recession. Companies
could plan for full employment by introducing such techniques as work
sharing instead of laying off the last hired during slow periods. In
California employees who are put on four-day weeks during slumps are
now eligible for unemployment compensation for the day of work they are
laid off. This is beneficial for workers because it allows them to retain their
fringe benefits, and for employers because it saves rehiring and retraining
costs.

· Introduce *leisure sharing.* A new state program being tried in California offers incentives to employers to encourage workers to take time off
without pay in order to create job slots for additional employees.

· Increase the number of *apprenticeships,* perhaps by making appren-
tices eligible for the current targeted-jobs tax credit. Ironically in the midst

of increasing unemployment there is a shortage of certain skilled workers. For example, the nation needs hundreds of screw-machine operators, jobs that pay $10 an hour at the journeyman level. Because the job is noisy and dirty, few young white Americans have learned the craft (the median age of screw-machine operators is fifty-five), and there is insufficient incentive for employers to train the minority workers who could benefit from these high-paying jobs. The consequence is a productivity squeeze—machines are idle and employers are bidding for the services of the dwindling pool of operators. So the production of screw-machine parts is being exported, along with potential jobs for Americans.

· Create greater incentives for the *investment of risk capital.* Since 66 percent of all new jobs are created in firms with twenty or fewer employees, tax laws might be revised to encourage investment in small firms.[14] The one thousand largest U.S. companies created seventy-five thousand new jobs between 1979–1978, while all other business combined created nearly 9.6 million jobs. Yet the one thousand largest companies used 80 percent of the investment tax credit.[15]

· Maintain *successful small businesses.* The National Development Council arranges for long-term financing for small businesses in innercity areas. These loans are said to produce a job at the cost of $10,000 (all of which is paid back), which is cheaper than creating a CETA job (for which none of the investment is paid back).[16]

· Permit cities to *charter and operate banks.* These banks would underwrite loans to individuals or groups wishing to start nonprofit or cooperatively owned businesses that would meet the employment needs of an underserved group or community. For example, businesses would be eligible if they offered meaningful employment to the aged, young, or minorities, or if they provided such groups with training to do meaningful but rare types of work, such as skilled crafts and repairs.

· Provide *human-depreciation tax allowances* or employment tax credits linked to the ratio of employment to fixed plant and equipment. Both policies (or others like them) would encourage the use of labor-intensive processes in industry.

· Encourage the creation of *community councils* designed to: (1) match people with work and educational opportunities; (2) counsel employers in the redesign of jobs; (3) lobby for the creation of part-time and flexible jobs; and (4) engage in local manpower planning.[17]

· Provide more part-time jobs and job sharing. Several practical examples of this reform are presented in Chapter 5. More radically, Britain's Patrick Goldring[18] suggests that if everyone were permitted to hold two jobs, the worker in a bad job might find some satisfaction in another, better position; stressful executives could unwind in manual jobs; and potentially redundant workers could spend part of their work time preparing for a future job.

This list of possible programs could be twice as long (I am also certain that many of the items included are neither desirable nor feasible). What is important is that we can and should start thinking in terms of such alternatives to traditional approaches. Although each program has a cost, its potential benefits must be considered, not only in economic terms, but also in terms of their effect on mental and physial health, crime, family cohesion, and social and political alienation. Moreover one has to weigh the inflationary aspects of the alternative macroeconomic policies and the costs of not acting at all in terms of lost income, taxes, and production.

Clearly the problems of unemployment deserve first priority on the nation's domestic agenda. But less pressing problems involving the under-utilization of human resources also require national attention. Two of these problems are (1) discrimination against some women and black workers, and (2) the work-related difficulties of the growing population of older Americans (in particular, the threat to the future solvency of their public and private pension funds). Like the problems of unemployment, these problems can be approached through nontraditional policies. While these policies are not likely to lead to perfect solutions, I illustrate below that they are likely to be *improvements* over existing policies.

WOMEN: IN PURSUIT OF EROS AND ANANAKE[19]

Women constitute the largest single demographic group in America. Their numbers, their education and training, and their knowledge of how to make the system work for them guarantee that ultimately they can have equality with men in the work place.[20] Indeed affirmative action has worked so well for women, *particularly for those in management and the professions,* that it is possible to forecast the day when these women will no longer need the special help of affirmative action to combat discrimination.

Today the greater constraint on women who wish to pursue professional careers is not on-the-job discrimination but social and cultural conflicts with the men in their private lives over the division of domestic labor. If each partner in a marriage pursues a professional career, it is nearly impossible for them also to do a first-rate job of raising children. If each is expected to be at work from 8:30 A.M. to 6:00 P.M. Monday through Friday (and on an occasional Saturday), with a half-hour commute tacked onto each end of the day, there is simply insufficient time for the feeding, bathing, clothing, cuddling, and playing that very small children require if they are not to grow up monsters. Even for children in elementary school there are not enough hours in the day for two working parents, however conscientious, to take kids to scouting, piano lessons, doctor appointments, skating, and football practice. And should a child become ill—well, the dictates of the typically structured professional, managerial, or technical career are such that the kid had bloody well better be able to take her own temperature and make his own chicken soup.

The obvious answer to this problem is for the couple to hire a "wife" who will cook, shop, sew, clean, and shove cherry-flavored cough syrup down Junior's throat at four-hour intervals. But few families can afford to hire a full-time wife—even if they could find a qualified individual (male or female) who would be willing to take on this culturally despised job. And the few dual-career couples with the wherewithal to afford a hired hand find it hard to overcome the guilt of spending only two hours a day with the kids who are, after all, *their* children. A babushka overcomes these money and guilt problems, but most 1980s grandmoms have their own agendas —or extract too high an emotional price for pitching in and helping their kids over their career/family crisis.

Thus in 1980 a key feminist issue is how to make it possible for women to have careers *and* families. Freud once asked what women want. Now we know. They want to have their cake and eat it, too. Which is, unfortunately, exactly what men want. I say "unfortunately" because if *both* men and women want work and love, something must give: Men don't want to stay home full time and watch the kids; women don't want to stay home full time and watch the kids; most men and women want kids. For all but Supermom and Superdad, these are the makings of great tension, conflict, and frequent unhappiness. For against all odds, millions of middle-class men and women are trying to raise children while they pursue their careers. As a result, the divorce rate is up and child and wife beating seem to be on the increase. Millions more who are witness to this great national sadness called the family decide to go AWOL from the eternal and winless war between the sexes. It is simpler not to get married. Or, if married, not to have children. (In this context we must not ignore the growing numbers of people who were once perfectly functioning heterosexuals who are now *choosing* homosexuality.) Add all these noncombatants together, and one finds that over 60 percent of American households contain no children.

The declining birth rate among the middle class is troubling, for it is from these classes that the nation takes its vitality. American culture is supported and transmitted by the middle class. We must recognize that if the middle classes *of all colors* fail to reproduce themselves at a self-sustaining rate, there will be enormous societal, political, and economic implications.

Of more immediate concern is the development of children in dual-career marriages. The prestigious National Academy of Sciences' National Research Council has established a committee on "parental employment and child rearing" to investigate these problems. Some people, of course, argue that the only way to save the American family is to destroy it. These critics advocate communal "marriages," homosexual "marriages," and other living arrangements among nonrelated individuals for the purpose of allowing women to work and have "families." But one wonders how such arrangements would respond to the issue that most experts recognize as central to healthy child development: the need for *fathers* to take a more active and participative role in all aspects of child rearing.[21] It would seem, then, that if we care about the problems of children, we should leave the family alone and change work so that both men and women can share family and job roles. If men and women both want Eros and Ananke, then it would seem sensible to provide the following working conditions for both sexes:

Flexible hours.
Part-time jobs (with appropriate benefits).
Job sharing.
No mandatory overtime.
Maternity/paternity leaves.
No mandatory out-of-town transfers.
Day-care centers.

Some unions are beginning to bargain for such conditions—but they have a long way to go. (Many unions are still dominated by illiberal, machismo males in their late sixties.) And some employers are beginning to offer such conditions—but not out of the goodness of their hearts. They are changing because they have to. In order to attract the brightest young workers, employers are finding it increasingly necessary to offer flexible working conditions to those who wish to spend more time with their families. Indeed in the last decade many of the best and brightest young Americans have turned their backs on jobs in large inflexible organizations. Since these are the same organizations that control the fate of our economy, the provision of working conditions that would allow young couples to have careers *and* families is now a national issue. The danger is that if more employers don't act on their own, the government will legislate in this field.

RACISM AT WORK

Most white Americans have grown noticeably tired of being accused of racism whenever things don't turn out the way black Americans would like. It is *not* racism when a black secretary who cannot spell or type gets passed over for promotion. It is *not* racism when America supports white Israel and condemns black Uganda. Yet every day black leaders tell white Americans that they are guilty of racism. Blacks see the racism, but liberal whites don't. After all, we whites marched for civil rights; we send our kids to integrated schools; we are careful to call black men "mister"; and we give to the NAACP. Aren't blacks being "oversensitive"?

Unhappily there is objective evidence to support the allegation of white racism at work. Let me cite just one example: a profession in which blacks—through hard work and without special favors from whites—have come to excel, only to have whites reject their success. The occupation is professional basketball. Thanks to this occupation, and without affirmative action, quotas, subsidies, or handouts from whites, a hundred or so poor black men have pulled themselves out of ghettos and into upper-middle-class economic status (a few have even become millionaires). Their story is classic Horatio Alger: a meritocratic rise to the top in a highly competitive industry. So successful have blacks become that they now represent over 80 percent of all players in the National Basketball Association. On at least two teams *all* the players are black. Even when white players are on squads, it is not unusual to find that in a given game all ten players on the floor are black (because the white players are marginal benchwarmers).

In early 1981 the top ten scorers in the NBA were black. This success is recent. A decade ago the majority of pro basketball players were white. During the eras of Bob Cousy and Jerry West pro basketball was an extremely popular sport. There were regularly televised games, much as there are today with football and baseball. But as the sport got blacker, the interest of whites in the game diminished. Attendance dwindled (particularly in those cities with teams without a white star). In the late 1970s the NBA lost its network television contract for weekly games. Whites said that the game had become "boring," that the rules made it "uninteresting." But the truth of the matter is that most whites just weren't interested in watching ten black men, no matter how skilled, compete with one another. Ironically, in this clear instance where blacks played the career game by white rules and succeeded without any special treatment, whites turned their backs and failed to offer the support needed to keep the enterprise viable. The evidence of racism here is dramatic. I suggest that if we were to be objective we would find similar evidence of racism—if not so blatant—in other aspects of work.[22]

My conclusion is thus an unhappy one. Since meritocratic systems of hiring and promotion function as they should only in the absence of unfair discrimination, it would seem that blacks will not be treated fairly in those work place systems that are designed to reflect merit only. For as long as there is a subtle racism at work that whites fail to recognize and overcome, it will be necessary to pursue affirmative action and other compensatory employment practices.

OLDER WORKERS

American lives don't have a second act.
—F. Scott Fitzgerald

Historically America was a nation of young people. In the past most Americans died before they reached age sixty-five; those who were among the lucky minority that survived the ravages of disease and war worked into their seventies. Because the old weren't always with us, mass retirement is an untested social phenomenon.

Now the Census Bureau forecasts that between 1965 and 2020 the median age of Americans will increase from twenty-seven to thirty-seven. Since caring for the elderly is expensive—in 1978 about a quarter of the total federal budget went to programs for people over age sixty-five—the graying of America will have profound economic consequences. Former HEW Secretary Joseph Califano suggests that federal expenditures for the aged will account for 40 percent of the federal budget by early in the next century.[23]

Experts in the new field of gerontology have brought to public attention the problems of ill-health, boredom, and loneliness that old people suffer. The abolition of mandatory retirement—while creating costs for young workers—was a humane national response to these problems. But most of all, older people have a problem of too little money. This problem is compounded by inflation, which at current runaway rates erodes savings and pensions faster than interest payments build these funds up. While the indexing of Social Security payments puts a Band-Aid on this problem in the short run, it merely increases the likelihood of total insolvency of the system in the long run.

In fact, the nation is totally unprepared for its demographic future. With the possible exception of the abolition of mandatory retirement, America has dealt unimaginatively with the social and economic problems of its increasing population of old people. And it hasn't even begun to think through the implications of the superannuation of the Boom Babies. The key questions raised by the new demographics are put succinctly by the economist Robert J. Samuelson:

> How much responsibility should government assume for the elderly? What, if any, standard of living should it guarantee? How much should it provide in services, and how much should family and friends provide? How much should government do to assure retirement income, and how much should it leave to people to plan their own retirement?
>
> Those questions go to the heart of government: the division between collective and individual responsibility, between collective and individual choice.[24]

American political institutions are not capable of addressing such philosophical questions. (If they were, Americans might get better public policies.) Instead the society debates the pros and cons of *programs*. And the key programmatic concern relating to the aged is the public and private pension mess.

Pensions (or those paragraphs least likely to be read)

Beginning in 1978 a distinguished group of actuaries, accountants, and lawyers met regularly in Los Angeles to discuss ways to reform that city's public employee pension plans.[25] After a year of conscientious study and discussion these experts still could not agree on the *facts* of how the plans were structured, let alone on what ought to be done to change them. Some of the arcane issues that confounded their deliberations were: vesting, accrued liabilities, unfunded prior service costs, plan integration with Social Security, and interest and wage assumptions. Given such difficult issues, we should forgive the experts' confusion. For pensions is a subject that no one really seems to understand—or at least can explain clearly. What everyone can understand is that pension funds aren't peanuts. There are forty million American workers covered by fifty thousand private pension plans with total assets of $600 billion. In 1979, the Social Security system *paid out* $107 billion.

Since the subject of pensions is as important as it is difficult, it cannot be ignored in these pages, though it would be convenient to do so. As the energy crisis dominated the 1970s, a pension crisis might dominate the

1990s. And, like the energy situation in the 1970s, this impending crisis can be avoided, or at least muted, by foresight and planning in the 1980s.

The pension mess has political, economic, and social ramifications. For example, it was pension costs more than any other factor that drove up the cost of local government in California in the 1970s; in the city of Los Angeles alone pension commitments absorbed approximately one-half of all property tax revenue in 1978. Thus pensions were the hidden factor that created the climate for the passage of Proposition 13. In the private sector the financial difficulties at Chrysler are complicated by the fact that the company's pension fund has over $1 billion in *un*funded liabilities, representing over one-third of the company's net worth. If Chrysler were to default, this might also mean the bankruptcy of the Pension Benefit Guaranty Corporation, a federal agency created to "insure" pension plans.

No doubt pensions are important politically and financially. But our prime concern here is with their *social* effects, in particular with their relationship to such issues as demographics, productivity, mobility, responsibility, security, participation, and flexibility. For pensions are as intertwined with the key concerns of this book as they are with issues of high finance, as the brief review below illustrates.

Demographics. In 1950 there were 7.5 workers aged sixteen to sixty-four for every retired person over age sixty-five. In 1980 the ratio is 5.4 workers for every retired person. By the time the entire Baby Boom generation has retired in the first third of the next millennium, the ratio will be down to only three workers to support each retired person. This is significant because there is no money invested to pay for the retirement of future generations. Social Security is not a pension "fund" but a pay-as-you-go program. And the costs are rising rapidly; the system paid out $1 billion in 1950, $104 billion in 1979, and will pay out $192 billion in 1984. Consequently Social Security taxes—already an onerous burden—will have to be raised by at least 50 percent over the next five decades to provide the Boom Babies with the same relative level of benefits that current retirees enjoy.

Productivity. The above assumption is based on the return to healthy levels of productivity growth. Economist Martin Feldstein warns that continued low productivity would necessitate raising the Social Security tax rate even higher.[26] And since most of the money expended for Social Security goes for consumption rather than investment, there is a vicious cycle in which productivity is *further* lowered by each increase in the share of the gross national income that goes to Social Security.

Mobility. Although Social Security benefits are fully portable—that is, a worker takes all the benefits with her that she has accrued when she changes jobs—almost no private pensions have this excellent feature. The typical worker covered by a private pension will lose all (or most) of his benefits if he changes jobs before having worked a minimum of ten years with the same employer. This period is called the "vesting" requirement. (A notable exception is a worker who belongs to TIAA/CREF, a pension fund that represents about thirty-three hundred of the nation's universities and such other nonprofit institutions as museums and research organizations. As long as a worker stays within this universe of thirty-three hundred employers, his benefits are fully portable.) Not only is the absence of portability unfair to most workers, it is a disincentive to the labor force mobility that is needed for productivity and individual fulfillment and growth.

Responsibility. About six million state, county, city, and federal workers do not participate in the Social Security system. A great many of these workers belong to pension systems that are more generous than the most generous plans found in the private sector (even when these private plans are combined with Social Security). For example, under the Los Angeles City fire and police plan benefits are based on the salary paid to a worker on his *last day* before retirement. Not only is this out of line with standard private pension practices that establish benefits as an average of a worker's salary over the *last three to five years* before retirement, but it also courts the abuse of eleventh-hour promotions in order to increase benefits. As I argued earlier, it encourages immoral and irresponsible behavior on the part of the police.

Another problem with these plans is "double dipping" (collecting two pensions). Many public pension plans allow for early retirement at full benefits after only twenty years of service. A military or police officer, for example, could "retire" on a full pension at age forty, take another job for a minimum of ten years to become eligible for Social Security (and a private pension), and "retire" again at age fifty, more than secure for life. Even more egregiously, elected officials in the state of California have arranged a system whereby they can retire after as few as eight years in office with retirement incomes that exceed the highest pay they ever received while working. And almost *all* Los Angeles County employees can retire with incomes higher than they ever received on the job— although, unlike the politicians, they have to work thirty years for the privilege.

Public employee retirement systems all too often encourage the macroequivalent of clock watching: calendar watching. Too many public employees are encouraged to keep their chairs warm for exactly the twenty years it takes to become eligible for retirement. This encourages not only low productivity but also a contempt for the public, who are seen as fools

for paying for the system. In his *Dictionary* Samuel Johnson defined a
pension as "pay given to a state hireling for treason to his country." While
the nature of the treason has changed from sycophancy to bureaucracy,
Johnson's definition is still applicable in all too many instances. There
should be no question of paying public employees less than employees in
the private sector, but logic and justice offer no reason why benefits for
public service should exceed those available to employees in the private
sector who are also, significantly, taxpayers who are not benefiting
themselves from the overgenerous public pensions.

Security. At the other extreme from public-sector employees are
millions of individuals who have no retirement incomes at all. About 7
percent of Americans over age sixty-five fall through the cracks in the
Social Security law and are ineligible for old-age or survivor benefits.
(These are mainly divorced or widowed housewives who have not worked
themselves for the required ten years and whose marriages lasted less than
ten years.) In the private sector only about one-half of all workers are
covered by pensions (many of those who are *not* covered are doctors,
lawyers, and other wealthy self-employed individuals for whom we should
shed no tears). But more significantly only one-half of those who are
covered will actually see any benefits. This is mainly because of the
ten-to-twenty year "vesting" requirements that most private plans impose.
It is also the result of plans folding. (After the passage of ERISA, and
partly as the *result* of ERISA, twenty thousand private plans folded, often
leaving workers with no benefits at all.)

Flexibility. Social Security penalizes people who choose to continue
working after age sixty-five. Even more damaging, private vesting requirements discourage midcareer change. Thus pensions encourage a monolithic career path consisting of one job for life followed by retirement at age
sixty-five.

Participation. Over a third of all shares of common stock are owned
by pension funds. However, as noted earlier, this does not mean that
American workers "own" one-third of American industry. In fact, managers of pension funds and bank trust funds *control* these stocks, and most
often they vote these shares in support of existing corporate management. It is usually in the self-interest of pension participants that fund
managers follow this conservative strategy—but not always. Occasionally,
for example, a pension fund will own stock in a company that uses
its resources to invest in foreign operations. This can lead to a loss of jobs
by the very same workers who own the stock. To take another case, a
municipal employee pension fund might own stock in a company that is
using its resources to move operations out of the same city where these

employees work—reducing the city's tax base in the process. Union leaders are beginning to question the wisdom of investing the savings of their members in corporations that act in ways contrary to the perceived self-interest of the workers. Says William W. Winpinsinger, the radical president of the International Association of Machinists and Aerospace Workers:

> An employee can enjoy the exclusive benefit of his pension fund only if he has a job secure enough and long enough to collect his deferred income pension. There is nothing that requires him to finance his own job loss.[27]

Winpinsinger goes so far as to threaten to take all the money invested in his union's pension fund and lend it to his workers as home mortgages. If the money were lent out at 10 percent, this would be a 3 percent better rate than workers could get on the open market in early 1980, and would return over 2 percent more than the fund realized in the same time period from investments in common stock (by early 1981, the economics favored the Winpinsinger approach even more).

Leaving the question of who *should* control pension funds to politicians, there is nevertheless an analytical question that concerns us: How *can* this money be used to maximize the macro-performance criteria? For example, can pension funds be used to increase employment, enfranchisement, equality, and efficiency? At present, Social Security does little for employment or efficiency because, as noted above, the money goes to consumption, not to investment. And most private pensions have the same shortcomings because they invest in large corporations that are not directly involved in job creation. The danger in creating "socially useful" pension funds is that the economic criterion will be completely disregarded, instead of merely being put in its proper place. In that event, pensioners might be faced with bankrupt plans—or society would become liable, neither of which is a happy alternative. Clearly how to use these funds to satisfy the performance criteria is an important question—the kind that economists never seem able to answer to anyone's satisfaction—and is likely to increase in importance as the size of pension funds grows during this decade.

Without claiming to have a solution to problems that I am eager to admit I don't fully understand, I nevertheless think that it is possible to make some changes in public policy that might bring the pension system into closer harmony with the performance criteria. As they say, fools rush in . . .

· It might be helpful to develop *tax incentives* to make private pensions carry more of the retirement burden; since private pensions contribute about 20 percent of the new capital used for investment, this would also help to create jobs.

· It might be helpful to establish a private, nonprofit *national pension corporation* (or several such corporations) to which workers would have the legal option of directing their own and their employers' contributions. Modeled on TIAA/CREF, the corporation would *not* be designed to replace Social Security, but rather to provide greater portability and security for private pensions.

· It might be helpful to establish a real *Social Security trust fund* to prepare for the day when the Boom Babies start to retire. Modeled perhaps after the Swedish social security system, this fund could be used as a source for capital investment and risk capital.

· It might be useful to *bring all government employees into the Social Security* system to deal with the problems of doubledipping, underfunding, and other inequities associated with the current public employee pension systems.

· It might be useful to *increase the Social Security retirement age to seventy.* And for all public and private plans it also might be useful to introduce a system of retirement benefits that are *phased in,* thus providing incentives for postponing retirement and for working after retirement. This would also serve the humanistic purpose of smoothing the always difficult transition between full-time work and full-time retirement. Abrupt, involuntary retirement is now widely viewed as inhumane, even homicidal (the number of sudden deaths shortly after retirement seems too large to be purely coincidental). The Europeans have responded to this problem by introducing flexible, phased retirement. In Sweden workers sixty-five to seventy are entitled to work from seventeen to thirty-five hours a week and still draw the Swedish equivalent of Social Security benefits to bring them up to 90 percent of their pre-"retirement" income. Between the ages of sixty and sixty-five many Dutch employees are entitled to extra leave time per week, ranging from a half day at age sixty to two and a half days just before retirement. The firm of Gilette-France offers full pay to older workers with the following provisions for work reduction:

Between ages sixty-one and sixty-two—two weeks additional leave in the winter.

Between ages sixty-two and sixty-three—two weeks additional leave in the winter and again in the spring.

Between ages sixty-three and sixty-four—four weeks in the winter, two weeks in the spring, four weeks in the summer, and two weeks in the autumn.

Between ages sixty-four and sixty-five—four weeks in the winter, two weeks in the spring, twelve weeks in the summer and two weeks in the autumn.[28]

One might even follow the example of the Chinese in this regard: Require retirees to pick up their pensions at the place where they last worked in order to maintain some ties with their old work mates.

  · It might be useful to establish a federal requirement for the *election of trustees* to all pension plans with over, say, $100 million in liabilities. At TIAA/CREF the participation of pension fund members is encouraged by the election of *all* fund trustees. In some cases such a total commitment to democracy may be impractical; nevertheless several outside or public trustees could be appointed or elected. In all cases the elected trustees could vote the stock for the members rather than leaving this important task to fund managers.

THE NEED TO CREATE IMAGINATIVE AND APPROPRIATE ALTERNATIVE POLICIES

Some readers may find it frustrating that I have only offered alternatives in this chapter and have not come to strong conclusions about what should be done to better utilize America's human resources. It is not because I am unable to choose among the many alternatives or to order my personal priorities that I have left this task unfinished. Rather it is because I believe that the working out of these details is the task of the citizens in a pluralist democracy. The goal of a fuller and more just use of human resources cannot be achieved by fiat. Moreover there is no single prescription that would be appropriate even if society were so foolish as to entrust a benign despot with the responsibility for achieving the goal. There are many roads to a more desirable future. And while it is possible to analytically identify which roads lead in circles (for example, following the path laid out by the discipline of economics will produce more of the same mess society currently enjoys), no one can presume to dictate for society which path *should* be taken.

It is legitimate to offer recommendations and alternatives, however. One can offer a map indicating the possible consequences of alternatives without telling society which way it should go or compelling it to take any particular path. The performance criteria proposed in Chapters 5 and 7 should be viewed as no more than guideposts on such a map. They are offered in the spirit of informing societal choice, not with the idea that what is proposed is the only or even the best road to pursue. Undoubtedly many other alternative national policies are also worthy of consideration. The danger is not in considering a spectrum of alternatives, but in closing our eyes too quickly to new ideas because economists and other pseudo-scientists armed with "the facts" tell us out of hand that some crazy new idea won't work. (Recall that in 1973 Irving Kristol condemned worker participation as "neo-Marxist" hogwash;[29] before the decade was out, General Motors was betting on worker participation as a means of restoring the productivity needed to compete with foreign automakers. Perhaps Chrysler executives made the mistake of listening to Mr. Kristol's "expert" advice.)

The greatest threat to America's future comes from the lack of foresight and imagination found in the narrowly trained experts upon whom the nation has come to depend too thoroughly and unquestioningly. These experts have learned to attack and ridicule new ideas by pointing out the obvious fact that no idea is perfect, by showing the inevitable fact that any new idea entails some new costs and necessitates some new trade-offs and sacrifices. Never mind that *the new idea is better than what we have*—the experts seek to get it rejected by measuring it against perfection instead of against the mess at hand.

Such expert nit-picking comes from the left as well as from the right. (Marxist economists, in fact, are the most vigorous in rejecting reforms that come without utopian guarantees.) For example, it is a foregone conclusion that some strict environmentalists and others on the new Left will ridicule the E Factors outlined here and dismiss them as merely "another growth model." That is, if work comes to organize along the principles that I suggest, it is likely that economic growth would ensue. To this charge I plead guilty in one respect: America needs a certain amount of *appropriate* growth. For example, there is an unqualified need for growth in employment opportunities for poor black men and women. To the extent that my proposals would lead to fuller employment, then yes, the E factors would produce some economic growth. But I suggest that full employment based on these new criteria would be *qualitatively different* from full employment achieved through policies designed solely to maximize economic efficiency.

At the firm level, the companies that adopted the micro-criteria might also grow. But why would this be bad per se? More to the point, the micro-criteria would lead to worker motivation, loyalty, commitment, and responsibility *even when there is no growth* to finance new fringe benefits, new entitlements, or higher salaries. The philosophy and organization of work proposed in these pages is appropriate for an era of slow or no growth because it offers meaningful rewards to workers instead of bribes in the form of meaningless and expensive fringe benefits that increase the overall cost of labor without increasing either productivity or the quality of working life.

Using the macro E factors and the micro-performance criteria as guides to the future should help to produce sustainable growth in America, for the new philosophy of work would stress the use of America's greatest asset: the skills, intelligence, education, abilities, and ingenuity of its work force. Growth in the use of these resources is appropriately nonpolluting, energy conserving, and ecologically sound. Fully tapping these resources might even give the United States a new competitive advantage in the world economy in the long run. Then America might be able to sustain its standard of living without sacrificing its quality of life. America might be able to increase equality without sacrificing liberty.

But the fuller utilization of human resources requires more than changing the organization of work and national employment policies; it also requires changing a hidebound educational system that misprepares people for the jobs that need to be done in the 1980s and beyond.

9

APPROPRIATE EDUCATION
FOR THE NEW WORK PLACE

THE unstated issues underlying the current debate about the connection between work and education was stated dramatically by G. B. Shaw many decades ago:

> Today a surgeon who is too lazy or too uppish to put on his boots and pull off his trousers can find a valet who will do both for him, and will submit to be sworn at and addressed on all occasions as an inferior, for a sufficient consideration. I am afraid this luxury will be untenable under an equalitarian constitution. All able-bodied persons will have to valet themselves; and the ladies who ring for a maid in the middle of the night to pick up a book they have dropped out of bed, will have to get up and pick up the book for themselves, or take more care not to drop it. But though the surgeon may have to put on his own boots, it does not follow that he will have to clean them. A state of society in which a surgeon would have to clean the boots and knives; make the beds; lay and light the fires; and answer the door, is as unthinkable as one in which the housemaids would have to cut off their own legs. What is quite thinkable is that the surgeon and person who makes the surgeon's bed should have the same income and be equally polite to one another. As it is, the hospital nurse is sometimes better bred, as we call it, than the surgeon; and there are periods of their respective careers in which she has a larger income. There is certainly no reason why she should at any time have a smaller one.[1]

In other words: Who should do the good work in society, and who should do the dirty work? What is a just distribution of rewards among those privileged to do the former and those condemned to do the latter? These questions are timeless (Aristotle raised them two millennia before Shaw); they are also timely. On one level of specificity, the controversial *Bakke* case decided by the Supreme Court was concerned with how society should choose who gets to be the doctor, who gets to be the nurse, and who should change the bedpans. On a more abstract level, the case was about achieving a just distribution of labor, status, and wealth in a free society.

For most of the time humans have inhabited the world such issues have been moot. Traditionally one's sex, age, class, caste, or race determined the work one would do in society. In Aristotle's Greece the division of labor was mainly ascriptive. Even in the Victorian England that Shaw describes, entry into certain desirable professions was for all practical purposes reserved for the sons of the upper classes. But by the time Victoria had ascended the throne the traditional process had been altered in one key respect: Good jobs were now reserved for the upper classes by virtue not of their class but of their class's stranglehold on access to the "public" schools and universities. This was a reform of sorts. But contemporary Americans find it almost as intolerable as the barbaric caste ascription of India and the racial ascription of South Africa.

In modern America neither education nor employment is reserved for any group on the basis of sex, class, race, or age. Nevertheless the distribution of jobs in the United States is still viewed as unjust by many (if not the majority). Although ascription is supposed to be dead, there still seem to be "too many" upper-middle-class white male doctors and business leaders and "too many" black laborers and "too many" women secretaries. Significantly this state of affairs persists despite nearly a decade of experiment in America with the radical corrective redistributive system advocated by Shaw and his fellow Fabian socialists: a meritocracy based on equality of opportunity. Paradoxically, giving all Americans equal access to education and jobs has not altered radically, as of yet, the traditional patterns of stratification in society. Why this should be so is as problematic as it is controversial.

The issue of justice in the work force is so complicated today that Shaw's proposal for a radical redistribution of income is no longer seen as an effective policy. It was Shaw's assumption that his nurse would find the division of labor equitable if she were simply paid as much as the surgeon. But in the future an American nurse is likely to have much the same skills and training as a doctor. Then will not the nurse find it unjust that the doctor has more autonomy, challenge, and authority in his work? Will not the nurse find it unjust that the doctor could go to AMA conventions in Hawaii and take Wednesday afternoons off for golf? Will not the situation be particularly galling if the nurse had the same qualifications for medical school as the doctor, but was rejected merely on the grounds that there were not enough places in the entering class? (Or if the nurse were actually more qualified than the doctor at the time of entry, but he was chosen because he was a man and she was rejected because she was a woman? Or *she* was chosen because she was black and *he* was rejected because he was white?) Equal pay for unequal work is not likely to remedy such perceived and real injustices.

In attempting to solve such problems society can, of course, increase the number of its doctors. But how many doctors can society reasonably afford? (Paradoxically the evidence is that increasing the supply of doctors drives up the cost of medical care.) Perhaps society can redesign the jobs of doctors and nurses so that the surgeon takes her turn giving shots while the nurse has his turn with the scalpel. (And what of the orderly—does he get his turn cutting off legs while the doctor changes bedpans?) This topsy-turvy social engineering quickly becomes absurd, but it does illustrate that there are organizational limits to how far society can get away from the hierarchical division of labor and still function efficiently and productively. Of course there are meliorative actions that can be taken: Performance certification, job redesign, continuing education, and many other workplace and school-place reforms are no doubt worth trying. But experience indicates that none of these is likely to make the nurse or the orderly perceive his or her occupational status as just vis-à-vis the doctor's— particularly when the nurse has a master's degree and the orderly has earned an A.A. or B.A. degree. Higher entitlement expectations will inevitably flow from higher educational degrees.

Indeed modern America's problem is even more complex than the one posed by Shaw in early industrial England: In an era of rising affluence, educational attainment, and expectations, will anyone be willing to clean the bedpans? Is it moral or prudent to continue the current unspoken policy of importing Latin and Asian labor to do these dirty jobs? Is it moral or prudent to advocate vocational education for black and other disadvantaged Americans to prepare them to do these jobs (especially when the advocates would not choose such a course of study for themselves or for their own children)?

Perhaps the answer to the problem lies in technology: Shaw's surgeon is already able to clean his own knives (with an ultraviolet sterilizer), lay his own fire (with pushbutton heating), and answer his own door (now a tape recorder answers his telephone). But how far can society go in automating the bad jobs out of existence? The greater the ratio of service and knowledge workers to production workers, the worse the problems of inflation and unemployment among the disadvantaged seem to become. Is it a solution to transfer people from bad jobs to the welfare rolls?

It is my belief that all these problems are likely to get worse. Others disagree. They argue, for instance, that this is merely a "transition period" on the road to a just and workable meritocracy, a temporary phase during which society must simply invent ad hoc mechanisms like affirmative action to compensate for the effects of past inequities. But I fear that the issues raised by *Bakke* are likely to be permanent unless something (what?) is done to make the conditions of life equal at birth. The problem of finding a just division of work will not go away because the persistent and insatiable desire for equality won't go away. Of course, since Western civilization has muddled through for two thousand years without coming up with a fair way to decide who should be the doctor and who should change bedpans, the cynic could easily argue that America will survive the current *Bakke* fuss. I too have no doubt that America will survive its current problems, but I am not sanguine that the nation will come through the period of rising egalitarian expectations in education and jobs with its sense of order, justice, and liberty intact.

This is not Classical Greece or Victorian England. For the first time in history 50 percent of the population (the women) view the division of labor in society as unjust. For the first time in history workers have the choice of not working (and living on unemployment compensation and welfare) if they don't find satisfactory work. For the first time education is not paying off in higher income and job status. For the first time in American history the nation's productivity relative to that of other advanced nations is declining. And, most significantly, for the first time in history all authority is being severely challenged. Unlike those in Shaw's day, the nurse and the orderly are now in a position to tell the doctor where he can shove the bedpan.

This changing environment can be seen as an opportunity rather than as a problem. American can continue to focus on a discrete series of work-force problems (e.g., alienation, teenage unemployment, falling rates of return on educational investment) *or* it can focus on the opportunity to more fully develop its human resources. This overaching, proactive, and positive alternative perspective may be useful in two ways. First, it recognizes that there is much work that needs to be done and plenty of human talent to do it. Second, it promises a situation that *might* be perceived as just by all workers: a future in which each individual's contribution to providing the goods, services, and brain power needed by the world is recognized and utilized. That is, the goal of all work places and school places would be to develop and tap the potential of each individual. Stated as such, this sounds like idealistic mush, for exactly how the human resource can and should be developed remains unclear.

What is clear is that the nation's schools and colleges are failing in this regard—ironically, not from want of trying, but from trying much too determinedly to make education relevant to work. Their efforts in this direction are understandable. Educational institutions face growing hostility from students, parents, and government officials, as manifested in the refusal of voters to support school and community college bond issues and in declining support from state and local funding agencies. And scrutiny of all levels of education has increased in the popular press. The cover of *Newsweek* asks: "Who needs College?"—a question in tone and inflection akin to "Who needs a Jewish mother?" *Time* follows with a cover story that lays the blame for the problems of primary and secondary education squarely in the laps of schoolteachers and administrators.

But in crisis there is creativity. To get their enterprise back on its feet, educators are willing to try anything—*except* spend more time with students, give up the practice of tenure, or betray a few dozen other inviolable principles of academia. Apparently conditions are merely critical, they are *not* desperate. No, this is a time for inventive *marketing,* not for reform. To this end, the managers of the nation's high schools, colleges, and universities have discovered the institution of work. Work, they claim, is either the cause of the current depression in education *or* it is the solution to the depression. This insight (as it were) is the foundation of the newest theme in education: "making education more relevant to the world of work." In great and growing numbers educators are convinced that if they can just set this line to a catchy tune, consumers will again beat a path to their doors.

As with all instances of common wisdom, there is more than a modicum of truth in the discovery that work and education are related.

WHERE VOCATIONALISTS GO WRONG

In fact, it is *easy* to demonstrate that work affects education, and education affects work. And that is enough for America's educators. They have used this particle of truth as a springboard to take a prodigious leap of logic: *Ergo,* they conclude, we must improve the fit between education and work. This goal is pursued in many and various ways, including career education in the elementary schools, vocational education in the high schools, professional education in undergraduate colleges, and dozens of "nontraditional" efforts to import work-place concerns into classrooms at all levels. Since none of these activities has worked terribly well, educators far and near are now intensifying their efforts. "We *will* make education relevant to work," they are saying with Germanic resolve.

But how? Vocationalism has a long and inglorious history of failure, and the reasons for these well-documented failures are hardly addressed by increasing the commitment to do more of the same. After decades of trying, it still seems nearly impossible to train young people appropriately in schools and colleges for specific jobs because:

1. *It is impossible to forecast labor-market demand more than a few months into the future.* Thus when schools gear up to train anvil salesmen, all the available jobs in this field are filled before the first A.A.'s in Anvils have their degrees.
2. *There are tens of thousands of different types of jobs, and it is unclear which skills are needed to do most of these jobs successfully.* Consequently it is also unclear how schools should go about training people for most jobs. What, for example, is the proper academic curriculum for one who aspires to repair roofs?
3. *Most skills needed in nontechnical jobs are taught on the job in a matter of weeks.* Hence students who intend to look for such jobs upon graduation do not require specific skills training in educational institutions. For such semiskilled jobs as roof repairing, a year's fully paid apprenticeship will leave one an expert on every house covering from tiles to tarpaper, while eighteen years of unpaid formal education will leave one falling off the roof. Most upper-level jobs that undeniably require specific skills training are learned at the graduate level, where professional schools are already fully geared to the world of work.
4. *By reduction, this leaves the two-year college as the locus for vocational training.* Unfortunately what is left over in this case is unpromising institutional residue. In a recent seminal study of junior college vocational education, Wellford Wilms found the following:[2]

· Such programs fail to equalize the advantages of those who have followed an academic track. Moreover they have damaging effects for low-income people, tracking those already disadvantaged by race and social class into second-class institutions. And since vocational credits cannot be transferred to academic programs, vocational training often ends up being the terminal educational experience for the poor.
· Employers require a command of English, math, and the other basic skills not taught in vocational programs.
· A key factor in job success is ego development: the ability to be autonomous, conscientious, self-confident, and to work well with others. Vocational programs are "miseducative in this regard."
· In the few instances where preemployment skills training is needed,

proprietary schools are a more cost-effective alternative than community colleges.

5. *For the small, residual category of technical, nonprofessional jobs that might require some formal classroom training, proprietary schools are the best bet.* But, in fact, almost none of these licensed, nonprofessional jobs actually *require* any specific training. For example, anybody with a decent high school education can learn almost all she needs to know about selling real estate by reading a single short book. Phony educational qualifications for selling real estate are mandated in some states solely to protect those already in the industry from too much competition, not for the altruistic purpose of "protecting consumers by ensuring highly trained real estate agents." As far as I can tell, the only real value of real estate schools is as compensatory education for those who didn't learn how to read well enough in high school or college to get through the how-to manual on the occupation.

"But . . . but . . . ," the reply of the vocationalist can be heard even before the argument is completed. "But if what you say is true, why is there so much youth unemployment?" The answer to that question is to be found in demographic, not educational, data. The figures show that the nation is now beginning a two-decade period during which the number of young people entering the labor market will decline drastically as a percentage of the entire labor force. Since it was basically the demographics of the baby *boom* that created the current employment problems of young Americans, it can be reasonably expected that the new demographic picture will turn the problem around for the baby *bust* generation. What must be recognized is that there has never been a problem of "fitting education to the world of work" during periods of labor shortages. During World War II, for example, minorities, youth, and women went productively to work on the nation's assembly lines *without* the benefit of vocational training. Clearly then, the problems young people have had in getting entry-level jobs during the last fifteen years have not been the result of lack of skills training in the schools. When youths start finding jobs more easily during the next decade education will not deserve the credit, for this will be the inevitable result of demographic change.

THE PURPOSES OF EDUCATION

The major *educational* problem relating to work is that educators have lost sight of the prime purposes of their enterprise. Peter Drucker argues convincingly that the key question every company must put to itself periodically is: What business are we in? When is the last time a respected group of educators seriously and analytically examined the question: What are the *purposes* of education? Admittedly this question is old hat. It lacks pizzazz. But has it been seriously raised in recent years by the educational community? There is evidence that it has not. Recall that all those excellent volumes produced by the Carnegie Commission during the last decade thoroughly questioned the programs, policies, and processes of higher education, but did not systematically question its purposes.

Now *society* is questioning the purposes of education. The question on the lips of students, parents, employers, and government officials is: What has education done for me lately? Put thus, the question is crude and misdirected. Still, it cannot be ignored. Just as society is now demanding accountability from institutions of government, business, and labor, it is rightly also demanding accountability from educational institutions. For a concatenation of reasons (supply your own list), educators are now being asked to calculate and justify the payoff of higher learning to the individual, the society, and the economy. What have you done for me lately? is a legitimate question. Unfortunately it is difficult to answer because of the myopic insistence of economists that the payoff be demonstrated in dollar terms only.

Whatever the measure, society has made continued support of education contingent on a cost/benefit analysis of its value. And here is the rub. Just when society is putting pressure on education to justify its costs, educators are less clear about its benefits than at any recent time. (As an anonymous British mathematician put it, "The only advantage of a classical brain is that it will enable you to despise the wealth it will prevent you from earning.")

It is significant that society has chosen to question the value of education in terms of its relationship to work. Perhaps that is not the way in which educators would have chosen to undertake such an important reckoning; nevertheless work may not be a totally inappropriate measure for analyzing the purposes of education. After all, work is of cross-cutting and transcendent concern, important to all institutions of learning, to all interest groups, and to minorities, men and women, liberals and conservatives, old and young. Work probably encompasses most of the basic questions that need to be analyzed in exploring the purposes of education: What are the proper relationships among work, leisure, and learning? What is a just distribution of labor? These questions deal with the kind of society we want in the future.

Having said all this, I have admitted a part of the vocationalist's argument: Education is failing to adequately prepare young Americans for workaday life. But, significantly, this failure occurs *not* in vocational concerns but in the prime educational functions of teaching young people to read, write, compute, think critically and analytically, and behave ethically and responsibly as workers, citizens, parents, and friends. Accomplishing these functions would provide more than adequate preparation for any kind of work that one could imagine. Moreover one might venture the scandalous hypothesis that it is this failure of education to accomplish its prime tasks that has created the demand for it to take on the spurious task of specific job preparation. Since employers can't find young employees who have learned how to read, write, think, and exercise initiative and responsibility at work, they are saying that they will settle for illiterate robots who at least have been trained to obediently flip switch X and turn handle Y.

The problem feeds on itself: (a) Failure to truly educate students creates (b) demands for vocationalism, which in turn act as (c) constraints on achieving the educational reforms needed to make education do its prime tasks well enough (d) to make graduates successful at work. Clearly something must be done to alter this conundrum. And intensifying vocationalism hardly seems a logical way out.

Instead of *intensifying* the very actions that have led to the current depression in education, it would seem more prudent and appropriate for educators to *change* their policies. In the short run it will be necessary to appease the public and their elected followers in the Congress and the state legislatures by directly confronting the problem of the shortage of jobs for youth. (Demographics will take care of this problem in the long run, but some short-term actions may be necessary.)

As a step toward dealing with these problems of youth unemployment, educators may have to join the call for national service. This should be something quite different from the current unpopular effort to reinstate the draft. By itself, the draft is morally repugnant to as many as half of America's young men and women. What is needed, instead, is a system that allows young people to choose a variety of alternative forms of national service, nonmilitary as well as military. This system should be an educative experience for youth and not just a way for the armed forces to reduce their manpower costs. Educators might work to create a system in which the vast majority of young men and women worked a year or two for their country after high school. This postponement of entrance into college for two years would have the following kinds of benefits:

1. It would relieve the problems of youth unemployment at ages seventeen to nineteen, the most difficult years to find jobs. While finding educative work for several million youths would not be easy, it would not be impossible. Even one as philosophically opposed to government-provided employment as William F. Buckley has suggested that taking care of elderly Americans would be a useful way to employ countless teenagers.
2. It would give young people some actual work experience, and thus create in them realistic expectations about work. In addition, it would help underprivileged youth to develop appropriate habits of punctuality and self-discipline, the lack of which we are told are the prime reasons they cannot get or retain jobs.
3. It would help young people when they went looking for jobs after they completed national service. Richard Bolles has shown that a whole resumé can be written around one work experience, no matter how trivial.[3]
4. It would provide a single clear social responsibility to all young Americans that would appropriately counterbalance the growing list of rights of citizenship.
5. It would improve the performance of young people once they went to college after the two-year interregnum. There is little question that older students get more out of the experience of college than those who enter directly out of high school. It seems that a little life and work after high school gives students the maturity and experience on which to hinge their conceptual studies.

Those who would dismiss these ideas as impractical might first ask if they are more impractical than turning all of education into a training ground for industry?

Once national service is taking care of the problems of youth unemployment and underemployment, formal education would be free to concentrate on its prime tasks. Educators could then demonstrate to the public that reading, writing, computing, analytical thinking, and all the essential enculturating aspects of general education *are* relevant to work.

This reform would not be as difficult as it may sound, for it is starting to dawn on corporate leaders that they need broadly and liberally educated employees. In the last two decades corporate recruiters and personnel managers have been hiring narrowly trained specialists to fill lower-level openings. While these people meet the immediate needs of a firm, as time goes along, it becomes clear that they are not promotable. Thus American corporations are now forced to spend hundreds of millions of dollars on employee education in a not terribly successful effort to prepare lower- and middle-level employees to assume greater responsibility. Corporations are finding it deucedly difficult to broaden the horizons of, for example, forty- and fifty-year-old engineers. That broadening would have occurred more naturally had these people pursued liberal undergraduate educations instead of specializing in engineering from their freshman year.

What Employers are Looking for in College Graduates

The most common misperception about the education/work interface is that corporations only wish to hire people with specialized or technical skills. No doubt many corporations are looking for people with engineering and accounting degrees, but demand for people with such specialized backgrounds is limited to the finite number of jobs that require such narrow skills. Accountants can do accounting and engineers engineering —their training is of little use for much else, as we professors of management find when we assign such specialists to analyze general business cases that demand sensitivity to human or social issues or flexibility in coping with nonroutine problems. Top corporate executives know that it is as hard as eating cream puffs with a mustache to make general managers out of narrowly trained people. Here's what four famous chief executive officers say they are looking for in young would-be managers[4]:

C. Peter McColough
Chairman, Xerox Corporation

I look for breadth of interest. Individuals with broad interests are best able to perform within a company today. We face many societal changes, and the broad outlook and encompassing overview are more pertinent than the traditional, circumscribed career preparation.

Henry Ford II
Chairman, Ford Motor Company

For starters I'd list honesty, candor, good judgment, intelligence, imagination, and the ability to write clear, concise memos.

Donald M. Kendall
Chairman, PepsiCo, Incorporated

The only place success comes before work is in the dictionary. The first qualification for success, in my view, is a strong work ethic. That's motive power. Without it nothing moves—planes, trains, or humans. Leadership capability, the capacity to get others to follow you, and what is more important, to *want* to, is key. Closely allied to leadership is integrity; without it no one can gain the respect of others.

While continuing to hold a deep commitment to his or her job, the young executive must become involved in the community. Corporations are no longer islands unto themselves, and managers moving up must utilize their skills and experience to improve the life about them.

J. Paul Sticht
Chief Executive Officer and Chairman,
R. J. Reynolds Industries, Incorporated

The first thing I look for is a sense of personal worth. It's a subjective quality and hard to define, but I generally know it when I see it. These individuals are decent, honest, and by their nature inspire confidence in others. They reflect self-respect and a belief in themselves.

Such persons are not only assets to their companies but become stalwarts in their communities. As they move up, they are ideally equipped to interpret the role of business to the public at large.

To be sure, these are the opinions of people who, no matter how powerful, don't do the hiring in their firms. One might argue that what the personnel directors of average-size companies are looking for is a more relevant gauge of job market realities. According to Seymour Lusterman's Conference Board poll of personnel officers (in 610 firms with 500 employees or more), "typical" corporate recruiters

are critical of the performance of the nation's schools and colleges in preparing people for work, and deplore particularly the lacks they find in language, or communications, and mathematical skills among younger employees. This is no longer news, I know. What may be worth stressing, however, is that in their observations about each of the kinds and levels of institutions, the complaints of business executives have to do much less with technical or professional preparation than with general competencies—with the ability, even of those highly schooled, to organize and present information and ideas, to relate to other people sensitively and effectively, to plan and make decisions, and to connect theory with practice.[5]

Lusterman's findings are echoed in Northwestern University's 1977 *Endicott Report,* which polled personnel people in 215 companies. This report found that the biggest problems college graduates faced in making the transition to work were not lack of technical skills but:

· Switching from the classroom to the job, and relating theory to practical situations.

- Adjusting to routine, regular hours and schedules.
- Understanding corporate structure and the business environment.
- Adjusting expectations to reality and setting realistic goals.
- Learning to work effectively with many different types of people.
- Accepting responsibility, getting the job done, and determining what is most important in making decisions.
- Understanding the philosophy of a profit-oriented organization and what motivates managers.
- Reexamining interests, abilities, and values, and generally "finding oneself."
- Adjusting to a new location or community.
- Learning to communicate effectively and overcoming inadequate writing skills.[6]

This kind of evidence is usually dismissed as "elitist." In truth, it applies to rich as well as poor, blacks as well as whites, college educated and non-college educated. Members of the White House Task Force on Youth Employment interviewed hundreds of employers to find what they were looking for in young workers. "They told us two things," the executive director of the task force reports. "First that they couldn't find enough kids who could read and write and, second, that they wanted to have kids with a track record of employment in the private sector."[7]

Throughout this book I allude to the fact that many American corporations are undergoing competitive crises. Because they have not been able to respond adequately to the changing needs of society, they are losing business to domestic and foreign competitors. Part of the problem is that these corporations are run by managers who have been narrowly and illiberally trained. When the world changes, the specialist has a harder time than the generalist in adapting to the change. These inflexibly trained people are easily threatened by change, and they act defensively, exactly the wrong mental state when what are demanded are innovation and initiative. Moreover threatened managers often behave in ways that society deems irresponsible. Too often it was narrowly trained engineers, scientists, and people with undergraduate degrees in business who panicked at places like Lockheed and paid bribes to foreign officials, who panicked at places like Allied Chemical and dumped Kepone into the James River, and who panicked at places like General Motors and spied on Ralph Nader when he challenged the safety of the Corvair. Of course there were also liberally educated people involved in these and other instances of corporate irresponsibility. The point is not that liberally educated people are more moral or ethical than narrowly trained specialists; rather it is that corporate leaders are now finding that they must devote 50 percent of their time to social issues—complex, ambiguous, sensitive, human issues that technicians are less prepared than generalists to handle.

While once it was the broadly and liberally trained educator who seemed to inhabit an ivory tower, today it is the super-specialist in fields ranging from economics to physics who is most out of touch with workaday reality. While contemporary work-place problems are ignorant of the departmental structures of universities, today's overspecialized scholar is blissfully unaware of what his or her colleagues are up to—even in closely related fields. Indeed young scholars revel in their provincial ignorance, holding it up as a sign of their "scientific" professionalism. When asked how their work relates to another discipline or to a practical issue, they joyously declare, "Who cares?"

Perhaps the common complaint of employers that college graduates are oblivious of the realities of workaday life stems from the fact that graduates have spent four years under the tutelage of *idiots savants*. The graduates, like their professors, have not been informed that the problems people encounter at work do not come in neat little packages addressed solely to one discipline or sub-sub field of that discipline. One wonders how the know-nothings and care-nothings of academia can train young people for work—at least for any work other than academic research.

Somehow amidst all the brouhaha about work relevance the message hasn't gotten through to educators that the problems most people face at work are complex, interdependent, and above all have to do with working with people cooperatively and ethically. Most of the difficult problems that people encounter at work are not technical—the computer can solve those. Indeed, the tough questions are not problems at all, if a problem is defined as having a single solution. For there are no solutions to the intransigent policy and organizational problems of work. There is only a spectrum of alternative responses, some more appropriate than others, but none either simply right or wrong. Problems of this nature have deep precedents in the history of social affairs and a broadly educated, truly enculturated professional manager is best equipped to analyze them. Because today's work places are social as well as economic institutions, America needs managers and professionals who can think critically and be ethically discerning. If there is a "skill shortage" among American managers it is not in the areas of finance or accounting; it is in moral discourse. If managers cannot ask what *ought* to be, they cannot create a just and productive work environment.

Lower down the occupational ladder, vocationally trained workers are ill equipped for the most democratic forms of self-management that must inevitably become the norm in American industry. Most futurists are forecasting that almost all routine work will be done by machines in the coming decades. This means that all "people work" will be nonroutine. In the future, then, the success or failure of American enterprises will rest on the willingness and ability of workers to take the initiative in those increasingly frequent situations that cannot be routinely handled. This means that workers will have to take responsibility for the welfare of customers, suppliers, and fellow workers. In short, as I argue in Chapter 3, they will have to care about their work. What will be required is humane individuals with analytical and entrepreneurial skills, people who know how to work in groups, who know how to identify and define complex problems, and who will not panic when something untoward occurs at places like Three Mile Island.

People who are vocationally trained to unquestioningly perform a single task are manifestly unprepared to design their own work, participate in decision making, assume control over their own working conditions, work as members of a community of equals, or take responsibility for the quantity and quality of their own work when a boss is not looking over their shoulders. Like narrowly trained managers, these workers feel easily threatened by change and act defensively, inflexibly, and in ways society deems irresponsible when circumstances require them to adapt.

WHAT SHOULD BE DONE?

Ironically, then, the well-intentioned efforts of educators to professionalize undergraduate education and to vocationalize the high schools have made education *less* relevant to work than it would have been had these efforts not been made. This situation cannot be put right merely by abandoning all manifestations of vocationalism, career education, and professionalization in the schools and colleges.

Beginning at the primary level, a radical reorganization of the entire educational enterprise is needed to make education relevant to the work place of the future. From ages six through seventeen, all young people should receive the same basic education, one that stresses the development of skills that will be appropriate on any job in the future: namely, reading, writing, computing, speaking, problem solving, basic science, along with some understanding of the nation's history and culture and the place these have in the context of the governing ideas and values of Western civilization. Some vocational skills might be taught as well—for example, typing, tool use, and the repair of home plumbing and electrical wiring— but they would be taught to *all* students, regardless of sex, social class, or aptitude. Specific vocational training would not begin until after the two-year term of national service, during which work skills and attitudes would be learned in the most effective way, through experience. This specific training should be separated from the humanizing, enculturating, general education, the kind of education all workers will need in what I suspect will be the increasingly complex, democratic, and morally confusing work place of the future.

In a nutshell, my brief against vocational education is that wherever it has been tried—in England, China, Germany, and the United States—it has always ended up ossifying the social class structure. Nothing is inherently more unfair and more socially divisive than the early separation of the young into two educational tracks: One for the privileged who are being prepared for high-level employment, and one for those condemned to labor at the lowest levels. Perhaps worst of all, such a system denies the fact that almost every human is capable of attaining a basic level of general learning. It is a pathetic waste of human resources to deny this learning to a condemned class—condemned all too often on the basis of race or income.

The ultimate advantage of the alternative approach described here is it would satisfy not only the needs of work places but of workers as well. If we were to treat everyone equally in the schools, everyone would have the opportunity to fully realize his or her potential. In helping to overcome counterproductive class stratification in the schools and work places, this system would give some hope of creating a distribution of labor that would be perceived as more just by the doctor, the nurse, and the orderly alike.

10

THE BOTTOM LINE: CULTURE *NOT* ECONOMIC POLICY

IF America is to be made to work as effectively as its foreign competitors, leaders in the public and private sectors must recognize that the root causes of low productivity and declining innovation are to be found in our culture, and not in national economic policies. While many changes in American tax and regulatory laws are called for, the evidence is overwhelming that culture is a more fundamental determinate of economic performance than public policy. One need only check the economic data to see that the Federal Republic of Germany has the most successful economy in the capitalist Common Market, and that the German Democratic Republic has the most successful economy in the communist Comecon. There is little doubt that the reason why West Germany is more successful than East Germany is the superiority of a market economy over a centrally planned one. Nonetheless, the fact that *both* Germanies outpace the economic performance of their allies on their respective sides of the Iron Curtain reveals something even more essential: Germanic culture encourages efficiency and productivity regardless of the rules under which Germans must work. Similarly, Chinese people—whether they live and work in Singapore, Hong Kong, or Taiwan—invariably find ways to be successful entrepreneurs. Even when laboring in the straightjacket of Marxist policies in the People's Republic, Chinese workers and managers out-produce their Asian counterparts in India, Pakistan, Bangladesh, Vietnam, Cambodia and Indonesia. Thus, being Chinese (or German, Jewish, Lebanese, Ibo, Kikuyu, or Japanese) is a more important factor in economic success than the tax and regulatory policies—or even the political/economic systems—under which peoples of these highly efficient cultures might labor.

One depressing conclusion that might be drawn from this argument is that Americans will never be able to compete equally with the Japanese because the simple fact that they are Japanese makes them more effective and efficient as managers and workers than we Americans. While there is probably some truth to this conclusion, the argument can be carried too far. More accurately, the argument suggests that America should not attempt wholesale borrowing of the Japanese philosophy and organization at work. These simply would not mesh well with our culture. It also means that America must find a new philosophy and organization of work that is compatible with the radical changes that our culture has undergone during the last two decades. The Japanese have developed practices such as consensus management, quality control circles, and lifetime job security that are compatible with *their* culture. Now, America must do the same. While our current managerial policies and practices *were* compatible with American culture in the 1940s and 1950s, these became out-of-synch as a result of the turbulent social shifts that occurred in the 1960s and 1970s: The Vietnam War; the permissiveness of schools, courts and parents; the women's movement; environmentalism and consumerism—all mixed with the potent catalyst of affluence—conspired to alter the values of the nation and subtly but ineluctably change the rules under which people are willing to work hard or are committed to their jobs. These new rules are reflected in the benefit package that a large suburban hospital in Los Angeles has been forced to offer *starting* nurses—a year-end bonus of 10 percent of annual salary, twenty-days paid time-off that a nurse can use, sell or save, twelve days of paid "R & R" for those who volunteer for the night shift, well pay, time-and-a-half for working weekends, flexible working hours, no mandatory overtime, and participation in decision-making. Eighty years after Shaw's prophetic statement (chapter 9), hospitals are finding that young Americans are simply unwilling to do the work of nurses. If this necessary job is to be filled, hospitals must voluntarily offer work conditions that even the toughest unions have never won through collective bargaining.

Clearly, if managers wish to motivate today's workers, they are forced to find practices that are congruent with changes in the broader culture. They must find ways to build on the positive aspects of the new work values—e.g., the growing willingness of young workers to change, experiment, innovate, and participate in decision-making—while minimizing the effects of such negative values as entitlementarianism, narcissism, and irresponsibility. To create policies that are appropriate to this end, managers must first understand the nature of the changes that are occurring in the family, in education, and in attitudes towards authority. That is why, for example, pains were taken in the last chapter to overcome the easy conclusion that the trend towards early vocationalism in schools and colleges is good for business in the long run. Managers must understand that the type of education must also be consistent with the emerging culture. In essence, managers must understand that they are dealing *not* with superficial changes in the society, but with fundamental ones. That is why the concepts used in this book—responsibility, rights, quality, ownership and participation—are basic terms rather than the flashy jargon used by those at the forefront of the social sciences. It is necessary to come down from the airy heights of current economic and psychological theory and reexamine the basics—for that is the level at which the problems of economic decline have their genesis.

What is unfortunate is that managers must start this reexamination where they are most uncomfortable—with introspection. They must begin by identifying their own patterns of values, beliefs, and behavior. They must do this if they are to alter their organizational cultures to become compatible with changes in the broader culture. Indeed, the unwillingness of American managers to closely, critically, and objectively reexamine their basic operating assumptions, may be at the root of what *appears* to be a crisis of mismanagement in America. But, in fact, it is something other than mismanagement that is at the core of the nation's economic malaise. More accurately, the problem is that corporations have persisted for too long with policies and practices which were successful in the past. While these policies and practices are not objectively "wrong" today, they are out-of-tune with the emerging post-industrial culture, and with the realities of America's diminished economic and political role in world affairs.

In general, most large U.S. corporations have been unable to develop adequate sensors of social, political, economic, competitive, and technological change. Even in those instances where corporations have adequately anticipated environmental change, few have been able to translate this information into appropriate policy changes. For example, in the early and mid-1970s American industry misread the environment and downplayed 1) the seriousness of the challenge of foreign competition, 2) the full extent and lasting nature of the energy crunch, and 3) the power and influence of environmentalists and consumerists. Moreover, very few American corporations have been able to respond quickly and appropriately to such social changes as the women's movement and the new work and social values of the under-35 generation.

Sadly, in my ten years of dealings with executives in large corporations, I have found that they tend to become defensive when faced with these new facts of life. Their initial reaction is to look for someone else to blame for the nation's industrial woes—their prime candidates are "meddling" courts, "unfair" foreign competition, "lazy" workers, "unreasonable" unions, "self-serving" consumerists, "prying" journalists, "radical" professors, and especially "power-hungry" government bureaucrats. Ironically, at the same time, managers look to changes in government policy to save American industry: They actively seek revised tax and depreciation rates, elimination of anti-trust activity, and reduction of regulation. Perhaps most of these things that are being sought from government would be helpful in revitalizing the economy, but they tend nonetheless to avert the gaze of managers from the one source of change that can most immediately respond to the shifts that have occurred in society: that is, *themselves.*

Only changes in the philosophy and organization of work can overcome America's economic decline. And such changes can occur only when managers are willing to identify the values and assumptions that underlie the culture of their organizations, what the productive and behavioral consequences of those cultures are, and what the cultures *should* be. Only then will they see the need for change and be able to create in the work place the conditions of diversity, flexibility, choice, mobility, participation, security, and rights tied to responsibilities, which are necessary in making the culture of organizations congruent with the larger culture—conditions that would go a long way towards making America work again.

NOTES

CHAPTER 2

1. Robert Heilbroner, *The Worldly Philosophers* (New York: Simon & Schuster, 1961), p. 2.
2. Sidney Weintraub, "The Human Factor in Inflation," *New York Times Magazine,* November 25, 1979.
3. Irving S. Friedman, "We Can End Inflation," *Industry Week,* Nov. 10, 1980, pp. 64–71.
4. Edward F. Denison, "The Puzzling Drop in Productivity," *The Brookings Bulletin* 15 (1978): 10–12.
5. Tom Wolfe, *The Right Stuff* (New York: Farrar, Straus & Giroux, 1979).
6. "Labor Letter," *Wall Street Journal,* January 7, 1981.
7. Louis Harris, "The Steelcase National Survey of Office Environments: Do They Work?" (Steelcase, Inc., 1978).
8. National Commission on Productivity, *Second Annual Report* (Washington, D.C.: Government Printing Office, March 1973).
9. "Workers Held Working only 55% of Shift," *Los Angeles Times,* October 17, 1979.
10. Gay Talese, *Thy Neighbor's Wife* (New York: Doubleday, 1980).
11. *Los Angeles Times,* November 23, 1979.

CHAPTER 3

1. Arthur Okun, *Equality and Efficiency: The Big Tradeoff* (Washington, D.C.: Brookings Institution, 1975).
2. Ibid., pp. 18–19.
3. U.S. Chamber of Commerce, "Employee Benefits, 1977" (Washington, D.C.: Chamber of Commerce, 1979).
4. Ibid.
5. Ibid.

6. Burnham P. Beckwith, "Free! Free! Free! The Priceless World of Tomorrow," *Futurist,* October 1978, pp. 307–312.
7. A 1978 study undertaken by Theodore Geiger, director of International Studies, National Planning Association, Washington, D.C.
8. Okun, *Equality and Efficiency,* p. 6.
9. Ibid., p. 7.
10. Ibid., p. 8.
11. Ibid., pp. 91–95.
12. Daniel Yankelovich, "New Approaches to Worker Productivity," an address before the National Conference on Human Resources System, October 25, 1978, in Dallas, Texas.
13. *The Yankelovich Monitor* (1977).
14. *Quality of Employment Survey* (Ann Arbor: Survey Research Center, Institute for Social Researching, University of Michigan, 1977).
15. Fred Best, "Exchanging Earnings for Leisure" (Washington, D.C.: National Commission for Employment Policy, January 15, 1979).
16. The Boom Babies were born between 1945 and 1957 some demographers say; others say they were born between 1946 and 1962. Even in the hard science of demographics, not every subjective decision can be eliminated! Between 1968 and 1978 two million workers were added to the labor force annually (six million were added in 1975–1977 alone). The Baby Boom peaked in 1979, when there were 4.3 million eighteen–year–olds. In 1998 there will only be 3.3 million eighteen–year–olds.

   *This is what the Baby Boom (and now the Baby Bust) looks like graphically:

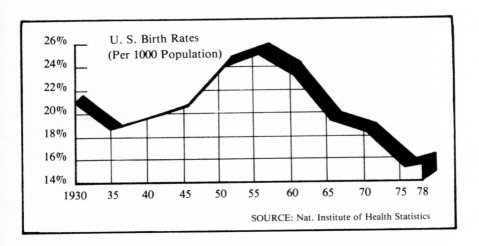

U. S. Birth Rates (Per 1000 Population)

SOURCE: Nat. Institute of Health Statistics

17. David W. Ewing, "What Business Thinks about Employee Rights," *Harvard Business Review,* September–October 1977, pp. 81–96.

18. Aaron Wildavsky, "The Guiding Force in America Today? Chicken Little," *Los Angeles Times,* March 4, 1979.
19. In an era of high inflation, this is a socially expensive form of risk reduction. Each time the consumer price index increases, there is a corresponding and automatic increase in the wages of 9 million union members and in the benefits of 34 million Social Security recipients, 3 million retired federal and military personnel, and 16 million recipients of food stamps.
20. Workers' compensation is an example of a system that discourages responsible behavior on the part of both employees and employers. At the beginning of this century workers had little protection against loss of income resulting from injury at work. The worker's only recourse was to sue his employer and prove that the injury was caused by employer negligence. Since such negligence is hard to prove, injured workers often received nothing in compensation for their injuries. Over sixty years ago states began to introduce workers' compensation as a reform of this unfair system. Workers' compensation insurance was to be no-fault, assuring some compensation for every injury (in exchange for this guaranteed compensation workers gave up their right to sue in the courts). The system also was designed to encourage safety by basing employers' premiums on their claims history.

   While this sounds like a just and practical reform, in practice today the system provides neither adequate compensation nor adequate incentives for safety. Both the rate of injuries and the cost of insurance are soaring. As Daniel Kasper explains:

   > Since workers' compensation limits the victim's recovery to an amount substantially less then his actual losses, the employer escapes the full brunt of his carelessness. More important, since his production costs do not reflect the social costs of his carelessness, the employer has less economic incentive to improve plant safety. (Daniel Kasper, "For a Better Workers' Compensation System," *Harvard Business Review,* March–April 1977. p. 2)

   Kasper recommends putting a bit of fault back in the system. In brief, he argues that *both* employers and employees should insure themselves against the *full* income loss and medical expenses caused by accidents. Fault then would be determined through negotiation between the competing insurance companies (with the provision for arbitration or appeal to an administrative court referee). Since premiums would reflect the total and true costs of accidents, both employees and employers would have real incentives to make work places safe.
21. The Unemployment Insurance (UI) system actually encourages companies to lay off workers by minimizing the financial impact of unemployment on employees (giving them, in effect, paid vacations), and by placing a ceiling on the premiums paid by companies (giving cyclical industries like autos, steel, construction, and textiles what amounts to a subsidy from industries that maintain full employment all year round). Consider an extreme alternative to the current overgenerous system: If there were no UI, workers would demand higher wages from their employers or demand other forms of job security. In Japan, which offers the least UI coverage among the industrialized nations,

unemployment rates are extremely low because workers demand that their employers plan for full employment, even in cyclical industries.

The effects of UI on employee behavior are similarly counterproductive. Several recent studies have shown that the recipients of UI spend less time looking for work, and remain unemployed longer, than those who aren't covered. One such study found that UI recipients spent 20 percent less time looking for work and remained unemployed almost eight weeks longer than those who didn't draw benefits. ("Labor Letter," *Wall Street Journal,* January 16, 1977.)

Reforming UI would not be easy. The German approach is to schedule short work weeks (*kurzarbeit*) and to use UI to make up 68 percent of the difference between wages earned in the short week and what would have been earned in a 40–hour week. Martin Feldstein argues that any American reform should include taxing companies on the basis of their experience rating, and taxing worker benefits (to create a real difference between the income generated while working and not working). The Feldstein approach would provide incentives for employees to demand full-employment practices from their employers. (Martin Feldstein, "Unemployment Insurance: Time for Reform," *Harvard Business Review,* March–April 1975, pp. 51–61).

22. Christopher Lasch, *The Culture of Narcissism* (New York: W. W. Norton, 1978).

23. Peter Steinhart, "Children: Victims in the Culture of Narcissism," *Los Angeles Times,* May 20, 1979.

24. Although the vast majority of young workers are engaged in services, it is clear that they have *not* been trained for these jobs, and these jobs (and the accompanying systems of compensation) are so poorly designed as to cause workers to take out their frustrations on customers. A growing number of observers, in turn, are themselves becoming frustrated by the lack of a service ethic in a society with a predominately services economy. Roy Walters, editor of the *Behavioral Sciences Newsletter,* was driven to expound on the subject after

> a recent spate of maddening experiences with "service" people who were incompetent, apathetic, or rude (usually, all three) in response to our attempts to get various services we were paying for. . . .
>
> The motto of superior service used to be, "The customer is always right." That's not true, of course. Customers can be wrong about specific facts, dumb in general, unrealistic, and arrogant. But the law of averages makes it unlikely that the customers will always be wrong. Yet that is the way some "service" people operate. (Roy Walters, "The Untrained Society," *Behavioral Sciences Newsletter,* Book VIII, Vol. 19, October 8, 1979, p. 1)

When I really want to find out what is eating Americans, I sometimes turn to Abigail Van Buren in addition to Messrs. Gallup and Harris. Here is an excerpt from a letter from an irate Milwaukeean to "Dear Abby":

HOW TO MAKE A CUSTOMER'S DAY

If a customer approaches, run and hide in the back room.
Continue to chat with other salespersons about what you did last night.

Never smile. A deadpan stare (or frown) will discourage customers from bothering you.

Never offer assistance. Wait for the customer to ask for help.

Never serve customers in the order they enter the shop. Wait on whoever has the nerve to elbow their way up to the front.

Don't stop stocking and taking inventory to serve customers. The fact that their purchases pay your salary is immaterial.

Forget the motto, "The customer is always right." They are always *wrong*, so don't let them put anything over on you.

If you do all the above, the customer will surely shop somewhere else and you won't be bothered writing up any sales. ("Dear Abby," *Los Angeles Times*, November 11, 1979, Part II, p. 2.)

25. Barbara W. Tuchman, "The Decline of Quality," *The New York Times Magazine*, November 2, 1980.
26. Studs Terkel, *Working* (New York: Avon Books, 1974), pp. 259–260.
27. Ibid., p. 265.
28. Ivar Berg, *Managers and Work Reform* (New York: The Free Press, 1978).
29. Robert Schrank, *Ten Thousand Working Days* (Cambridge, Mass.: The MIT Press, 1978).
30. "Business Perks That Rile the White House," *U.S. News and World Report*, March 27, 1979, pp. 33–34.
31. Ascherman v. Saint Francis Memorial Hospital, 45 C.A. 3d507; 119 Cal. Rptr. 507 (1975).
32. Christopher Stone, *Should Trees Have Standing?* (Los Altos, Calif.: W. Kaufman, Inc., 1974).
33. "Italy Calls in Sick," *Industry Week*, November 12, 1979, pp. 99–101.
34. E. F. Schumacher, *Good Work* (New York: Harper and Row, 1979).

CHAPTER 4

1. *Survey of Working Conditions* (Ann Arbor: Survey Research Center, Institute for Social Research, University of Michigan).
2. Daniel Yankelovich and Bernard Lefkowitz, "The Public Debate on Growth: Preparing for Resolution," a paper presented at Third Biennial Woodlands Conference on Growth Policy, October 28–31, 1979, in Houston, Texas.
3. *The Pension Balloon* (Los Angeles: Town Hall of California, 1979).

CHAPTER 5

1. "The Factory Workers Who May Win a Nobel Peace Prize," *Next*, Preview Issue, 1979.
2. Robert Schrank, *Ten Thousand Working Days* (Cambridge, Mass.: The MIT Press, 1978).
3. Richard E. Walton, "Teaching an Old Dog New Tricks," *Wharton Magazine*, Winter 1978, pp. 38–48.
4. It is with some personal anguish that I set the record straight on these issues. In 1973, I was responsible for the *Work in America* report to the Secretary of

Health, Education and Welfare which, among other things, advocated the reform of the American work place based on social science research that has since been ignominiously discredited. *Mea Culpa.* For a state-of-the art summary of this subject, see *Job Redesign* by J. Richard Hackman and Greg Oldham (Reading, Mass.: Addison-Wesley, 1980).

5. The presidential panel that reviewed the events at Three Mile Island wrote that "the most serious 'mindset,' is the preoccupation. . . . with the safety of equipment, resulting in the downplaying of the importance of the human element in nuclear power generation. The NRC and the industry have failed to recognize sufficiently that the human beings who manage and operate the plants constitute an important safety system." *(Behavioral Sciences Newsletter,* Book VIII, Vol. 21, November 12, 1979, p. 1.)

6. Robert Zager, "Managing Guaranteed Employment," *Harvard Business Review,* May–June 1978, pp. 103–115.

7. "Participative Management at Work," *Harvard Business Review,* January–February 1977, pp. 117–127.

8. Nick Kotz, "Worker–Community Group Sees Dream of Saving Steel Mill Fade," *Los Angeles Times,* July 9, 1979.

9. Daniel Zwerdling, "Workers Seize Plant!" *Working Papers,* Fall 1974, p. 17.

10. Agis Salpukas, "Work Ideas Lift Steel Output," *New York Times,* October 17, 1980.

11. Lawrence Stessin and Arnold Naidich, "Labor and Management: Cutting Costs to Save Jobs," *New York Times,* October 7, 1979.

12. Jonathan Kwitny, "Tube Part, Six Hundred Jobs Saved in Indianapolis—In the Nick of Time," *Wall Street Journal,* March 22, 1978.

13. These numbers may seem unimpressive. But management consultant William J. Exton estimates that an average clerical error costs $56 to correct. If a clerical worker's error rate is only 5 percent, he would make 720 errors in a year, costing $40,000. Even supposing that Exton is off by a factor of four, and errors only cost $28, and the typical worker only makes 360 errors annually, if we multiply $10,000 times Prudential's 40,000 employees, we are still, to paraphrase the late Senator Everett Dirksen, talking real money! See "The Cost of Clerical Errors," *Behavioral Sciences Newsletter,* Book VIII, Vol. 14.

14. J. Patrick Wright, *On a Clear Day You Can See General Motors* (Grosse Pointe, Mich.: Wright Enterprises, 1979).

15. Schrank, *Ten Thousand Working Days.*

16. Robert H. Guest, "Quality of Work Life—Learning from Tarrytown," *Harvard Business Review,* July–August 1979, pp. 76–87.

17. G. L. Staines, S. E. Seashore, and J. H. Pleck, "Evaluating the Quality of Employment," *Economic Outlook USA,* Spring 1979, pp. 34–39.

18. "Firm Finds Pay Scheme That Works: Employees Vote on Each Other's Raises," *Los Angeles Times,* January 10, 1979.

19. Edward Lawler, "Workers Can Set Their Own Wages—Responsibly," *Psychology Today,* February 1977, pp. 109–112.

20. Martin Koughan, "Boss Has Brainstorm: Workers Set Own Pay," *Boston Globe,* February 16, 1975.

21. Thomas C. Hayes, "Dana: Few Rules, Many Sales," *New York Times,* October 19, 1979.

22. Barry A. Macy, "A Progress Report on the Bolivar Quality of Work Life Project," *Personnel Journal,* August 1979, pp. 527–599.
23. Robert D. Hulme and Richard V. Bevan, "The Blue–Collar Worker Goes on Salary," *Harvard Business Review* March–April 1975, p. 112.
24. Ibid., p. 104.
25. "A Low–Cost Fringe the Workers Appreciate," *Business Week,* March 13, 1978, p. 79.
26. "How to Earn Well Pay," *Business Week,* June 12, 1978, p. 143.
27. Robert E. Cole, *Work, Mobility and Participation* (Berkeley: University of California Press, 1979).
28. Stanley D. Nollen and Virginia H. Martin, *Alternative Work Schedules,* 2 vols. (New York: American Management Associations, 1978).
29. Fred Best, "Work Sharing: Policy Options and Assessments" (Paris: Organization for Economic Cooperation and Development, September 4, 1979).
30. Ibid., p. 47.
31. "U.S. Problem not Labor but Managers—Sony Chief," *Los Angeles Times,* October 29, 1980.
32. In Private Conversation.

CHAPTER 6

1. Daniel Zwerdling, *Democracy at Work* (Washington, D.C.: Association for Self–Management, 1978), p. 124.
2. Statement of Janette Eadon Johannesen in U.S. House of Representatives, Committee on Banking, Finance and Urban Affairs, Subcommittee on Economic Stabilization, *Employee Stock Ownership* (Washington, D.C.: U.S. Government Printing Office, 1979).
3. Michael Conte and Arnold S. Tannenbaum, "Employee–owned Companies: Is the Difference Measurable?" *Monthly Labor Review,* July 1978, pp. 23–28.
4. Louis O. Kelso and Mortimer J. Adler, *The Capitalist Manifesto* (New York: Random House, 1958).
5. John Kenneth Galbraith, *The New Industrial State* (New York: Mentor Books, 1972), esp. chapters 12 and 13.
6. Zwerdling, *Democracy,* p. 11.
7. Ibid., pp. 113–130.
8. Paul Bernstein, "Run Your Own Business," *Working Papers,* Summer 1974, pp. 24–35.
9. Ibid.
10. In Private Conversation.
11. "An Employee–Owned Firm" (Ann Arbor: Survey Research Center, Institute for Social Research, University of Michigan, January 17, 1977).
12. *Time,* October 4, 1976, p. 80.
13. Thomas M. Rohan, "Tool firm's 'owners' hit the bricks," *Industry Week,* November 24, 1980, p. 103.
14. Quoted in Zwerdling, *Democracy,* p. 69.
15. Statement of Johannesen, op. cit.
16. R. O. Christianson, "An Analysis of Employee Attitude and Employee Stock Ownership," unpublished manuscript (St. Cloud University, 1978).

17. Statement of John Deak in U.S. House of Representatives, *Employee Stock Ownership Plans,* op. cit.
18. Peter Drucker, *The Unseen Revolution* (New York: Harper and Row, 1976).
19. Roger Strang and Roy Herberger, "Privately–Held Firms: Neglected Force in the Free Enterprise System," unpublished manuscript (University of Southern California, 1978).
20. Quoted in Ben Achtenberg, "Working Capital," *Working Papers,* Winter 1975, p. 7.
21. "Distrust of Capitalism Found in U.S.," *Los Angeles Times,* August 31, 1975.
22. Louis Harris, The Steelcase National Survey of Office Environments: Do They Work?" (Steelcase, 1978).
23. *Congressional Record,* No. 27, March 1, 1978.
24. "Wealth to the Workers," *The Economist,* October 16, 1976.
25. Ann Crittenden, "Italy's Red–Led Co–Ops Prosper," *New York Times,* June 18, 1978.

CHAPTER 7

1. The participants were: Warren Bennis, former president of University of Cincinnati, currently at University of Southern California; Morton Darrow, Prudential Insurance Company; Paul S. Goodman, Carnegie–Mellon University; J. Richard Hackman, Yale University; Rasabeth Moss Kanter, Yale University; Edward Lawler, University of Michigan, currently at University of Southern California; Elliot Liebow, Center for Studies of Metropolitan Problems, N.I.M.H.; Michael Maccoby, Harvard Project on Technology, Work, and Character; Will McWhinney, consultant; Raymond Miles, University of California at Berkeley; S. M. Miller, Boston University; James O'Toole, University of Southern California; Abe Raskin, former labor editor at the *New York Times;* Robert Schrank, Ford Foundation; Richard Walton, Harvard University; Peter Weitz, German Marshall Fund; Basil Whiting, OSHA; William F. Whyte, Cornell University; Robert Zager, Work in America Institute, Inc.; Sam Zagoria, Labor Management Relations Service; Shoshana Zuboff, Harvard University.
2. Michael Maccoby, *The Gamesman: The New Corporate Leaders* (New York: Simon & Schuster, 1976).
3. William H. Whyte, Jr., *The Organization Man* (New York: Simon & Schuster, 1956).
4. John Beatte, *Other Cultures* (London: Routledge and Kegan Paul, 1966).
5. J. Patrick Wright, *On a Clear Day You Can See General Motors: John Z. De Lorean's Look Inside the Automotive Giant* (Grosse Point, Mich.: Wright Enterprises, 1979).
6. Robert Townsend, *Up the Organization* (New York: Knopf, 1970).
7. Wright, *On A Clear Day,* p. 216.
8. "Stereotypes, Statistics and Some Surprises," *Forbes,* May 15, 1974, pp. 118–125.
9. Arjay Miller, Review of Maccoby's *The Gamesman, Wall Street Journal,* January 27, 1977.
10. Maccoby, *Gamesman,* p. 100.

11. "What's Ahead for the Business–Government Relationship," *Harvard Business Review* (March–April 1979), pp. 94–105.
12. Wright, *On a Clear Day,* p. 5.
13. *Twinning* is the name of the process by which cattle farmers seek to double the size of their herds either by causing two eggs to be fertilized in the cow, or by causing a fertilized egg to split, thus producing identical twins instead of a single calf. In organizations the process is done through recruiting and promoting one's *doppelgangers.*
14. Bennis made this suggestion at the Conference on Education, Work, and the Quality of Life, Summer 1974, at Aspen, Colorado.

CHAPTER 8

1.   UNEMPLOYMENT, VARYING ESTIMATES (1973)

		Number (thousands)	Percent of labor force
1.	Unemployment severity index (days per person)	—	2.7
2.	Recipients of unemployment compensation, weekly	1,783	2.3
3.	Variable unemployment, monthly	4,304	4.5
4.	Official unemployment, monthly	4,304	4.9
5.	Four above, plus discouraged workers	4,983	5.6
6.	Recipients of unemployment compensation, annual total	6,200	8.5
7.	Alternative unemployment measure, 1st quarter, 1972	6,541	7.6
8.	Five above, plus part-time workers wanting full-time work	7,502	8.5
9.	Eight above, plus labor force dropouts, December 1970	8,100	9.4
10.	Unemployment and earnings inadequacy, 1972	9,942	11.5
11.	Official unemployment, annual	15,287	15.4
12.	Real unemployment	25,600	24.6
13.	Labor reserve of experienced unemployed, 1970 census	26,500	—
14.	Subemployment, lower-level income, 1970 census	—	30.5
15.	Exclusion index	36,827	40.1
16.	Subemployment, higher-level income, 1970 census	—	61.2

Explanations of various measures:
1. Measures the number of days of unemployment per person in the officially defined labor force.
2. From BLS figures.

3. Adjusts official unemployment to changes in sex and age composition of labor force since 1955.
4. From BLS figures.
5. Includes workers not in labor force because "they think they cannot get a job."
6. From BLS figures.
7. Adds to official unemployment an estimate of those who would seek jobs if full employment existed.
8. From BLS figures.
9. From BLS figures.
10. Same as 5 above, *less* those over 65, 16–21, and currently unemployed with above-average income for year, but *plus* the currently unemployed below a "poverty threshold."
11. Total persons experiencing some unemployment (as defined in 4 above) during year.
12. Includes rough estimates of job wanters among so-called unemployables, housepersons, men 25–54, older persons, students, and manpower trainees.
13. Persons not in labor force who worked for pay in last 10 years.
14. Includes 9 above, plus those currently employed at less than $4,000 a year.
15. Includes those unemployed, employed part-time but desiring full-time work, desiring work but not looking for a job currently, and employed in jobs with substandard wages.
16. Same as 14 above for workers earning less than $7,000 a year.

Source: Stanley Moses, "Labor Supply Concepts: The Political Economy of Conceptual Change," *The Annals of The American Academy of Political and Social Science,* No. 418, March 1975, pp. 38–39.

2.   EIGHTY YEARS OF UNEMPLOYMENT

In thousands of persons 14 years and over for 1900 through 1960. In thousands of persons 16 years and over for subsequent years. Annual averages.

Year	Unem-ployed	% of -civilian -labor -force	Year	Unem-ployed	% of -civilian -labor -force	Year	Unem-ployed	% of -civilian -labor -force
1900	1,420	5.0	1917	1,848	4.6	1934	11,340	22.0
1901	1,205	4.0	1918	536	1.4	1935	10,610	20.3
1902	1,097	3.7	1919	546	1.4	1936	9,030	17.0
1903	1,204	3.9	1920	2,132	5.2	1937	7,700	14.3
1904	1,691	5.4	1921	4,918	11.7	1938	10,390	19.1
1905	1,381	4.3	1922	2,859	6.7	1939	9,480	17.2
1906	574	1.7	1923	1,049	2.4	1940	8,120	14.6
1907	945	2.8	1924	2,190	5.0	1941	5,560	9.9
1908	2,780	8.0	1925	1,453	3.2	1942	2,660	4.7
1909	1,824	5.1	1926	801	1.8	1943	1,070	1.9
1910	2,150	5.9	1927	1,519	3.3	1944	670	1.2
1911	2,518	6.7	1928	1,982	4.2	1945	1,040	1.9
1912	1,759	4.6	1929	1,550	3.2	1946	2,270	3.9
1913	1,671	4.3	1930	4,340	8.9	1947	2,356	3.9
1914	3,120	7.9	1931	8,020	16.3	1948	2,325	3.8
1915	3,377	8.5	1932	12,060	24.1	1949	3,682	5.9
1916	2,043	5.1	1933	12,830	25.2	1950	3,351	5.3

Year	Unemployed	% of -civilian -labor -force	Year	Unemployed	% of -civilian -labor -force	Year	Unemployed	% of -civilian -labor -force
1951	2,099	3.3	1961	4,714	6.7	1971	4,993	5.9
1952	1,932	3.1	1962	3,911	5.5	1972	4,840	5.6
1953	1,870	2.9	1963	4,070	5.7	1973	4,304	4.9
1954	3,578	5.6	1964	3,786	5.2	1974	5,076	5.6
1955	2,904	4.4	1965	3,366	4.5	1975	7,830	8.5
1956	2,822	4.2	1966	2,875	3.8	1976	7,288	7.7
1957	2,936	4.3	1967	2,975	3.8	1977	6,855	7.0
1958	4,681	6.8	1968	2,817	3.6	1978	6,047	6.0
1959	3,813	5.5	1969	2,831	3.5	1979	5,963	5.8
1960	3,931	5.6	1970	4,088	4.9			

Note: In 1957, definitions of employed and unemployed were changed slightly. In years subsequent to 1957 the number and percentage of unemployed is thus somewhat higher than in previous years.

3. Thanks to the invention of the E–P ratio, there is now a seventeenth way of viewing unemployment:

THE HALF-FULL GLASS:

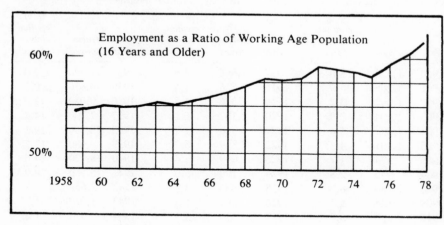

THE HALF-EMPTY GLASS:

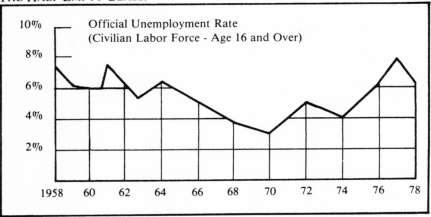

4. Prior to 1975 there were more professional and technical jobs than there were college graduates to fill them. Since the middle 1970s, however, there have been more college graduates than "appropriate" jobs for them to fill.

Year	College Graduates as a Percent of Total Civilian Labor Force	Professional-Technical Jobs as Percent of Total Civilian Jobs
1960	10.0	11.0
1965	11.7	13.0
1970	13.2	14.2
1975	16.9	15.0
1985 (projected)	20–21	14.9–15.4

5. James W. Singer, "When the Public Sector Doesn't Work, Give the Private Sector a Chance," *National Journal,* September 29, 1979, p. 1608.
6. Arthur Okun, *Equality and Efficiency* (Washington, D.C.: Brookings Institution, 1979).
7. E. F. Schumacher, *Small is Beautiful* (New York: Harper and Row, 1973).
8. John Kenneth Galbraith, *The New Industrial State* (New York: Mentor Books, 1971).
9. See James O'Toole, "What's Ahead for the Business–Government Relationship," *Harvard Business Review,* March–April 1979.
10. For an explanation, see James O'Toole, *Work, Learning, and the American Future* (San Francisco: Jossey–Bass, 1977), p. 211.
11. Idea presented at a Workshop on Work, Education and Leisure, Preconference Woodlands Workshop, 1979, at the University of Houston, from Berg's current research on "structural unemployment."
12. A new concept called "supported work" is showing that a large percentage of chronically unemployable people—including ex-addicts, alcoholics, ex-

offenders, high school dropouts, and welfare mothers—can become productive employees. With such techniques as peer support, immediate feedback on performance, carefully designed job structures, and frequent raises, bonuses, and promotions, many people society had written off have shown that they can develop the work discipline needed to hold unsheltered jobs. While the percentage of such "saves" has been low in public-sector training and employment programs, several recent private-sector experiments have proved more successful. For example, at New York's Chemical Bank thirteen former addicts were hired to work in the check-processing department. A year later eight were still with the bank, and three had been promoted to teller. None of the five who left had been fired for misconduct. This turnover rate was roughly the same as for the bank's typical entry-level workers. Says Norborne Berkeley, Jr., president of Chemical Bank:

> If we—as bankers with a reputation for caution—can demonstrate to the business community that this is a viable program, if we can persuade other businessmen by our example that the risk is small and the gains are great in terms of maintaining our society and our marketplace—then we are talking about hundreds of companies who could provide thousands of job opportunities.

Lucy N. Friedman and Carl B. Weisbrod, "A Way to Move Welfare Recipients into the Work Force," *Harvard Business Review*, January–February 1978, p. 12.

13. This raises the question of how much a job costs, and if it is cheaper to "buy" a job in the private or public sector.

Creating a new job in the private sector in 1978 cost anywhere from $5,000 (at Gino's Pizzas) to $443,000 (at Commonwealth Edison). These figures represent the amount of money invested per worker in plant and equipment. Investment per workers is highest in the oil industry and in utilities. Significantly the money invested per employee in such declining industries as steel ($60,000 at U.S. Steel) is considerably higher than in the new, growing high-technology industries ($18,000 at Texas Instruments). ("Who are the Biggest Employers?" *Forbes*, May 15, 1978, pp. 286–292.) This is a significant finding because it may mean there is enough capital available to create full employment *if* it is invested in areas where America has a competitive advantage. The bad news is that it may be prohibitively expensive to raise employment and productivity in the older heavy industries. In effect, any "reindustrialization" of America would have to be a selective process.

There is a broad variation in the cost of job creation in the public sector, too. In 1976 a billion-dollar federal expenditure would have bought fifty-five thousand jobs in the defense industry, sixty thousand CETA jobs, eighty-five thousand jobs in water-pollution abatement, and ninety thousand jobs in education. (O'Toole, *Work, Learning and the American Future* [San Francisco: Jossey-Bass, 1977], pp. 82–83.)

A cost/benefit analysis of job creation in the private versus the public sector is tricky. For example, a comparison of the $16,000 needed for a CETA job and the $18,000 needed for a job at Texas Instruments must take into account the fact that the worker's $10,000 salary must be *added* to the investment cost at Texas Instruments. If we stop there, a job in the public sector looks like a relative bargain. But wait, the $18,000 private investment is a *one-time expenditure*. After it is made, the worker's output more than pays for his own salary; indeed over time it will pay back the money invested. Thus the job in the private sector is *permanent* for the life of the investment. In contrast, the $16,000 public expenditure must be made every year, and only a part of it is paid back (as taxes and as whatever output in services the employee renders).

14. Singer, "When the Public Sector Doesn't Work."
15. Edward M. Kennedy, "Creating Jobs Through Energy Policy," Opening statement to the Subcommittee on Energy, Joint Economic Committee, March 16, 1978.

Between 1969 and 1976 total employment in the United States increased by 9.6 million jobs. According to Congressman John B. Breckinridge, 99 percent of this increase occurred in firms not large enough to make the *Fortune* list of the one thousand largest industrial firms. (Breckinridge, Speech before the Small Business Legislative Council, February 8, 1978).

JOB CREATION AT THE FORTUNE 1,000 INDUSTRIAL FIRMS

Year	First Fortune 500 Firms	Second Fortune 500 Firms	Civilian Labor Force
1976	14,836,163	1,874,614	94,773,000
1975	14,412,992	1,861,352	92,613,000
1974	15,255,946	1,993,976	91,011,000
1973	15,531,683	1,966,814	88,714,000
1972	14,676,849	1,845,502	86,542,000
1971	14,324,890	1,765,418	84,113,000
1970	14,607,581	1,719,805	82,715,000
1969	14,813,809	1,822,071	80,734,000
Total Increase	22,354	52,543	14,039,000
Total % Increase	0.15	2.8	14.8
Average Annual % Increase	0.02	0.42	2.3

16. "Keeping Small Business in Town," *Business Week,* July 17, 1978.
17. Willard Wirtz, *The Boundless Resource* (Washington, D.C.: New Republic Book Co., 1975).
18. Patrick Goldring, *Multi-Purpose Man* (New York: Taplinger, 1974).
19. See Sigmund Freud, *Civilization and Its Discontents* (New York: W. W.

Norton, 1962), in which Freud argues that the two most compelling human drives are eros (love, or sex) and ananake (work, or necessity).

20. Many radical feminists argue that affirmative action isn't working. They cite all kinds of impressive figures that show little or no progress in terms of mobility or salary among women workers. But this data is counterintuitive. Every business, professional office and university department can plainly be seen to have women in positions of authority, where none were present before. Why don't the figures reflect this change? Here is the puzzle: In 1978 women who were employed full time and year round earned only 60 percent of what males earned (which is exactly the same ratio that prevailed in 1939). Yet it is illegal for employers to pay men more than women for equal work. Why, then, has this large discrepancy in relative incomes persisted?

Part of the explanation is that women tend to be disproportionately represented in low-paying clerical and services work. Additionally, "full time, year round" covers a broad spectrum of average hours worked per week, and men tend to work more hours per week than women—even those who are considered full-time employees. It is also obvious that some employers are breaking the law. But are these reasons sufficient to explain the observed inequalities in income? I'll leave it to econometricians at the RAND Corporation or some other seat of advanced learning to push the regressions in search of scientific truth on this matter. But I have a hunch that the real reasons for the failure of women to close the income gap are more subtle and complex than are likely to be picked up in a typical statistical scrutiny of the national employment data.

Let me demonstrate by removing all occupations from consideration but one: the legal profession. This profession presents a neat little paradox. While the rate of increase of women lawyers probably has been greater than in any other profession (in 1971 only 7.3 percent of all law degrees were awarded to women; five years later the figure was 19.2 percent), statistically women lawyers seem not to have made headway in their incomes relative to men lawyers. Men lawyers—who are only good at mathematics when it comes to preparing their bills—are unable to explain the phenomenon. Women lawyers—no doubt still suffering from the math anxiety that prevented them from getting into medical school—are likewise unable to explain the galling fact.

The answer to the puzzle may lie in a strange and unintended consequence of affirmative action: If pay in a profession increases with seniority, and if affirmative action programs constantly increase the percentage of women in entry-level positions, then the ratio of male-to-female salaries will tend to increase for many years. In effect, the successes in opening up more legal jobs for women has led to the statistical anomaly of increasing sexual inequality in compensation. To clarify, let's look at the rosters of two well-known New York law firms.

The chart shows that Noncompis, Shyster, and Swine has sixteen attorneys, including one woman who graduated from law school in 1974 (and married the firm's senior partner later that year). The ratio of male-to-female salaries in this firm is approximately 1:1, statistically making it a paragon of equality. The chart also shows that Darrow, Brandeis, and Holmes hired no women at all until 1976, when collective guilt struck the firm. At that time it pledged not to hire another man until there were as many women as men in the firm. Today

	FIRM OF DARROW, BRANDEIS, AND HOLMES	FIRM OF NONCOMPIS, SHYSTER, AND SWINE
Year Attorneys Graduated from Law School	Number and Sex of Attorneys at Each Salary Level	Number and Sex of Attorneys at Each Salary Level
Before 1971	2 men at $100,000 p.a.	2 men at $100,000 p.a.
1972	2 men at $90,000	2 men at $90,000
1973	2 men at $80,000	2 men at $80,000
1974	2 men at $70,000	1 man and *1 woman* at $70,000
1975	2 men at $60,000	2 men at $60,000
1976	*2 women* at $50,000	2 men at $50,000
1977	*2 women* at $40,000	2 men at $40,000
1978	*2 women* at $80,000	2 men at $30,000
Average Male Salary	$80,000	$64,666
Average Female Salary	$45,000	$70,000

the firm has ten men and six women attorneys; the ratio of male-to-female salaries in this firm is approximately 2:1, statistically making Darrow et al. an exemplar of discrimination.

This hypothetical example suggests the possibility that the observed difference in the ratio of male to female income in professional, technical, and managerial occupations may be the result of *the success of affirmative action programs at the entry level.* Ironically the fastest way for a firm or company to achieve equality in male/female incomes would be to stop hiring women at the entry level for the next five years. Unfortunately such unfair and counterproductive game playing is now encouraged by insistence on measuring the results of efforts to reduce discrimination solely by use of simple statistics that no longer reflect the reality and complexity of the problems that women are now encountering.

21. Even feminist activists seem to be coming around to this position, as the following statement by Betty Friedan illustrates: "To some it may sound strange for a feminist like myself to be arguing so passionately for the importance of families. Such arguments have been dismissed by some radical feminists as 'reactionary family chauvinism.' But it may very well be that the family, which has always been considered the bastion of conservatism, is already somehow being transformed by women's equality into a progressive political force. For when men start assigning a higher priority to their families and self-fulfillment, and women a higher priority to independence and active participation in 'man's world,' what happens to the supremacy of the corporate, bureaucratic system?

"Some recent management studies, for instance, indicate that the corporate policy of frequently transferring executives and demanding that they work night and weekends is not really necessary for the work of the corporation, but that, by estranging them from their communities and families, it serves to make executives corporate creatures, 'company men.' Will women renounce their bonds and their power within the family in order to become 'company women'? Some already have, but in most instances, women's equality, in the home and in the workplace, strengthens the family and enable it better to resist dehumanization." (Betty Friedan, "Feminism Takes a New Turn," *New York Times Sunday Magazine,* November 18, 1979.)

22. A review of the data below concerning the 1977 status of several racial groups in the civilian labor force reveals that whites are relatively overrepresented in managerial and technical jobs, blacks are overrepresented in service work and unskilled laboring, and Hispanics are overrepresented in factory and farm jobs. Both blacks and Hispanics are overrepresented in unemployment lines.

Labor Force and Occupational Status	White	Black	Hispanic Origin
I. White-collar workers	(51.7)	(32.5)	(31.8)
Professional and technical	15.5	10.1	7.5
Managers and administrators, except farm	11.4	4.1	5.7
Sales workers	6.8	2.4	3.7
Clerical workers	18.0	15.9	15.0
II. Blue-collar workers	(32.9)	(39.4)	(46.6)
Craft and kindred workers	13.6	9.1	13.8
Operatives, except transport	11.0	15.6	21.1
Transport equipment operatives	3.7	5.8	4.1
Nonfarm laborers	4.6	9.0	7.7
III. Service workers	12.3	26.0	17.1
IV. Farmworkers	3.2	2.2	4.5
V. Unemployment rate	6.2	13.9	10.0

23. Robert H. Binstock, "Federal Policy toward the Aging," *National Journal,* November 11, 1978, p. 1838.

24. Robert Samuelson, "Aging America—Who Will Shoulder the Growing Burden?" *National Journal,* October 28, 1978, p. 1717.

25. *The Pension Balloon* (Los Angeles: Town Hall of California, 1979).

26. M. Feldstein, "Facing the Social Security Crisis," *The Public Interest,* No. 47, Spring 1977, p. 89.

27. Neal R. Pierce and Jerry Hagstrom, "Unions, Frostbelt Seek More Control over Pension Fund Investment," *National Journal,* January 27, 1979, p. 145.

28. Bernhard Teriet, "Gliding Out: The European Approach to Retirement," *Personnel Journal,* July 1978, pp. 368–370.

29. Irving Kristol, "Is the American Worker 'Alienated'?" *Wall Street Journal,* January 18, 1973.

CHAPTER 9

1. From Shaw's *Redistribution of Income,* quoted in Mortimer Adler and Charles Van Doren, *Great Treasury of Western Thought* (New York: Bowker, 1977), pp. 917–918.

2. Wellford Wilms, "Vocational Education and Social Mobility: A Study of Public and Proprietary School Dropouts and Graduates," (Los Angeles: U.C.L.A. School of Education, June 1980).
3. R. Bolles, *What Color Is Your Parachute?* (Berkeley, Cal.: Ten Speed Press, 1978), rev. ed.
4. Milton Rockmore, "Management Shopping List," *American Way,* October 1979, pp. 51–54.
5. Seymour Lusterman, "Education in Industry," in Dyckman Vermilye, ed., *Relating Work and Education* (San Francisco: Jossey–Bass, 1977), p. 85.
6. *Behavioral Sciences Newsletter,* Book IV, Vol. 4, February 28, 1977, pp. 3–4.
7. Philip Shabecoff, "Jobs for Youth: New Proposals for an Old Problem," *New York Times,* March 9, 1980.

INDEX

Nader, Ralph, 119, 180
NASA, 18
National Consumer Cooperative Bank, 106
National health insurance, cost of, 29
National policy. *See* Public policy
National service, 176–77
Natural resources: as entitlement, 40;
limited, social justice and, 12
Net income, as percentage of sales of
privately and publicly held firms, 101
New Japan Steel Corporation, 81
New Labor Economics, 145–54; and
Buddhist economics, 147–49; compared
with traditional assumptions, 145–46;
performance criteria for, 146–47; and
unemployment, 149–54
New School for Democratic Management,
San Francisco, 105
Nontraditionalists: attitudes toward
entitlements, 30–32; and work reform
guidelines, 57
Northwestern University, *Endicott Report,*
179–80

Office employees, on benefits of increased
productivity, 20
Oil, Chemical and Atomic Workers International, foreword to contract with Shell,
Canada, 71–72
Oil prices, 46–47; and productivity/labor
cost ratio, 23
Okun, Arthur, 26, 27, 29–30, 145
Older workers, 158–65; demographic data,
160; forecasts on numbers of, 158; and
involuntary employment, 142; and
pensions and Social Security, 159–65;
problems of, 157
Olga Company, 81
On-the-job training, 173
Organization Man, 116, 120
Organizational change, 111–39; anthropological approach to, 138–39; characteristics of successful and unsuccessful,
111–16; and individual managerial
behavior, 116. *See also* Organizational
culture
Organizational culture: changed managerial
type and, 120–22; changes threatening,
137–38; defined, 117–18; dysfunctional
values, 125–28; of General Motors,
118–19; identification of, 128–35; and
individual differences and similarities,
119–20; institutional biography for
identification of characteristics of,

128–35; reasons for changing, 135–39;
and risk-taking characteristics, 136;
tyrannical, 137–38; values characterizing,
123–28; and work-place reform, 117–39
Organizational psychologists, individual
managerial behavior and, 116–17
Organizational theorists, economic growth
and, 14
Output per hour worked, in measures of
productivity, 16–17. *See also* Dollar value
of output
Overhead, entitlements and, 29
Ownership: principle of, 100–101; risks of,
102–104

Parenting, decrease in, 34
Parsons Pine Products, 77
Participative management, 6–8. *See also*
Worker decision-making
Part-time work, 79, 153–54; and employ-
ment security, 81; increase in, 74
Pay cuts, prevention of lay offs and, 65
Penney, James Cash, 136
Pension Benefit Guaranty Corporation, 160
Pension plans, 49, 159–65; mobility and,
160–61; problems with, 159–60; pro-
posals on, 163–65
Per capita income, in U.S. compared with
other nations, 26
Perquisites. *See* Executive perks
Personal liberties, as entitlements, 26
Personal productivity, perceptions of,
19–20
Personal time, lost productivity and, 20, 21
Personality; culture and, 122; of managers,
as focus for organizational change,
116–17
Personnel officers, polls on qualifications of
college graduates, 179–80
Pessimism, "culture of narcissism and,"
33–34
Philip Morris, 137
Physicians, changing attitudes of, 15
Pitney Bowes, 79
Plant closures: economy and, 106; and
financing mechanisms for worker-
ownership, 104; prevention of, 64–67, 71,
89; and worker capitalism, 105, 107
Plant relocations, right to vote on, 28
Plant size, productivity and, 66–67
Plywood factories, worker-owned, 95–96
Polaroid, 76
Political events, changed values and, 44–46
Political freedom, 28

Work-place democracy, as goal of worker capitalism, 90

Work-place reform: attitude of middle management to, 68; case reports, 58–84; and fringe benefits, 82; as goal of worker capitalism, 89–90; goals of, 50–51, 68–69; guidelines for, 56–59; and Maslow hierarchy of needs, 56–57; and organizational culture, 117–39; performance criteria and, 82–84; resistance of management to, 115–16. *See also* New Labor Economics: Organizational change; Worker capitalism

Work quotas. *See* Task system

Work rules, peer-established, 75

Work schedule. *See* Flexible working hours

Work sharing, 152

Worker capitalism: abroad, 108–10; as alternative to government ownership, 96–97; benefits of, 95–96; case reports, 85–86; evaluation of successes and failures of, 98–102; failed expectations for, 92–98; federal support for technical assistance to, 105–106; future of, 104–108; goal conflicts, 91–92; goals of, 89–92; labeled as socialist, 108; lack of preparation for, 98–99; meeting expectations, 95–98; and ownership principle, 100–101; problems of, 84–87; and productivity, 62; and responsibility principle, 102; and risks of ownership, 102–104; and sale of companies by worker-owners, 94. *See also* Cooperatives; Joint partnerships; Trusts

Worker decision-making, 4, 8, 10, 28; and feelings of powerlessness, 112; management reversal of, 86; and profit sharing,

62–64; on salaries and raises, 75; on work rules, 75

Worker expectations: and "culture of narcissism," 33–34; and employee ownership, 92–98; as entitlements, 25–26; productivity and, 25. *See also* Entitlements

Worker ownership. *See* Worker capitalism

Worker responsibilities. *See* Responsibilities

Worker retraining, 152

Worker self-management, 62–64; adverse managerial reaction to, 54; productivity and, 4; and vocational education, 181–82

Worker stock ownership. *See* Stock ownership by workers

Workers: and affluence, 23; demands for pure social entitlements, 28; initiative, management rejection of, 53–54; motivation, as goal of worker capitalism, 90–91; needs of, 55–56; in participative management plant, 6–8; perceptions of personal productivity, 19–20; productivity of, *see* Productivity; responsibilities of, 36–38

Workers' compensation, 190*n*

Working schedules. *See* Flexible working hours; Job sharing

Yankelovich, Daniel, 30–32, 47–48

Young workers, employer attitudes toward, 34–35; as "marginal workers," 19. *See also* Baby boom generation

Youngstown Sheet and Tube plant, 64, 104

Yugoslavia: cooperatives in, 110; worker-owned firms in, 104

Zero risk, 32–33

Zwerdling, Daniel, 93–94, 99